Role of a Lifetime

Role of a Lifetime

Four Professional Actors and How They Built Their Careers

ROBERT SIMONSON

BACK STAGE BOOKS
An imprint of Watson-Guptill Publications/New York

To Sarah

Copyright © 1999, by Robert Simonson

Published in 1999 by Back Stage Books,
an imprint of Watson-Guptill Publications,
a division of BPI Communications, Inc.,
1515 Broadway, New York, NY 10036-8986

Editor for Back Stage Books: Dale Ramsey
Book design: Bob Fillie, Graphiti Design, Inc.
Production manager: Ellen Greene

Library of Congress Cataloging-in-Publication Data
Simonson, Robert.
    Role of a lifetime: four professional actors and how
they built their careers / Robert Simonson.
        p. cm.
    Includes index.
    ISBN 0-8230-7832-9
    1. Actors—United States—Biography. I. Title.
PN2285.S535   1999
792'.028'092273—dc21   98–52788
[B]   CIP

Manufactured in the United States of America
1 2 3 4 5 6 7 8 9 /03 02 01 00 99

Acknowledgments

Role of a Lifetime was written with the help of numerous people to whom I extend many thanks: Jon Robin Baitz; Amy Bartram; Louis Botto; Zoe Caldwell; Robert Cashill; Katina Commings; Olympia Dukakis; Dr. Bella Itkin; George Lane; David Sheward; Iva Rifkin; and Sam Whitehead. I am also very grateful to the staff members who assisted me at the New York Public Library for the Performing Arts; the Harold Washington Public Library, in Chicago; the Metropolitan Museum of Art; and Photofest; the publicity staffs of the Mark Taper Forum, the Goodman Theatre, the Long Wharf Theatre, Center Stage, the McCarter Theatre, Steppenwolf Theatre Company, the Bay Street Theatre, and the Yale Dramatic Association; and, in particular, the staff and interns of the Williamstown Theatre Festival.

I especially appreciate the encouragement I received from my family: my mother Doris, my father Bob, Karin, Alan, Eric, Britta, and Dennis. I also thank my patient and skilled editor, Dale Ramsey, without whom this book would not be.

And, of course, I owe a great debt of thanks to Gloria Foster, Austin Pendleton, Ron Rifkin, and Lois Smith, who gave so generously of their time and their memories.

ROBERT SIMONSON

Contents

Preface

I n 1995, I conducted a series of interviews with actor Austin Pendleton in preparation for a magazine profile. Most actors keep the length of such press ren-
dezvous to a minimum—a lunch, a dinner, an hour in a dressing room, and
they're off, glad to be rid of the experience.

Pendleton was different, to say the least. He was very giving of his time.
After talking with him for two hours, I was surprised to find him open to the idea
of another interview. A couple of weeks after the second date, he called me up and
asked if I'd like to get together for a third session. All told, I interviewed him four
times, a total of ten hours.

Pendleton related, in detail, the many fascinating episodes of his career—the
roles he created in *Oh Dad, Poor Dad, Fiddler on the Roof, The Last Sweet Days of Isaac,*
and others; his directing career; his venture into playwriting; what felt like his vir-
tual banishment from the industry in New York, in the late 1970s; and his long,
slow climb back. Listening to the trajectory of his full life, I was struck by what a
perfect subject he was for a biography.

Once the profile was published, I asked him for permission to pursue such a
project. Even as I asked, however, I knew that no publisher would ever buy *The
Life of Austin Pendleton.* With all due respect to the man, the average person knows
nothing of Austin Pendleton. Sure, people may know the face and, if their memory is jogged, they may recognize a role or two. But he is not a *name.* He is not a *star.*

That said, here is *Role of a Lifetime,* a book profiling Pendleton, along with
three other equally talented and interesting actors: Gloria Foster, Ron Rifkin, and
Lois Smith. The fact that their life stories wouldn't justify, in terms of today's publishing mill, a book-length biography is the same reason why their lives *are* worth
telling. Foster, Pendleton, Rifkin, and Smith are steadily employed professional
actors—successful, respected, lifelong semi-knowns. It is not despite, but because
they have achieved considerable, while not phenomenal, success that they are, in a
way, ideal—that is, representative—actors.

Confronting the origins of this quartet, it is wondrous that they managed to
become actors at all, let alone prosperous ones. Consider the following thumbnail
sketches: An awkward, bespectacled English major, slight of stature and burdened
with a stutter. A black woman, schooled before the Civil Rights movement and
raised by grandparents in the rural Midwest, who nevertheless insisted that the
classic roles of drama be made available to her, simply because that's what she had
been taught in college. The Kansas-bred daughter whose parents were descended

from a religious sect which forbade dancing and movies. And a New York native, raised as an orthodox Jew in the Williamsburg section of Brooklyn, who saw virtually no theater until he was a teenager.

We could expect that such circumstances would produce not one actor, let alone four. Yet each survived, and at times thrived, and came to embody every factor an actor's life can embrace. Between them, they have experienced widespread critical adulation and acceptance and equally widespread dismissal; artistic death and rebirth; early stardom and late stardom; roles in historic productions and infamous disasters; professional rejection and rediscovery; jobs in theater, radio, film, and television; opportunities to work as an actor, a director, and a playwright; religious and racial prejudice; marriage, children, and divorce; ensemble work and solo vehicles; long periods of unemployment; and, last, but not least, the challenge of working at every stage of life.

Each of them has often been referred to as an "actor's actor," a somewhat backhanded compliment with an unspoken subtext. Actor's actors aren't glamorous or famous. They don't reap the recognition or salaries that "audience's actors" do. They reap respect and professional admiration, which, in America, verge on being slight, if not disappointing, rewards.

But that brings us again to the point of this book. Just as there is little to learn from the story of a failed actor, there is perhaps even less to learn from the story of a fabulously famous one. The first tale is all too common; the second all too rare—and neither can tell an aspiring actor how to navigate the routinely successful career.

These four actors' accounts, their stories, can telegraph that and much more simply in the telling. Taken together, they comprise a paradigm of the modern American actor's life, one of cheerful versatility (Pendleton), strong principles (Foster), philosophical melancholy (Rifkin), and grounded common sense (Smith). They are lives that cannot help but interest and provoke any curious mind, and cannot fail to edify anyone sharing their challenging profession.

Austin Pendleton

A Broad Spectrum of Effort

ARLY ONE SUMMER MORNING in 1957, seventeen-year-old Austin Pendleton was jostled from his sleep. Putting on his glasses, he made out the figure of a fellow Williamstown Theatre Festival intern standing over him. "It's Nikos," said the messenger, naming the theater's artistic director, Nikos Psacharopoulos. "He wants you in his office right away."

Two minutes later, Pendleton—disheveled, half-awake—was sitting in Psacharopoulos' book-lined office just off the lobby of the theater. Pendleton searched his mind for the reason behind the dawn summons. Had he done something wrong?

Psacharopoulos stared doubtfully across his desk at Pendleton. Finally, he spoke. The final WTF production was Shaw's *Caesar and Cleopatra,* he told the intern, and he had no one to play the young king, Ptolemy Dionysus, brother of Cleopatra. He had called every actor he knew in New York to no avail. It was now Saturday morning. The show was opening in 84 hours.

Pendleton glimpsed a ray of hope—a role. A speaking role. A Shavian speaking role. It was his first year as an intern, and the season had nearly passed without his being called upon to take the stage in any Williamstown production. This was his big chance. He knew he could do it. Yes, there was his stutter to contend with, but if they could only see him in action.

"You've acted in high school, you say," Psacharopoulos began tentatively, "and you. . ."—he searched for the appropriate euphemistic term—*"managed* all right?" Pendleton, as eager as Ruby Keeler in *42nd Street,* assured him that he had. Psacharopoulos paused for what seemed like a lifetime. Finally, he sighed and sent the teenager off to the theater. Three days later, *Caesar and Cleopatra* opened. The show, and Pendleton, were a success.

Since that fateful morning, when Nikos Psacharopoulos gave him, arguably, the biggest break of his career, Pendleton has returned to Williamstown for seventeen summers, acting in nearly two dozen plays and directing nearly a dozen more. After Psacharopoulos' death, in 1989, he was even briefly considered as his one-time doubting mentor's successor. The stuttering English major from Ohio has never worked outside the performing arts since.

Psacharopoulos was not narrow-minded. He had every justification for questioning young Pendleton's ambitions. As an aspiring actor, he cut a figure bespeaking anything but. Awkward, scrawny, bespectacled, a stutterer since age seven, there was little in the teenager that would communicate: Actor. But Psacharopoulos didn't take into account one signifying fact about his young Ptolemy. Austin Pendleton was virtually born in a theater.

Born in a Theater   Austin Pendleton was born on March 27, 1940, in Youngstown, Ohio, and raised in nearby Warren, both heavy-industry centers that have since grown together. Austin's father, Thorn Pendleton, was the owner of the Warren Tool Company, a maker of implements such as pickaxes and sledgehammers. He married twenty-six-year-old Michigan native Frances Manchester in 1938. She had spent a year as an actor at the Cleveland Play House, and had lived for a while in New York City.

The Pendletons went on to have two other children: Alec, in 1941, and Margaret, in 1945. With World War II over and her last child born, Frances returned to what would prove a lifelong interest in the theater. She became involved in a new community group, the Trumbull New Theatre, named for the county and called TNT for short. The company's first two productions were Noël Coward's *Hay Fever* and Philip Barry's *Hotel Universe*. Both productions were rehearsed and performed in the Pendleton home on West Market Street. "They would hang up a curtain in the living room," remembered Pendleton. "All the furniture would be cleared out, they would put in folding chairs, and you could seat maybe fifty people. On the other side of the curtain was the playing area."

Frances directed *Hotel Universe*, a drama which had proved a flop for Barry when it premiered on Broadway in 1930. (Her interest in the work persisted; she would mount it again seven years later with the same group.) Every night, the cast of nine would congregate in the Pendleton house to attempt art. The goings-on had a profound effect on the six-year-old Austin.

"What would impress me," recalled Pendleton, "is that for weeks they would rehearse, and often in our house. And, in fact, these rehearsals continued even after they began to perform the plays in other places. It was just thrilling to me. They probably worked in the mills, they worked as secretaries in offices, they were receptionists for doctors, or they were doctors or lawyers, and they would come over after dinner and there would be coffee and they'd rehearse for three hours in the course of the evening.

"We would be sent up to bed, and I would sneak down, as would Alec, and we'd hide and watch the rehearsals. And of course, on the nights of the performances, we'd stay up and watch them."

The following season, TNT began to rent auditoriums, and there were no more opening nights on West Market Street. But the damage had been done: "From that moment on," Pendleton said, "I had no doubt at all that I wanted to go into the theater."

An Emerging Determination Pendleton's first instruction in acting came at the hands of his mother. Every Christmas, the theater would spoof an old-fashioned melodrama. One victim was called *Gold in the Hills*, in which Pendleton landed his first TNT role, playing an orphan alongside his mother and father. At age ten, he knew only that he wanted to act. He did not know *how* to act.

"Before we would go into rehearsals, I remember, my mother would coach me, because I didn't know anything about acting. She would ask me things like:

'Where are you coming from?,' 'Is it cold, is it warm?,' 'Who are you?,' 'What just happened before you came on?' I had no clue that any of that was important. Before I knew all that, I didn't know how to function at rehearsal."

In 1954, his parents moved to the other side of town to a house on Atlantic Street, and young Austin's theatrical ambitions entered a new phase. Rather than depend on the fluctuating need for child actors at TNT, he and his friends formed their own company, taking turns acting in and directing productions in the Pendletons' basement. They called themselves the Atlantic Players.

The group of about a half-dozen or so rehearsed often and staged what Pendleton termed "a series of shows of escalating ambition." They inaugurated the company with an evening of one-acts, featuring a deadly serious adaptation of Edgar Allan Poe's "The Tell-Tale Heart" and the third act of Thornton Wilder's *Our Town*. They would go on to mount Agatha Christie's *Ten Little Indians*, George S. Kaufman and Moss Hart's *You Can't Take It With You* (directed by Mrs. Pendleton), Patrick Hamilton's *Angel Street*, and Tennessee Williams's *The Glass Menagerie*.

Pendleton's stutter had emerged at age seven and had not abated by high school. It proved trying at rehearsals, but the heightened sensation of performance usually caused it to disappear. He proved a capable performer. He was not, however, always lucky. In *Angel Street*, a melodrama which had premiered on Broadway just two days before Pearl Harbor, he played the lengthy lead role of a detective. Unlike his experience in previous plays, his stammer did not evaporate upon meeting an audience.

"Only in the third act, where the detective kind of loses it, was I fluent," said Pendleton. "The first two acts, which are endless questioning and exposition, were more endless in this production. And no one knew what to do. The director, who was a friend of mine, a sweet guy, didn't know what to do. And everyone kept thinking, 'It will go away once the audience comes,' because there had been instances when that had happened. But it didn't. It was a nightmare.

"I was obsessed with theater from when I was in *Gold in the Hills*," explained Pendleton. "My parents were very concerned for me. It's not that they didn't want me to [pursue theater]. But I had this awful speech defect. Really, I mean I was inarticulate. But I was just determined I was going to be an actor. It's like the person who's crippled who's decided he was going to be a track runner.

"I usually did well [onstage], which, of course, fueled my desire to be an actor. I would get up there and somehow—even if I'd had trouble in rehearsal—it would go away. That's still what drives me to act as much as I do. It's still like an obsession, and it has its origins in that."

An Apprenticeship Pendleton attended the Warren public school system through the ninth grade, after which he spent the workweeks at University School, a high-toned prep school in the posh Cleveland suburb of Shaker Heights. True to its no-nonsense name, University School had a reputation for getting its students into the university of their choice. Of course, you had to know what your choice was. So in the spring of his junior year, Pendleton journeyed east, along with his father and brother Alec to inspect prospective alma maters.

The trip was brief and resolute. Once the car stopped in New Haven, Connecticut, Pendleton did not need to look further. "The moment I walked on the campus of Yale, I knew I wanted to go." He was given an interview with the dean, and it was there he realized that the value of the Atlantic Players stretched far beyond Trumbull County.

"A real shift happened in the second half of the 1950s, where they would ask you things having to do as much with your extracurricular activities as with your grades," said Pendleton. "They were trying to break down the hierarchical system. They were looking for a diversification in people. [The dean] asked me about the Atlantic Players, this group I had been in, and he got really interested in that. I got okay grades at University School, but it was that combined with the players that interested him. That had a lot to do with my being accepted at Yale."

The budding Yalie had one other significant encounter that trip. As the caravan stopped in Williamstown, Massachusetts, to inspect Williams College—where his father had earned his degree and his brother would go to school—the family spied a bill on the wall of the Adams Memorial Theatre. It was a poster for the Williamstown Theatre Festival, which had begun only the previous season. "There were pictures of their productions," Pendleton remembered. "Ambitious things, not like summer theater. We saw that the artistic director was this man by the name of Nikos Psacharopoulos. My father asked someone at the theater if they had apprentices." Williamstown was non-Equity in 1956, so it was not allowed to foster apprentices. The next year, however, the theater was "going union" and would begin an apprentice program. Austin resolved to go.

In the spring of 1957, Pendleton traveled east once again, this time to Manhattan for the Williamstown apprentice tryouts. Along for the ride were a friend of his mother's, serving as chaperone, and Lila Corbin, a cousin and fellow Atlantic Player who also had dreams of becoming an actor. They lodged for the week at the then-affordable Algonquin Hotel. During the day, they strained at their audition pieces for hours on end. At night, for inspiration, they feasted on Broadway: *The Most Happy Fella, Separate Tables, My Fair Lady, Long Day's Journey into Night*; and, off-Broadway, *The Threepenny Opera*, at the Theatre de Lys.

To young Austin and Lila, their first professional audition was a triumph. Each delivered a classical monologue, and, as Tom and Amanda, they enacted a scene from that Atlantic Players' triumph, *The Glass Menagerie*.

"We thought we had done splendidly," Pendleton recalled. "We were on a false high. We had major fantasies. This was in the heyday of Broadway; this was in the day of *Theater Arts* magazine, which would arrive in Warren every month— and we would just devour it. We just thought we were going to be found. We thought that they weren't just going to accept us as apprentices, but were going to say 'Oh, my God!,' and soon the word would get around New York. We were going to land on Broadway fairly soon."

After the Saturday morning audition, the Warren warriors turned their car around and sped back home, arriving in time to catch the final performance of the Atlantic Players' rendering of *The King of Hearts*—which would turn out to be the troupe's swan song.

Acclaim from the east was slow in coming. Day after day, Austin and Lila emptied mailboxes bereft of Massachusetts postmarks. April passed. May. Reality slowly began to set in. Then, in early June, two weeks before the beginning of the Williamstown Theatre Festival's 1957 season, just as Pendleton was beginning to look forward to a carefree summer in Warren, a letter arrived accepting him as an apprentice. Lila was accepted as well.

There were eleven apprentices that year, matched by the same number of company members. In those first summers, Williamstown had only the one theater, a traditional proscenium stage facing a large, sloping auditorium. It was an eight-show season: John Patrick's *Teahouse of the August Moon*, Guy Bolton's *Anastasia*, William Douglas Home's *The Reluctant Debutante*, Arthur Miller's *A View from the Bridge*, Terence Rattigan's *The Sleeping Prince*, Jean Giraudoux's *The Enchanted*, Tennessee Williams's *Orpheus Descending*, and Shaw's *Caesar and Cleopatra*.

A new show opened every week of the season, and the apprentices contributed heavily to the mounting of each one. Pendleton saw the plays come and go, but he never took the stage in any one of them until the last.

After being rudely awakened that Saturday morning by Psacharopoulos' decree, he was rushed into rehearsal. Because the company was acutely afraid that, if exhausted, their Ptolemy might not be able to speak, Pendleton was given few other duties during those days. Opening night was cathartic for all, Pendleton remembered: "When I did well on the opening night, people were just sobbing. Psacharopoulos was very proud. It was the beginning of probably the most artistically significant relationship in my life."

Big Man on Campus As it happened, Psacharopoulos taught at Yale and was the director of the Yale Dramatic Association, the university's undergraduate extracurricular group, informally known as the Dramat. Through that serendipitous connection, Pendleton's small reputation preceded him before he set foot on the campus in the fall of 1957. And enough was made of his appearance in *Caesar and Cleopatra* that he was soon approached about appearing in the Freshman One-Acts, an annual evening of original plays directed by upperclassmen and cast entirely with freshmen. One of those upperclassmen was Broadway lyricist and director-to-be Richard Maltby, Jr., who cast Pendleton in the title role in a Western parody called "Stranger in These Parts." According to the *Yale Daily News*, it was a smashing debut.

"Stranger in These Parts" played only twice, but it established Pendleton at Yale. He was asked to take part in scenes presented in directing classes. Psacharopoulos, who directed the Dramat's three mainstage productions, cast him in a small part in Wilder's *The Skin of Our Teeth,* and a musical adaptation of *Cyrano de Bergerac,* by Maltby and David Shire, another Yalie.

That summer, no longer a stuttering youth but Austin Pendleton of Yale, he returned to apprenticeship at Williamstown. He essayed several small roles. The number of apprentices had doubled. Among them was Katina Commings, his future wife. "It was clear, in 1958, that a lot more people had auditioned. I always suspected that the reason there were eleven apprentices the first year was that there were eleven who had auditioned."

The apprentice program now offered acting classes for the first time, the first he had taken in his life. As Leland Starnes taught the principles of Stanislavsky acting, Austin heard echoes of his mother's instruction at the Trumbull New Theatre: "Who are you?," "What just happened before you came on?"

The following summer, instead of Williamstown, Pendleton went to New York. He had been hired for his first professional job, the off-Broadway production of a British revue called *Share My Lettuce.* He roomed with Bill Hinnant, a Yale actor and a bit of a local legend. Following two years at college, Hinnant had netted a role on Broadway in *No Time for Sergeants* and did not return to finish his degree for another two years. He and Austin became friends, and when Pendleton got his own mid-college-career break, he bunked with the older actor.

Neither the roommate situation nor the play worked out. Hinnant and Pendleton parted company after two weeks, and Pendleton retreated to the YMCA. His stint in *Share My Lettuce* didn't last much longer. "I got fired from it," he remembered. "They were very sweet about it, but I don't remember the explanation." Pendleton had been on a roll that had started with *Caesar and Cleopatra.* Now it was ending.

Seeds of a Playwright
By 1958, Pendleton had become a big fan of the musical comedy genre and had resolved to write one himself. Teaming up with a composer and lyricist, he wrote the book for a show based on Fielding's classic novel, *Tom Jones.* The show was accepted by the Dramat and performed the following spring. The composer of *Tom Jones* graduated soon after, so, in his senior year, Pendleton paired up with a composer named Jim Massingale.

"Jim was a very quiet, shy, intense, talented guy. And I said, 'What do you want to write a show about?' He said, 'Well, I want to set it in nineteenth-century America.'" Pendleton recalled a Edwin Booth biography, *Prince of Players,* by Eleanor Ruggles, that he had read in high school. He found the book and reread the first sixty pages, which detailed Edwin's journeys around the country with his father, the thespian Junius Booth, and suggested it to Massingale.

Pendleton, Massingale, and lyricist Peter Bergman spent their senior year working on *Booth Is Back in Town*. The production was directed by Leland Starnes and designed by a young John Conklin. Edwin Booth was played by Philip Proctor. Halfway through Act II on opening night, as Pendleton stood at the back of the theater, Bergman (who, with Proctor, would go on to form the famed comedy team Fireside Theatre) sidled up to him and said, "I have terrible news for you. It's quarter to midnight." And the show went on another thirty minutes, ending at 12:15 A.M.

The three-and-a-half-hour show was a flop. "It was very dark," said Pendleton. "The music, which I still love, was a cross between Stephen Foster and Kurt Weill." But people left after the three-hour mark.

The show was at the end of Pendleton's college career, but his fascination with the material would continue. He would work fitfully on an Edwin Booth show for the next thirty years.

How to Audition for a Play   During his senior year, Pendleton read an article about a Phi Beta Kappa tyro from Harvard named Arthur Kopit, who had written an absurdist fever-dream of a play with the improbable title of *Oh Dad, Poor Dad, Mama's Hung You in the Closet and I'm Feelin' So Sad*.

In this play, the titular father arrives, deceased and in his coffin, at the Cuban holiday digs of the tyrannical, man-eating Madame Rosepettle as just another piece of her luggage. Madame keeps a piranha, venus flytraps, and one son, Jonathan, a bookish, cloistered, stuttering youth. When not being completely cowed by his mother, Jonathan is fighting off the predatory advances of the innocent-seeming babysitter, Rosalie.

"That kind of crazy writing was just coming into vogue," Pendleton recalled. "And those kinds of characters that were screwed up and eccentric made my name."

Kopit's play had sent normally sober producers into a feeding frenzy. Performed at Harvard, it was published by Hill & Wang in August of 1960. "The play was published before it had a production," remembered Pendleton, "which was unheard of." Roger Stevens and Hugh Beaumont eventually landed the producing rights and announced that they intended to stage it in New York. Then it was London, then New York again. The play was finally mounted at the Lyric Hammersmith, in London, starring Stella Adler and Andrew Ray. Frank Corsaro directed. It folded after only a week and a half.

Meanwhile, back in New York, Pendleton bought the playscript in a Grand Central Station bookshop and read it on the train to New Haven. "I knew that if I could ever get an audition for that part, I would get it," he recalled.

In the fall of 1961, an entirely new production of *Oh Dad* was announced, piloted by choreographer Jerome Robbins, in his play-directing debut. Pendleton set about getting an audition for the part he knew he could land.

"I started going to agents saying, 'Would you submit me for this play?'" Pendleton recounted. "And they kept saying 'Oh, we don't know your work, and we just can't send someone we don't know to Jerome Robbins. What have you done?'" He would then tick off his Yale and Williamstown credits, and the interview would end. "This went on all fall, on and off."

Then he got a call from actress Nancy Donahue, who had been an apprentice at Williamstown and had an agent named Deborah Coleman. She had just been to see Coleman, who said Robbins was having a difficult time casting the role of Jonathan. Donahue asked Coleman to meet with Pendleton. He showed up at the agent's door on Friday, December 1. Recalled Pendleton: "She said, 'Well, you look right for this part, and they can't cast it. I'm going to send you over to see [casting director] Terry Fay this afternoon.'"

He saw Fay at 5 o'clock. "She was exhausted. We talked for a little while, and she said, 'Oh, I'm just going to go on instinct here. I'm going to give you an audition. You seem right for it.'"

Pendleton's audition was for the following Tuesday. "All that weekend, I rehearsed it as if it were a production. I got two different actors to work with me. I learned up to three-quarters of the part. I rehearsed it hour after hour, as if the show were running and I was going into it."

On Tuesday afternoon, Pendleton reported to the set of *Mary, Mary*, at the Helen Hayes Theatre. He was early and sat near the stage door watching actors he recognized pass him on their way to the stage—dozens of the hundreds who would eventually audition before the choreographer of *West Side Story* for the role of Jonathan. His 3:15 slot came and went. Finally, around 5:30, Robbins' assistant, the actor William Daniels, came through the stage door and asked, "Who are you?" Pendleton said he had an appointment. "Let me run back in," said Daniels. "I think Arthur's gone but Jerry's putting on his coat." Pendleton was shown in. Robbins took off his coat.

"So we started," he remembered. "First of all, I had never acted with someone as good as Bill Daniels. Then, I noticed after a while we were well into the scene and it hadn't been stopped. Then, about two-thirds into the scene, Jonathan had this long speech. So I got into that, and by this time I was hardly looking at the script. When I looked at Bill Daniels, who was looking out into the audience nodding his head to Jerry—then I knew."

Afterwards, Robbins came onto the stage and said, in mock accusation, "That's the best audition I've ever seen for a play. Have you worked on it?"

"If you've learned the lines, you're not supposed to let them know that at an audition," commented Pendleton. "I said, 'Well, yeah, it's published.'" Then Robbins, impressed with the natural hesitancy of Pendleton's delivery, asked him if he stuttered. "I said a little bit. Which was a lie."

Robbins asked him to return in three days to audition for Arthur Kopit. "I was very excited. I thought, I've got this part. I auditioned two hours ago for Jerome Robbins; he said it was the best audition he had ever seen. I just couldn't believe it." Friday, however, did not go as well. Robbins came onstage afterward, again pleasant, but uneasy. Kopit was polite, but noncommittal.

Pendleton was convinced he had now lost the part. His instinct was to go out with a few of the five roommates with whom he shared an apartment at 108th Street and Riverside Drive and get drunk. The next day, he went to the laundromat, washed his clothes, and slowly got used to the fact that he wouldn't be starring off-Broadway as soon as he'd thought.

Back at the apartment, the phone rang. From the other end came the magic, almost unbelievable words: "This is Jerome Robbins. Could you come and see me?" Pendleton raced to the director's East 74th Street townhouse. "Look," said Robbins, "Arthur didn't like your audition. But we've got to try to convince him somehow." Robbins told him to work on the lines and report again the next Tuesday. After Pendleton's third audition, Robbins was again excited, but Kopit remained unswayed. Pendleton returned two more times, but made no headway with the young playwright.

Pendleton flew home to Ohio for Christmas and spent the holiday again convinced that he had lost the role. On the 27th, he got a call from Coleman, who was by now his *de facto* agent. "You have another audition tomorrow morning," reported Coleman. His parents drove him to Youngstown Airport that evening. The following morning, he read with Barbara Harris, who would go on to play the part of Rosalie. "That audition worked the way the first one worked," recalled Pendleton. As the actor left the stage, Robbins told him he had the part.

"The Worst Year of My Life"
Austin Pendleton—neophyte, unknown, discovery of Jerome Robbins—would remember his twelve months as a star of *Oh Dad* as the worst year of his life. Certainly, there was an excitement and ecstasy to making his New York debut, but there was also a tension that sang through the whole experience, most of it attributable to youth and inexperience. Pendleton's neuroses found their echoes in his co-stars: Jo Van Fleet, an actress with demons of her own; and Barbara Harris, a breakout performer squirming under a suddenly hot spotlight.

The company began rehearsing in January. Pendleton would frequently be handed over to William Daniels, who would coach him. Often the two put in extra hours after dinner. "It became apparent to me, and I think to the others, that I didn't know how to act yet," explained Pendleton. "I didn't have a fully developed craft. I would find moments and try to hang on to them, and they'd lose all their spontaneity. I made all kinds of primitive young-actors' errors. It was hard work. Bill was in effect having to teach me how to rehearse a role. I learned an awful lot from that experience."

Finding the essence of the show was as difficult as it no doubt had been in the play's previous, aborted productions. But during its ten previews at the

Photo courtesy of Photofest

Austin Pendleton and Jo Van Fleet in the original 1962 Phoenix Theatre production of Arthur Kopit's *Oh Dad, Poor Dad, Mama's Hung You in the Closet and I'm Feelin' So Sad.*

Phoenix Theatre on East 74th Street, the show proved a crowd pleaser. On Monday, February 26, at 7:30, the press arrived on a rain-soaked night primed with a year's worth of fanfare: Kopit, *wunderkind* playwright; the celebrated Robbins in his directorial debut; Van Fleet, recent Tony and Oscar recipient.

"Opening night sat there like an egg," said Pendleton, relating the anticlimax. "It was appalling. Nobody laughed. It just went off the tracks. It just didn't work. Nobody knew what to say afterwards."

Except, of course, the critics. The *Daily News* called it "a total bust." *Newsday*'s George Oppenheimer labeled it "an avant-garde comic strip . . . less the theater of the absurd than the theater of the absolutely ridiculous." The *Herald-Tribune*'s sage Walter Kerr termed the play "an anti-feminist demonstration scored for tin bugles, toy drums, and kazoos." The *New York Times*'s notice was favorable, calling it "halting and bemused," but added: "If you don't insist on a full measure of sense, Mr. Kopit has a fanciful, droll, lurid way with the theater." Not the reception an already-published play's ballyhooed, pre-sold production might expect.

Harris received the most praise, and Van Fleet got her measure. Pendleton was, in his words, "dismissed, but with respect." His reviews were positive, but meted out finely; most of them succinctly pronounced his performance "good" or "right." Kerr did note that Pendleton was, "in the guise of a teddy-bear with all the stuff let out, fine."

Pendleton had left the cast party for his own party at Sardi's East, an offshoot of the famed theatrical restaurant (it operated for only a couple of years in the early '60s). After a while, his friend Joe Mathewson—a future novelist and playwright but then a copy boy at the *Times*—came through the door with the reviews. "Then, to our horror, the door swung open, and in came the Arthur Kopit family," recalled Pendleton. "They had obviously come in to sit down, because it had been an even more catastrophic night for Arthur than for me." The atmosphere was strained; Pendleton was sharing the room with the man who refused him a role through four auditions. Then, spying Mathewson, Kopit asked him to read the notices—aloud. "It was awful," said Pendleton.

The cast had the next day off, and Pendleton stared out at the continuing rain, very depressed. "I thought I'd had my chance and blown it." But Wednesday night went as well as the previews had gone and the second batch of reviews, from the weeklies and magazines, were more sanguine. The show survived on the Phoenix subscription list for a while, then the word of mouth kicked in, aided by the astonishing announcement that Richard Rodgers and Alan Jay Lerner had decided to write a musical catered to the talents of Barbara Harris. (Rodgers dropped out, replaced by Burton Lane; the show became *On a Clear Day, You Can See Forever.*) *Oh Dad* would break off-Broadway records for box office grosses and continue running for 454 performances.

Though now an off-Broadway actor, Pendleton was in many ways still the Austin Pendleton of Atlantic Street. "About two or three weeks after we opened," related Pendleton, "in the early scene with Rosalie, I started to stutter. I got into one of those things I couldn't get out of. That began a thing that went on, where I never knew what was going to happen from night to night." Some nights he would soar in the role, other nights would be torture. A *Montreal Star* critic, viewing the show in late 1962, unwittingly tapped into the teetering nature of the actor's performance, writing, "Austin Pendleton stutters, shakes, and staggers with such extraordinary conviction that you have the uncomfortable feeling this may have been typecasting."

Because of the nervous nature of the role, the audience rarely understood the seriousness of the problem, but the unpredictability wreaked havoc with the cast and was murder on Pendleton. He would spend each day full of anxiety, not knowing what sort of performance he would give that evening.

"I was like a car on an icy road. I was smashing into trees. As a result, I think I was occasionally brilliant. But often, I was embarrassing. . . . I don't know if it was the content of the part, because Jonathan stuttered, or because it was the first time I'd played a part even remotely this long."

In June, after a series of particularly painful performances, the stage manager, Tom Stone, asked Pendleton, "What are you going to do about this? Why don't you get help?" Pendleton went to a speech clinic run by Alfred Dixon, who had been a stutterer. Working on the stutter had a positive psychological effect, but the speech defect still came and went throughout the summer.

Agent Deborah Coleman called and asked Pendleton if he wanted to audition for the training program at the newly found-  ed, as-yet-unbuilt Lincoln Center. The program would entail eight months of training, five days a week, eight hours a day. At the end of the eight months, certain people would be selected for the permanent company. He tried out and was accepted. He per- formed *Oh Dad* at night, and during the day took classes in acting with Robert Lewis, movement with Anna Sokolov, and voice with Arthur Lessac. "That helped enormously," said Pendleton, "because that just began to open up things about act- ing to me."

Still, Lessac was a voice teacher, not a speech therapist. At the end of Janu- ary 1963, the whole matter came to a head. After a Sunday night performance, Pro- ducer T. Edward Hambleton—who became a lifelong friend—called Pendleton in and said he was going to have to replace him with his understudy. The effect of this on Pendleton suggests that the fear of replacement was greater that the fear of stut- tering: "I came to the show the following Tuesday night and soared. I was brilliant and had no trouble at all. Performance after performance was like that. So I went to Hambleton and said, 'Look! I'm all right now!' He said, 'We've already promised your understudy he would go in.' He wouldn't let me stay on."

Pendleton left *Oh Dad* in February, replaced first by his understudy and then by Sam Waterston, in his first big break. "Even though the circumstances of my departure were very painful, it was a huge relief," he remembered.

The Tailor Motel Kamzoil
At the conclusion of the Lincoln Center training pro- gram—where his colleagues included Frank Langella, Faye Dunaway, and Bar- bara Loden—Pendleton received an audience with the head of the program, direc- tor Elia Kazan. "I was ambivalent about whether I wanted to join or not. The idea that I could ever appear on a New York stage again—I didn't think I could. I did- n't know what was the point of my being in the Lincoln Center company." Neither, apparently, did Kazan, who said, "Look, you're obviously not that interested in act- ing, but if you want to be an assistant stage manager or something. . . ." It was his tactful way of saying, "You can't reliably speak."

But even if Kazan had no faith in Pendleton, and Pendleton had lost much of his faith in himself, a man who remembered the best audition he'd ever seen had not. That fall, Jerome Robbins hired Pendleton for a musical, based on the stories of Yiddish writer Sholom Aleichem, to be called *Fiddler on the Roof.* The production was delayed a year as the producers waited on Zero Mostel's availability and Pendleton spent the spare time working on his speech with Lessac and taking act- ing classes with Uta Hagen.

Fiddler began rehearsals on June 8, 1964, and during the next seven weeks of rehearsal and eight weeks on the road, the cast had a total of three days off. Pendleton had originally auditioned for the role of the rebel Perchik, but then Robbins had him read one day for the meek tailor Motel Kamzoil and swiftly cast him. The musical opened at the Fisher Theatre, in Detroit, on July 26.

The review in *Variety* appeared two days later. "Everything is ordinary about *Fiddler on the Roof* except Zero Mostel," the notice read. "He's extraordinary." The review went on to dismiss the show in the most jaded of terms. The word "ordinary" was applied four separate times, though not in regard to the choreography, which was termed, instead, "pedestrian." The songs were unmemorable. Robbins had done a "workmanlike job." Finally, Pendleton "as the tailor, leaves much to be desired." *Variety* decreed that the show "may have a chance as a moderate success on Broadway."

"I remember the night the *Variety* review came out," Pendleton said. "Robbins was sitting at a bar across the street, and I said 'Jerry, what are you going to do?' He said, 'Fix ten things a day.'" That is, every day Robbins would solve ten of the show's problems. There was restaging, and a lot of cuts. The song "Do You Love Me?" was added. Little by little, the show attained clarity.

When it opened at the National Theatre, in Washington, D.C., the reviews were terrific. Still, Robbins continued to work. Pendleton's song, "Now I Have Everything" was given to Perchik, and replaced with a new number, "Miracle of Miracles."

The recurrent criticism was that the second act was too depressing. In response, Robbins conceived an elaborate chorus number near the end of the show called "A Little Bit of This." "We rehearsed and rehearsed this. We were going to put it in the first preview in New York, and it was going to pull the whole second act together—this accent. It was a brilliant Jerome Robbins number, the way it built, the life of it—it was breathtaking " The show arrived in New York, and, prior to the first preview, the cast gathered to rehearse. Robbins looked at his new number on which he had labored for weeks, and said "We're not going to do it. We don't need it. The show is what it is."

"I was awestruck," recalled Pendleton. And from then on, no one who saw the show complained about the second act.

Opening night, on September 22, at the Imperial Theatre was "rather bland," remembered Pendleton. "There was a tension in the audience. I thought the performance was perfectly OK." The reviews were good on the whole; the *Times* was positive, but Walter Kerr at the *Herald-Tribune* chided, "Fiddler dips below its own best possible level by touching character too casually, and sometimes soiling it, with the lesser energies of easy quips, lyrics that stray too far from the land, and occasional high-pressure outbursts that are merely marketable." Pendleton left the cast party thinking that perhaps *Variety* had been right back in Detroit. The next day, however, his path to the dressing room was blocked by a line of 300 people which stretched around the block. Producer Harold Prince announced an advance sale of $650,000, with reservations booked through February 13, 1965.

As with *Oh Dad*, Pendleton stayed with the show for near-ly a year. However, life while playing opposite Zero Mostel—arguably the most combustible personality ever to appear on the American stage—was never easy. Critics, while praising the show, often complained about Mostel's rampant improvisation. Yet, whatever their irritation with his unpredictability may have been, it was only a fraction of that suffered by the performers  onstage. In one scene in particular, when Motel petitions Tevye for his daughter's hand in marriage, Pendleton endured all manner of hijinks. Mostel would strangle him with his tape measure. He would lower his full weight upon the slight actor. "These were not," said Pendleton, "exactly naturalistic observations about Tevye the Dairyman.

"I was enthralled with the man—I just adored him. But a lot of the cast was enraged. There were times when he just stepped over the line. But even then I couldn't get mad at him. The only time I ever got mad at him was one night when we had a big scene and he grabbed me by the balls. I got very angry. Then he sent a member of the chorus to my dressing room, who said, 'Zero wants to know if you're angry at him for *any reason!*'"

Cheers and Boos As the deadline approached for the renewal of his *Fiddler* con-tract, Pendleton received a call from his mother, asking him if he would direct her in *The Glass Menagerie* at the Trumbull New Theatre—a role reversal of the Atlantic Players' triumph of years before.

"I was very secure in *Fiddler on the Roof*," said Pendleton. "It was a place to go every night, being part of this very secure institution. And it was, of course, a job, and, for the theater, an unusually steady job. I said to Harold Prince that I had an offer to go to this community theater and direct, and he lit up. He said, 'You've got to! You have to! You've got to direct!'"

To make the decision easy, Prince offered to take Pendleton back for another year after the directing stint. Pendleton finally decided to go and ended his contract the same night as Mostel. He then traveled back to Warren, to begin what would become a long directing career in the same place where he had discovered acting.

When he returned to New York, he had, for the first time since he had moved to the city, no prospects, and was unemployed all winter. In March, the phone finally rang. William Ball's newly formed American Conservatory Theatre had just played a season in Pittsburgh. While directing in Ohio, Pendleton had driven a couple times to see its productions. The company was now rehearsing in New York and planning to tour. Pendleton was asked to play a variety of utility parts, includ-ing Charley in *Charley's Aunt*, Bernard in *Death of a Salesman*, and Waffles in *Uncle Vanya*. "I said, 'When do you want me there?'"

The tour began in Westport, Connecticut, and ended in Chicago. Suddenly, within a span of months, Pendleton had tripled his professional stage credits.

"Those months with A.C.T.—all those classes—when you're in training as an actor you learn a lot of things with your voice that the usual person who has a speech impediment doesn't have access to. And being thrown onto the stage for a whole year, you just learn things on your feet. I had this whole new security."

And it showed, shortly after the A.C.T. tour, in *Hail, Scrawdyke!*, the first play by Englishman David Halliwell, in which Pendleton landed a role for the Broadway premiere. It told the sordid story of four foolish and slightly fascistic Norfolk, England, art students and their ineffectual yet disturbing rebellion against the establishment. Predating the student riots of the '60s, it stood as something of a bridge between Britain's "Angry Young Men" plays of the late '50s and the coming artistic anarchy. While the play hadn't done well in its English incarnations, the New York production had a certain cachet. The star Alan Arkin directed, and Victor Henry, who had made a splash in London the previous year, starred as Malcolm Scrawdyke. Even the Beatles and Brian Epstein had invested $5,000 in the show.

The reception, however, was not kind. Most notices were negative, and the play closed on December 5, 1966, after eight performances at the Booth Theatre. While barely making a dent in Broadway history, the production nonetheless became a milestone in Pendleton's career. Though the play had been panned, the reviews of his performance, as one of the four students, had been good. The true impact of this critical reception, however, was delayed and powerful. In an article reviewing the 1966–67 season, Walter Kerr, now with the *New York Times*, miraculously recalled Pendleton's performance as the shy, awkward Irwin Ingham: "He was not only infinitely appealing, he was the quiet, skimpy sort of actor who knows so well what he is about that he is able to make you attend to him while he seems to be erasing himself altogether." Kerr was a judge on the panel for that season's Clarence Derwent Award, given every year by Actors' Equity Association. That year's prize went to Pendleton.

"It was the first time I had taken a role and really been able to flourish in a reliable way artistically," explained Pendleton. "It was a turning point in the way I was perceived as an actor. I zoomed up in people's estimations."

At the end of its tour, the A.C.T. received residency invitations from both San Francisco and Chicago, and Ball eventually decided on San Francisco. He invited Pendleton back for A.C.T.'s first California season. After *Hail, Scrawdyke!* closed, the actor accepted, leaving for the coast in January of 1967. During that second year, he played Konstantin in *The Seagull*, Damis in *Tartuffe*, Dr. Einstein in *Arsenic and Old Lace*, and a role in George Kelly's *The Torchbearers*.

Pendleton was not liked by the Bay Area critics. "It was the first time I had been singled out as a bad actor," he remarked. "I didn't get all terrific reviews in those days, but I don't think I ever got a bad review. All of a sudden, I was this pariah with the press. As the years go by, that kind of thing gets easier to absorb. But when it first happens, it's completely shocking." The experience was, in Pendleton's words, "the great inoculation."

Fortunately, Pendleton's A.C.T. reviews were not on the desk of producer Saint Subber one tense day in May of 1967. The announcement picturing that year's Clarence Derwent award-winners was. Subber had a headache over the casting of a production of Lillian Hellman's *The Little Foxes* that wunderkind director Mike Nichols was putting together. They had offered the role of Oscar's malevolent son Leo to Dustin Hoffman. But Hoffman, newly a star thanks to Nichols' casting him in *The Graduate*, was vacillating.

Subber's phone rang. "Get me somebody else to play Leo," yelled Nichols. "What do you want?" asked Subber. "I want a young character actor." His head pounding, Subber's gaze drifted down to his desk and landed on the photo of the Derwent winner. "How about Austin Pendleton?" he offered. Nichols barked, "Take him!"

Fairy-tale stories don't always have fairy-tale endings. And not long after *The Little Foxes* began rehearsals, Nichols began to regret his casting of Pendleton sight unseen. "He thought I was miscast," recalled the actor. "He came up to me after the first day or two and said, 'You're really wrong for this. You're going to have to work hard on this.' So he spent a lot of rehearsals being unhappy with what I was doing and not knowing what to do about it. There was one time we had a run-through and he gave a lot of notes to everybody and he didn't give any to me. I went up to him afterwards, and said, 'You didn't give me any notes.' And he said, 'Well, it's all wrong. I don't know what to say.'"

Not knowing where to turn, Pendleton confided in Anne Bancroft, who was playing the lead role, Regina. The next day she returned with a piece of advice. "You walk wrong," declared Bancroft. "That's what's bothering him. Here's how you walk: You lead with your head because you're secure in your mind. Leo is stupid. He would lead with his groin. You walk right, other things will start to happen to you."

"So she made me practice in her dressing room," related Pendleton. "Then I went out on the stage to rehearse. Mike said, 'This is better.' He didn't know why, and I didn't want to tell him, because I didn't want him to know Anne was working with me."

Like many Nichols productions to come, *The Little Foxes* was star-driven. The cast included Bancroft, E.G. Marshall, George C. Scott, Maria Tucci, and Richard Dysart. It opened on October 26, 1967 to largely good reviews, including those for Pendleton. The *New York Post* called him "excellent," and the *Times*'s Clive Barnes praised his "stylish portrait of the rat-minded son." There were some visible remnants of the recent director–actor conflict, however. The *Morning Telegraph's* Whitney Bolton disliked Pendleton's sniveling Leo as a wrongheaded performance. He laid the blame, however, at the feet of what he deemed Nichols' indulgent, lax direction.

Skidoo Mike Nichols would bear no animosity toward Pendleton, and would, in fact, go on to cast him in the film *Catch-22*, the actor's second film. The first was *Skidoo*, in which Pendleton had the fortune — or misfortune, depending on how you view it — of being baptized in film by the famously despotic Otto Preminger, a director "with the personality of a producer," as one film critic put it.

Skidoo was the story of a counterculture mix of hippies and mobsters written by Bill Cannon, a friend of Pendleton's. The actor flew out to San Francisco for a screen test in the spring of 1968. He was picked up by Preminger outside his hotel and spent the half-hour ride to the set chatting with the director about politics. Once they arrived, however, Preminger dispensed with the audition. "Take Mr. Pendleton back to the hotel," he commanded the driver. "We don't need to do a test. I like you. I like talking to you. I want you to have the part."

Pendleton reported to Los Angeles a couple of weeks later and began filming. For the first week or so he was miserable, he remembered. Preminger "was very autocratic on the set. Whatever spontaneity I had was being killed, and I was very uncomfortable in film. I'd never done one."

Finally, one day, Preminger wheeled on the actor and thundered, "You are an amateur!" Pendleton, at wit's end, replied, "I know! What are we going to do about it?!"

"He turned on a dime," said Pendleton. "He said, 'Oh, I didn't mean you're an amateur, just that you are learning how to do film.' And from that point on, he was terrific with me, and I began to see why there had been so many good performances in Otto Preminger films."

The movie — Preminger's sole stab at screwball comedy — is famous for being a flop. Its odd-duck status is communicated simply by a roll call of its cast: Carol Channing, Jackie Gleason, Harry Nilsson, Mickey Rooney, Frankie Avalon, and Groucho Marx in his last performance. Its peculiarity has over the years earned it the rank of cult classic. "It's one of those undismissable disasters," Pendleton remarked.

Soon after came *Catch-22*, Nichols' film based on Joseph Heller's satiric antiwar bestseller. Pendleton shared all his scenes with that film royal, Orson Welles, by then long in decline and hovering somewhere between legend and has-been. "He was difficult," stated Pendleton. "He had wanted to direct a film of *Catch-22*, so that added to it. Every scene he had, had me in it; every scene I had, had him in it. When we were acting, he was impossible. He would interrupt a take if he didn't like the way you were doing something. He didn't act with you at all."

Bill Cannon had another script, *Brewster McCloud*, in which he wanted Pendleton to star. By the time he got Robert Altman interested, however, the director would not hear of casting an actor who, earlier, had turned down the role of Radar in *M*A*S*H* because he hadn't liked the script.

"That cut me out of that whole Robert Altman roster," said Pendleton. "I didn't know who Altman was at the time. And he was really angry at me for that, so when his next film was *Brewster McCloud* and Bill Cannon proposed me, he wouldn't even consider it. That was the biggest mistake I ever made. Not so much because I didn't get to play Radar, but because of all those Altman movies. He used the same people over and over again. I've always regretted it."

The Best Sweet Days of Austin Gretchen Cryer had lived in
New Haven at the same time as Pendleton while her husband was a divinity student. She had had an off-campus typing job and occasionally appeared in Yale stage productions, and there she met Pendleton. She had since begun a career in the theater, and had written (with composer Nancy Ford) and starred in an off-Broadway revue called *Now Is the Time for All Good Men.* She and Ford had a new musical called *The Last Sweet Days of Isaac,* and Pendleton was cast in the title role.

Pendleton's stature as an actor had grown over the decade, through praised performances in supporting roles. In *Isaac,* he would be asked to carry a show, and a musical, no less. Ford and Cryer's creation was very much of its time: two independent, but obliquely connected, one-acts. Austin's character is a fabulist, half-Romeo, half-pop philosopher who is obsessed with the manner in which he lives and hauls around a tape recorder and camera, intent on making art out of his recorded life. In the first act, "The Elevator," Isaac gets trapped between floors with Ingrid, a repressed secretary (played by Fredericka Weber and, later, Alice Playten) whom he gradually seduces into a *carpe diem* tryst. In the second piece, "I Want to Walk to San Francisco," Isaac is nineteen and put in jail for participation in an antiwar demonstration. There he watches television footage of the riot in which his camera strap gets tangled in a police car bumper and strangles him.

Isaac was set to open at the Eastside Playhouse, the same theater where *Oh Dad* had premiered. The director was Word Baker, who had directed *The Fantasticks*; a 1958 revival of *The Crucible* which had reversed the reputation of that play; and Ford and Cryer's *Now Is the Time for All Good Men.* He was, according to Pendleton, "in a harmless way a very temperamental kind of guy . . . [who] gave off the impression of not knowing what he was doing.

"The show was in big trouble in previews. Haila Stoddard, the producer, would say [of Baker]: 'He can't pull it together.' She ordered that the day after we opened the sets should be taken away, because the previews were so bad. The show had a very particular sense of humor to it, and it just wasn't happening. The audience didn't know what to think of it."

Baker, however, persevered. One night, just days before the press opening, he got the show to work, and the opening, on January 26, 1970, was as big a success as anyone could have hoped. Nearly every critic liked it. The *New York Times*'s Clive Barnes said, "I do not mean it dyslogistically, but Mr. Pendleton must be the most articulate inarticulate actor in the world today. He positively glitters with dimness and yet is radiant with understanding." John Simon of *New York* said, "I have undoubtedly overpraised *Isaac*; but this, in its funny way, is just what it deserved." Many reviewers mentioned a hilarious sequence in the elevator scene where Isaac tries to remove Ingrid's skirt with his toe. Martin Washburn of the *Village Voice* hailed Pendleton's performance as "played with much charm and a relieving note of nastiness."

Except for the Derwent award, Pendleton received all the acting awards he has gotten so far for *The Last Sweet Days of Isaac*: An Obie, a Drama Desk award, and the *Variety* Critics Poll award. "It was very exciting," he remembered. "And wildly disorienting. I kept thinking that I would not be able to keep up the performance. But I was now much more secure as an actor." He stayed with the show during its entire eighteen-month run, and, on November 16, 1970, during a month-long off-Broadway actors' strike, married his longtime sweetheart, Katina.

Shortly after *Isaac* closed, in May of 1971, Pendleton began work on what may possibly be his best known film performance. The film was *What's Up, Doc?*, and he asked its director, Peter Bogdanovich—who had met Pendleton on the set of *Catch-22*, where the director and film historian had interviewed Orson Welles—

Austin Pendleton and Alice Playten in Ford and Cryer's *The Last Sweet Days of Isaac,* in the spring of 1970.

Photo courtesy of Photofest.

if he could have an audition. Bogdanovich was hesitant: "I think of you more as the kind of character you played in *Catch-22*," he said. Pendleton mustered up his courage and fabricated a lie. "I did that as a favor to Mike," he told the incredulous Bogdanovich. "I don't like to play those kind of parts anymore, but for Mike, I did it." The director didn't challenge the claim, and the next week Pendleton read for and got the role of the effete foundation president, Mr. Larrabee.

What's Up, Doc? was Bogdanovich's attempt to recreate the energy of the screwball comedies of the 1930s—specifically the Howard Hawks classic, *Bringing Up Baby*. The filming process presented Pendleton with one of the severest acting challenges of his career and his most difficult film acting assignment ever. A familiar concern centered on "all that incredible rapid-fire dialogue," said Pendleton. "We could not do it fast enough. And he would do everything in long master shots, which is now completely out of fashion, as opposed to a bunch of close-ups. So the whole thing had to play in the long master because there was nothing to cut to. It was exhausting, grueling. And I was still insecure about my speech. We'd get in these grooves and I would be terrified. You'd get to the end of a flawless take and everyone was doing fine, and you'd stumble over a word."

Pendleton was at the beginning of one of the short, dense spates of film work that would prove a pattern in his career. This first flurry included *What's Up, Doc?*; *Every Little Crook and Nanny* (with Peter O'Toole and Lynn Redgrave); *The Thief Who Came to Dinner* (with Ryan O'Neal); and the Billy Wilder–directed remake of *The Front Page* (with Jack Lemmon and Walter Matthau). In the latter, Pendleton garnered the best film reviews of his career so far for his portrayal of an escaped convict.

A Change of Direction

As Pendleton's acting profile grew, he was also accumulating credits in another field, which, in just a few years, would come to equal and even overshadow his onstage accomplishments for a while. In 1969, roughly between *Skidoo* and *Isaac*, he and Nikos Psacharopoulos had discussed the roles he might play that season at Williamstown. The Greek director said, "Of course, there's the directing thing." Pendleton remembered, "It was the first time he had ever breathed a word about that." The actor had only one professional directing credit under his belt, directing his mother in *The Glass Menagerie*. But he accepted, suggesting *Tartuffe*, which proved a hit.

Pendleton could not make it to Williamstown the following two summers—in 1970 he was in *The Last Sweet Days of Isaac*; in 1971 he was shooting *What's Up, Doc?*—but he returned his first available summer and directed Chekhov's *Uncle Vanya*. It, too, was a success. "So the first two shows I directed were hits. If they had not been, I might not have continued."

Continue he did. After *Uncle Vanya*, the offers flew in. He was asked to direct an evening of two one-acts by Joanna Glass, "Canadian Gothic" and "American Modern," at a nascent off-Broadway company called Manhattan Theatre Club; an evening of Strindberg for New Haven's Long Wharf Theatre; and Nancy Ford and Gretchen Cryer's first effort since *Isaac*, a Broadway musical, *Shelter.*

The Glass production, performed at the Bohemian Hall on East 73rd Street, was one of MTC's first ventures, and it went well. *Shelter*, in scope and material, furnished Pendleton with his most consuming Broadway assignment to date. The plot, which hinged on society's preoccupation with media and technology, exceeded its predecessors in whimsy. At its center is a TV commercial writer who spends his nights in the studio, awash in an unreal environment created by his computer. Into his world floats an actress whose husband left her that morning. She spends the night. But come morning their idyllic bond is shattered by the arrival of a cleaning woman with whom the writer is having an affair, and, later, his wife.

Finding the correct tone for this unorthodox material harnessed much of Pendleton's energies. At one point, Jerome Robbins took a peek at the show. Afterward, he advised Austin, "You have to get the chemistry working. I don't know what else to say. If the cast has chemistry on opening night, the critics will like it. If they don't, they won't."

Pendleton was already aware that things weren't sparking between three leads, Marcia Rodd, Terry Kiser, and Susan Browning. "The kind of writing Gretchen does depends on a kind of chemistry between the actors," he noted. "Her plays are almost about that. In *The Last Sweet Days of Isaac* we had that. We couldn't make it happen in *Shelter.*" The producer, Richard Fields, was anxious, and during previews, brought in Peter Hunt to co-direct. Pendleton knew Hunt from many seasons at Williamstown, and so didn't mind the assistance—except that Fields made it appear to the cast that he had been replaced as director.

Pendleton, Hunt, and Fields never captured the elusive chemistry of which Robbins spoke. Finding it would become a mysterious problem Pendleton would face time and again in the future. "I learned a big lesson in *Shelter*," he attested. "You've got to get the people to work together or appear to be working together. That's 60 percent of direction. And to a certain degree, that's out of the director's hands."

Shelter ran for a month at the Golden Theatre, closing in March of 1973. While bearing his first directorial wounds over this, Pendleton actually received modestly positive notices for his contribution. The critics focused instead on the bizarre plot. "The book is too fantastic in its story line," charged Barnes in the *Times*. The *Wall Street Journal*'s Edwin Wilson, in a criticism nearly as confused as the show's plot, said, "The show does not add up—like a Scrabble board with six extra pieces where you can never make your word come out right." The *Village Voice*'s Julius Novick simply called it, "Uneven, inchoate, and confused, among other (bad) things."

Pendleton immediately went from the winter of *Shelter* to a Strindberg spring. He was directing two of the playwright's works at New Haven's Long Wharf

Theatre—*Miss Julie* and *Dance of Death*—comprising one long evening. The cast featured Christopher Walken, Joyce Ebert, Linda Hunt, Roberta Maxwell, and Katina. They worked happily away, rehearsing *Dance* in the afternoon, *Julie* after dinner. With high expectations, they took the stage for the first preview.

The evening began with *Miss Julie,* which ran an hour and a half. The show was going wonderfully. Then came the second act. Pendleton gaped in disbelief: "Every time there was a scene break in *Dance of Death*, fifty people would walk out," he recalled. "I couldn't believe it, because the show was so brilliant. At one point, at the beginning of a scene, Joyce Ebert had an entrance through the vomitory and had to fight the people passing through." He retreated into the lighting booth and lay down on the floor, bewildered and defeated. By evening's end, only a third of the audience remained; they, however, stood up and cheered.

Pendleton didn't know where to turn. The Long Wharf's artistic director, Arvin Brown, was out of town, so any decisions rested with him. He toyed with ideas, trying to smoke out the problem. He alternated the order, beginning with *Dance of Death; Miss Julie* had no scene breaks, he reasoned, so people would remain seated. But still they poured out. He then contemplated eliminating *Miss Julie* altogether, but could not bring himself to do so.

Finally, opening night came. No one walked out. The reviews were good. Finally, it occurred to Pendleton that audiences hadn't been forewarned of the considerable duration of the evening. He placed a sign in the lobby advertising the two plays' running times. While people still left, they only did so at intermission. "It turned out fine, but, boy, was it a trauma."

Recalling the experience, Pendleton mused, "In those early days, you always think so melodramatically about everything. You think, 'Oh, now my career is falling apart. Oh, now it's healing.' And what it is—is job after job after job. And all kinds of different factors enter into them. The thing that always amuses me is people who go into directing who are control freaks. There is a certain justification of that in film, because you can sit in the editing room and create out of other people's work exactly the thing you want. But in the theater, it's the opposite of being in control. You can develop your vision of it during rehearsal. But you're at the mercy of the actors and all kinds of indefinable factors that can send a production off into some direction you don't intend."

That summer, Pendleton returned to Williamstown to direct Molière's *The Misanthrope*, starring John Glover as Alceste. In the fall, he went back to Long Wharf to direct E.G. Marshall and Geraldine Fitzgerald in Ibsen's *The Master Builder*. He followed that with another Ibsen, *Little Eyolf*, at Manhattan Theatre Club, starring Nancy Donahue and Katina. The summer of 1974, he completed this northeastern circle once again by traveling to Williamstown to direct Sheridan's *The Rivals*.

A professional actor by trade, Pendleton had now opened up a new area in his career. He been directing almost exclusively for two straight years. He explained: "There was no plan to this, but it turned out that the directing things were just more interesting to do than the acting jobs I was getting. . . . I missed acting. It's always been more important to me. I've never had the ambition to become a major director, like a player. I always, on the deepest level, could take or leave directing, in a way I've never been able to do with acting. If it had all not worked out in directing, I wouldn't have been destroyed."

Over the Transom Pendleton's friend Joe Mathewson, who had read him his reviews on the rainy, dismal opening night of *Oh Dad*, had a friend named Milan Stitt, who had written a play. As a favor, Pendleton begrudgingly took the play, *The Runner Stumbles*, along with several other scripts, with him on a vacation in St. Thomas, in the spring of 1974. Stitt's script was by no means vacation material. Based on a 1911 Michigan trial of a priest accused of killing a nun, the play was unmitigatedly solemn. Pendleton picked it up a couple times but never lasted past page six.

"Once I got past the first few pages," he explained, "I really got into it. It was awkward and crude—not only in the writing but in the structure. The writing was very head-on, without a trace of irony at all; it was blunt. It had structural problems and there was something about the basic premise of it that was not entirely believable. But with all of that, it was haunting."

Pendleton took the play to Lynne Meadow, artistic director of Manhattan Theatre Club. She thought the work striking. Stitt, who had labored over the play for years, labored still more, sculpting new drafts with Pendleton's input. The play opened in December as a showcase production at MTC, with Nancy Donahue as Sister Rita, Alan Mixon as Father Rivard, and Sloane Shelton as the priest's housekeeper. A couple small reviews applauded Pendleton for his efforts, while deeming the play a promising work in progress.

The production was popular, and MTC extended it an extra weekend. One of these added performances was attended by Del and Margo Tenny, who were about to begin a theater in Stamford, Connecticut, called the Hartman Theatre Company. They wanted *The Runner Stumbles* for their first season. There were more rewrites and Mixon was replaced with Stephen Joyce, because of what Pendleton termed another case of actor "anti-chemistry," this time between the former Father Rivard and Donahue.

The Hartman production, which opened in December, 1975, was a huge success for the theater. Crowds packed the old converted Stamford film house every night. On New Year's Day, a producer named Wayne Adams came to the Hartman. After taking in the play, Adams, on his way back to New York, called Stitt from the freezing-cold platform of the Stamford train station. "I want to meet with you and your agent at 1 A.M. this morning, in an hour and a half," commanded the producer. "I'm bringing it to Broadway."

The play's opening was delayed so that Pendleton could keep commitments: One to act in Romulus Linney's *The Sorrows of Frederick* at St. Clement's in the winter, and another to direct Robert Lowell's *Benito Cereno* at American Place Theatre in the spring. Stitt typed out still more drafts. The script slowly improved, as did the performances. *The Runner Stumbles* finally opened at the Little Theatre (now named the Helen Hayes) on May 18.

The notices were mixed. Pendleton received widespread praise for his handling of the actors. John Simon, of *New York*, called it "an excellent example of that old-fashioned theatrical object, a gripping melodrama that holds the attention through a skillfully managed interplay of facts, ideas, conflicts, surprises, torments, and resolutions. . . . Much credit for this exceptional staging must go to Austin Pendleton. . . . This is strong, absorbing theater which shows what the give-and-take of team work can accomplish." *The New Yorker*'s Brendan Gill said, "Faultless direction—every sentence and every silence is given its full weight and attention."

The play itself was not given as full praise, but the reviews were laudatory enough for Adams to keep it open. Business was good all summer, but unaccountably dropped off after Labor Day and never recovered.

A Conversation with a Critic Up until the mid-1970s, Austin Pendleton had been fortunate in his relationship with the critical press. He had been the target of an occasional bad review, but on the whole the press had been generous and favorably disposed toward him. In 1975, though, Pendleton began to detect a change in the wind. That year, the Kennedy Center, in Washington, D.C., was putting on a series of old American plays to commemorate the nation's Bicentennial and asked him to direct *The Scarecrow* by Percy Mackaye, a 1908 drama based on a Nathaniel Hawthorne short story called "Feathertop," in which a pact between a witch and the Devil brings a scarecrow to life.

Just prior to the play's opening, Pendleton sat down to lunch at the Kennedy Center for a standard press interview with a critic from one of the major local papers. About twenty minutes of food and conversation later, remembered Pendleton, the critic stopped the interview.

"I'm very disappointed in you," said the critic.

Pendleton hesitated. "What do you mean?" he asked.

"Well, from your movies, I thought you were going to be this flaky, out-there guy. You're just an uptight, uninteresting, emotionally conservative person. You haven't said one interesting thing so far."

Pendleton paused. "Now I don't know what to say," he finally remarked.

"Well, we'll get through the lunch," sighed the critic. "I've been assigned this interview, so we'll get through it." The interview proceeded in this fatalistic fashion, until the writer inquired about Pendleton's approach to *The Scarecrow*. "Surely, you're going to camp it up," he suggested. The director said, no, he wasn't. "You can't be serious," the critic commented. "You're not going to do this play straight?"

"This is a very hard play to do," argued Pendleton. "Why would I go to all this trouble just to make fun of some old play that nobody even knows? Why would I do that? I'm not that frantic for a job."

"What is there to take seriously?" the critic demanded.

"First of all, it's adapted from Hawthorne, who, let's face it, is a *writer.* And the play, while it's not Hawthorne, still has a very serious heart, and it ends tragically. I want to take the audience there. That's a challenge."

The critic was not convinced. Indeed, he was angry. "He got so hostile about it," remembered Pendleton. "So contemptuously hostile." A few days later, the critic reviewed *The Scarecrow,* criticizing the production's wrongheadedly straightforward approach to the play. "It was so cynical," observed Pendleton. "He wasn't even pretending to come to it with an open mind."

An incident as singular as the Washington lunch never occurred again, but Pendleton has had his share of trouble with critics since then, critics who can see him only in the role of the nebbish, the eccentric, "everybody's wimp," as he put it. He even has had what might be termed a dedicated agitator in John Simon, the longtime theater critic of *New York.* While Simon has occasionally reviewed Pendleton approvingly, most of the time he has berated the actor in almost savage fashion. Simon once suggested in print that Pendleton retire. After reviewing Pendleton's play *Booth,* Simon floated the hope that playwriting might keep the actor from performing. When informed by this author that Simon had probably seen more Pendleton performances than any other critic, Simon deadpanned, "Some people are born lucky."

Pendleton, however, maintains a seasoned and thoroughly thoughtful attitude toward critics—including John Simon—rarely seen in actors. Much later, in the summer of 1995, when Pendleton had become the new artistic director of Circle Repertory Theatre, he lunched with Simon, who was frankly befuddled that the actor he had so often lambasted had agreed to meet with him.

"I said, 'Listen, John, you're a literate writer,'" related Pendleton. "'That's all I ask. Being attacked in print by someone who doesn't know what they're talking about, can't write, and is nowhere near as qualified for their job as I am for mine—that I resent. But a literate critic, who can write, who can analyze, and who has his own understanding of the theater—that's show business.'

"Everyone in the world reacts to actors the way John Simon does," the actor continued. "They just won't admit it. Actors have to take responsibility for the fact that when they walk on the stage they are going to affect people by the way they walk and talk. No matter how crafty actors are, they finally have no control over the way people react to their presence onstage. And actors don't want to know that. They want to think that with the right degree of craft, they can conquer all that. But they can't.

"The kind of criticism I have a problem with is when people pretend to this

Olympian detachment. I don't think anyone has that. At least with John Simon, you know; he makes very clear his own humanity, the prejudices you're dealing with. I'm beginning to treasure that more and more. Criticism needs to be a passionate act. I think we all get so self-pandering. I've done it. You get so, 'Oh, he hurt my feelings.' What can you possibly have thought was going to happen? There are people out there; you don't know anything about their lives, about their day. You don't know anything about anything."

After the ice was broken, that summer meeting between critic and artist went well. The two struck up a small friendship. That season, Simon came to review a play Pendleton directed at Circle Rep. However, he didn't like it.

Two "Sisters" In 1976, Pendleton returned to Williamstown to direct Olympia Dukakis in Tennessee Williams's *Orpheus Descending*, and to play Baron Tusenbach in Chekhov's *The Three Sisters*. The Williams did not go well, earning lukewarm reviews. The Chekhov was another matter.

Nikos Psacharopoulos, who had made a career out of directing Chekhov and filling his festival with the playwright's work, was having his third go at the *The Three Sisters*. The cast included Olympia Dukakis as Olga, Blythe Danner as Masha, Laurie Kennedy as Irina, Ken Howard as Vershinin, and John Glover as Solyony. Psacharopoulos avoided the pregnant pauses and studied pace the public often associates with Chekhov, and infused the play with emotion and momentum, charging the story and the characterizations with a natural fluidity.

By his own account, Pendleton was, that summer, perfectly attuned to the mental circumstances of the Baron, a man who is idealistic about love, work, and the future, and yet thwarted in all. The actor had recently been through some emotional and personal strains when Psacharopoulos asked him to play the role. "I was a raw, walking wound, and it all went into the cheerfulness of Tusenbach," said Pendleton.

The crew and ensemble were hailed, and none more so than Pendleton. The local critics, long affectionate in their feelings toward the actor, now embraced him. The *North Adams Transcript* said, "Austin Pendleton is refreshing in his brilliant interpretation of the stammering intellectual. [He] proved conclusively in this production that Chekhov did have an excellent sense of humor." A critic for the *Times Record* said his Tusenbach "remains in the memory as a performance of award stature. He has such superb timing, such impeccable stage manners, such a natural, spasm-inducing comic sensibility that you could hate the rest of the production, but still walk out satisfied by this bravura performance."

"In 1976, during *Three Sisters*, a lot came together for me as an actor," explained Pendleton. "My performance in that production was a huge leap forward. And, of course, Nikos had a lot to do with that. It was the best production of a play I have ever been in."

By coincidence, British director Frank Dunlop asked Pendleton to repeat the role of the Baron several months later in a production of *The Three Sisters* at the Brooklyn Academy of the Arts. Dunlop had been asked by BAM to put together a resident acting company, and the new venture—called the BAM Theatre Company—was in the middle of its first loosely-constructed season. The three sisters of this production, which opened in May of 1977, were Rosemary Harris, Ellen Burstyn, and Tovah Feldshuh. And if the production, in Pendleton's view, was not as accomplished as Psacharopoulos', the actor's reception was, incredibly, even more lavish.

The dailies were all positive, and Edith Oliver, in *The New Yorker*, called Pendleton "hands down, the best Baron Tusenbach I have ever seen or expect to

Photo by C. G. Wolfson.

Austin Pendleton and Olympia Dukakis in the Williamstown Theatre Festival production of Chekhov's *The Three Sisters* in 1976.

see." Walter Kerr, meanwhile, lauded Pendleton in the kind of review of which actors only dream. "It is conceivable," he wrote, "that Mr. Pendleton's work is the most striking of the evening. Playing Chekhov's quintessential character, impulsive, abashed, self-conscious, outspoken, extravagantly gay, extravagantly foolish, likable, and doomed, Mr. Pendleton claps his hands and stomps his boots in childlike enthusiasm for a better world he's never going to see. If the production hadn't been worth doing for a dozen other reasons, it would have been worth doing simply to put this one role into such dazzling perspective." Kerr then went on to dwell on the actor for another full paragraph, devoting, in total, fully one-fifth of the critique to Pendleton alone.

The *Three Sisters* reviews were among the best he had ever received. They were also among the last good reviews he would receive for years.

Turning Point If a line could be drawn dividing Austin Pendleton's career neatly in half, it would fall down the center of BAM's former Leperq Space. Pendleton was at the top of his form: skilled, respected, and sought after, and Dunlop promptly invited him to join the BAM Theatre Company for its 1978 season, its second. But the actor's career and reputation would never be the same after that season, in which he embraced some of the biggest challenges of his career and suffered, at the hands of the press, the public, and the theater community, some of his most ignominious defeats.

The season began promisingly. The roles Pendleton had always aspired to were coming his way. Dunlop offered him Albert Adam, the lovesick composer, in Ferenc Molnar's *The Play's the Thing,* Marc Antony in *Julius Caesar,* and Estragon in Beckett's *Waiting for Godot*—not, to put it mildly, the sort of parts for which Pendleton was routinely sought. And he was among good company. Other members of the troupe included Richard Dreyfuss, René Auberjonois, George Rose, Tom Hulce, and Carole Shelly. The company's first season had caused much excitement, and there was no reason to believe the coming season would not deliver on that promise.

The Molnar, which opened the season in February at BAM's Helen Carey Playhouse, under the direction of Dunlop, went without a hitch. There were dissenting voices from *New York* and *Variety,* but the dailies were positive on the play and Pendleton. The production was no great hit, but certainly no failure either.

Next came *Julius Caesar.* Once more, Dunlop directed. He staged the tragedy in the Leperq Space, a large room with a high ceiling. He placed the audience on bleachers on either side of a bare stage. The casting was unusual: George Rose as Caesar, René Auberjonois as Brutus, Richard Dreyfuss as Cassius, and Pendleton as Antony. Perhaps someone carefully examining Dunlop's quixotic casting of the play could have predicted an incredulous response, but no one could have predicted the hailstorm of criticism that followed.

"Frank Dunlop's production of *Julius Caesar* is not about acting," intoned the *Village Voice*'s Barbara Garson. "What it is about, as far as I could tell, is staging — and obtrusive staging, which if abstractly may have seemed attractive, was marked by pointless embellishment, alternating with pointless austerity." Virtually no one appreciated Dunlop's stark interpretation, and while that dislike laid the foundation of nearly every negative review, the detractors did not rest at that, but continued on to what they considered bizarre casting and worse performances. Auberjonois' Brutus was seen as nervous, edgy, ignoble. Many a joke was made at the expense of pudgy Dreyfuss as the "lean and hungry" Cassius. Most reviewers, however, saved the reserve of their bile for Marc Antony.

"To see the text bereft of all meaning, witness the Marc Antony of Austin Pendleton," charged *Time*. The *New York Times*'s Richard Eder complained, "The director can choose to cast against type. . . . But in Marc Antony, Mr. Dunlop has cast not against type but against character and the choice wrecks the play. Austin Pendleton, slight, unhealthy-looking, and with a small, strange, and supplicating smile, is the most unorthodox thing in the whole production." John Simon, as usual, was funniest: "Pendleton comes to bury Antony," he wrote, "not to play him."

By the time smaller publications like the gadfly *Soho Weekly News* appraised the show, Pendleton's disastrous reception had permeated every corner of the theater community. They wrote: "The purposeful miscasting of Austin Pendleton as Marc Antony is already legend." And so it would remain for some time.

"I went down in flames," recalled Pendleton. His agent tried to cheer him. Forget *Julius Caesar*; next comes *Godot* — that's your territory. It was true, he felt secure doing Beckett. He had played Estragon in college to great acclaim. If there remained any way to draw victory out of his defeat of Antony, *Godot* was it.

Waiting for Godot, however, was also an ordeal, and one that began not with opening night, but at the first rehearsal. The play was not a production, but rather a reproduction, based on a *Godot* which had been staged by Beckett himself at the Schiller Theater, in Berlin, during the 1974–75 season. Dunlop had wanted Beckett to come to BAM and direct the play with four of the company's actors. Beckett, however, did not travel to America as a rule. Instead, he sent his associate Walter Asmus, who had assisted on the Berlin production and has since restaged Godot all over Europe. (Pendleton called him "Beckett's representative on Earth.")

Two days after *Julius Caesar* closed, the cast and crew of *Godot* sat down to read the play. "Asmus virtually drummed his fingers on the table during the first read-through, while we were making what he regarded as hash out of the play," recalled Pendleton. "Immediately afterward, he set about directing it. The play begins with Estragon pulling off a shoe. [Asmus] started in orchestrating the grunts, the exact number of grunts, the pitch of them. This word goes up, this word goes down, you take six steps on this cross, and eight on this. He was re-creating the direction that Beckett had done in Germany. Well, I inwardly freaked out. The rehearsals were a nightmare."

He and Sam Waterston, who played Vladimir, constantly butted heads with Asmus' dictatorial approach. To them, Asmus was imposing upon them a conceit which had worked in a different language with two completely different actors several years before. "I got so I literally could not speak," said Pendleton. "It got so frightening. And this was hard on the heels of *Julius Caesar*, which was the first full-scale disaster I had ever had in New York. And now it was about to happen to *Waiting for Godot*."

It did. The critiques bore out the actors' criticisms concerning Asmus' set-in-stone production. That, however, did not save the performers themselves from abuse. Except for the *New York Post*, no major paper liked the show. Richard Eder in the *Times* said, "Mr. Pendleton's performance is dreadful. . . . [His] Estragon abjures human force, but he quite fails to take on any abstract or stylized force either. . . . [He] makes him a junior, petulant Puck." The *Soho Weekly News* quipped, "Pendleton is Dunlop's weapon in the war against type-casting."

Pendleton fell into a slough of despond. The day after *Godot* opened, he met with Lynn Redgrave over coffee. The cloud of that day's reviews threw a pall over the meeting, and Redgrave offered some advice. "I grew up in London, where my father and several other of the major actors of his day were, in their middle years, just savaged by the press," she said. "But in England that kind of thing isn't taken that seriously. You're going to have a problem here, because that kind of thing frightens people in this country."

Time would prove Redgrave right. In the meantime, Pendleton had to get through the run of *Godot*, and that was proving increasingly difficult. Finally, he felt he couldn't go on. "One night, about a week after we opened, I was onstage, and while Sam was talking, I was thinking that at the intermission I was going to tell the stage manager that I'm quitting after tonight's performance. The audience isn't enjoying this; I'm not enjoying this; it'll be a great break for my understudy; and it'll be the exact same performance."

Pendleton repaired to his dressing room during intermission with a fantastic sense of relief. Knowing he only had to get through the second act and the entire ordeal of *Godot*—and, indeed, of the entire BAM season—would be over, he took the stage imbued with a new sense of serenity.

"All of a sudden, I started to listen to Sam," he related. "The direction had been so exact that I'd fallen out of the habit of listening; I knew that no matter what I heard, there were things I had to do, and I was trying to remember them. And then the performance that Walter had been trying to get from me came through. Something happened. And I know it wasn't just me because the applause that night was much greater than we had ever had."

Returning backstage after the curtain call, the stage manager stopped Pendleton and asked, "What happened?" After that performance, people began to commend the actor, and wonder out loud about the veracity of the reviews. Pendleton never said a word about leaving. And he never forgot the lesson handed him at the unlikely hands of Walter Asmus. A dozen years later, performing in *Ivanov* at Yale Repertory Theatre, with William Hurt, he hit his head against a similar brick wall. A Russian director from the Moscow Art Theatre had been flown in to re-create his production of the Chekhov play. Once again, Pendleton found himself faced with a man who told him exactly what to do, this time through a translator. But he scored a triumph in *Ivanov* simply by connecting the dots.

Hurt, meanwhile, fought the direction at every turn. Finally, Hurt drew Pendleton aside. "Why are you doing so well?" he demanded. Pendleton replied, "Bill, I'm not doing anything but what he tells me. When a director is this controlling, you have to do what he says. You have no choice. It's not your work anymore. It's his. All you can do is turn yourself, in almost a Zen way, into a vessel. If you do that, you have a shot at it."

That performance in *Ivanov* led to other acting jobs. *Godot* and the other plays in the BAM season, meanwhile, led to a black hole. The theater community, though it might never admit it, takes reviews to heart, and worries about their effect on audiences and fund-raising. Pendleton's BAM notices had made him an artistic pariah. Prior to the BAM season, Pendleton had enjoyed a reputation as a successful, respected, and well-liked stage actor—the result of nearly twenty years of work in dozens of plays. That was now gone. Pendleton became, in his words, "*persona non grata* overnight."

He couldn't get auditions for roles he previously would have been offered outright. Theaters he had worked for in the past wouldn't return his calls. Circle in the Square Theatre was doing Gorky's *The Inspector General,* a play in which he felt he could fill any number of roles, including the lead. But they had not called. "So I called up the casting director and said, 'Could I have an audition for this?' And I got this kind of, 'Oh, uh, yeah . . . sure.' They were so embarrassed that I had made this call. So I went in for this audition that was agonizingly *pro forma*. The director wouldn't even look at my face. They just sat there looking at their watches. And remember, I was an actor—through the reputation I had built up until 1978—that everybody wanted."

A Theater Called Steppenwolf If Pendleton's acting career had been crippled by his BAM reviews, his directing career had not. The press surrounding *The Runner Stumbles* had given him the reputation of welcoming unsolicited scripts from unlikely corners. One such manuscript came from Ralph Pape, a student in an acting class Pendleton was teaching at New York's HB Studios.

The play, *Say Goodnight, Gracie,* set in 1976, examined the bond between five friends, all approaching thirty, who battle to hold off the grim realities of adulthood, the future, and their upcoming high school reunion. Intrigued by the characters, Pendleton attended a reading at Circle Repertory Company. He then committed to directing it and came into contact with André Bishop, at Play-

wrights Horizons, who arranged for a workshop of the play in November of 1978. Then Wayne Adams, the producer of *The Runner Stumbles,* stepped in and moved the play to the 78th Street Theatre Lab.

The reviews for the 78th Street production were not good, but the word of mouth was, and the play ran for sixteen sold-out weeks. *Say Goodnight, Gracie* made its final move, to the Actors Playhouse, in July, 1979. The reviews for that incarnation, though finding flaws in the play's aimless structure, were mainly positive, and their praise for Pendleton's work was unanimous. Indeed, in many circles, Pendleton, and his two-year investment in Pape and the actors, was credited with the play's success.

During *Gracie'*s long run at the Actors Playhouse, Michael Cullen, artistic director of Chicago's Travel Light Theatre, prodded by a couple of his company's board members, took in the play. Cullen met after the show with Austin, Adams, and Katina, who was then nine months pregnant. Cullen wanted the show. Adams agreed, but insisted that Pendleton direct the Chicago production. Cullen agreed — as long as they used a promising new group of actors who had been making their mark in a church basement in the Chicago suburb of Highland Park. "They're about to move into the Near North Side and they're sort of at large right now," said Cullen. "I want them to be in *Gracie.*"

The next night Katina gave birth to a baby girl, whom she and Austin named Audrey. After spending the day in the hospital, Pendleton told Adams he didn't want to leave his wife and child to direct the Chicago production. Adams tried to change his mind. "He showed me some publicity stills of the acting group," said Pendleton. "They had met on the campus of the University of Illinois, and they called themselves Steppenwolf! It all sounded so precious to me."

"I think you owe this to me," Adams finally said. Pendleton acquiesced, but agreed only to forfeit two weeks of his time. He flew to Chicago on a Sunday night in the fall of 1979 and met the Highland Park troupe. The next morning, he held tryouts at a warehouse. The actors auditioned one by one: John Malkovich, Joan Allen, Gary Sinise, Glenne Headly, Laurie Metcalfe, Terry Kinney. "It was astounding," recalled Pendleton. "These were very talented people. I'd never heard of any of them." Pendleton made out a cast list featuring Malkovich, Allen, Headley, and Francis Guinan. He offered the fifth part to Steppenwolf founder Jeff Perry, and listened in faint disbelief as he refused. He had played too many big roles of late, explained Perry. It wouldn't be fair to the other members.

Pendleton returned a few weeks later, regarding his task as one of re-creating the New York production. "I started to block it, and the kind of life they were creating was so original, so interesting, that a little way through the rehearsal I threw away the New York production — which I'd loved — and started all over."

Richard Christiansen of the *Chicago Tribune* stated that Gracie was so "surely, securely, convincingly directed and acted that it makes even the script's more repetitive and superficial spots seem achingly right and true." The production ran at Travel Light Theatre from December 5 to January 20 and then moved to the Ruth Page Auditorium, where it played for seven months. The production effectively put the three-year-old Steppenwolf on the theatrical map. The show also led the troupe to Wayne Adams. At first horrified that Pendleton had meddled with the New York staging, Adams was so impressed after seeing *Gracie* that he vowed he would one day bring a Steppenwolf production to New York. In 1982, he did so, producing the company's rendition of Sam Shepard's *True West* off-Broadway. The production launched the company's international reputation, as well as the careers of many of its actors. Later, Adams transferred C.P. Taylor's *And a Nightingale Sang* and Lanford Wilson's *Balm in Gilead.*

As for Pendleton, *Say Goodnight, Gracie* cemented a relationship between him and the Chicago company. He was invited back to direct Michael Weller's *Loose Ends* in 1982, *The Three Sisters* in 1984, and *Cat on a Hot Tin Roof* in 1986. He was finally invited to become a Steppenwolf ensemble member in 1987.

"Steppenwolf came into my life when I was beginning to feel depleted," said Pendleton. "It, and Audrey, reversed that feeling in two entirely different ways. Theatrically, I felt: 'My work isn't going anywhere.' Somehow, coming into contact with those people really recharged me."

Liz and Lillian In the fall of 1980, at the Washington, D.C., premiere of a revival of *Brigadoon*, Elizabeth Taylor, veteran of fifty-two movies, seven marriages, and no performances in stage plays, told producer Zev Bufman that she would like to act on the stage. Thus set off one of the largest publicity firestorms in the history of the New York theater. Liz was coming to Broadway. Critics dropped their pens. Theatergoers ran for their wallets.

By the time it was revealed that the play would be Lillian Hellman's *The Little Foxes*, with Taylor as Regina Giddens, Austin Pendleton was working at Circle in the Square, directing E.G. Marshall and Irene Worth in Ibsen's *John Gabriel Borkman*. As a director, he was well positioned; he had staged a production of Shaw's *Misalliance* in Chicago, starring Lynn Redgrave and Worth, which had won several awards; *Say Goodnight, Gracie* had been a success in two cities; and his 1980 Williamstown production of Shaw's *Candida*, starring Blythe Danner and Edward Herrmann, had been praised by Frank Rich, of the *New York Times*. "That all added up to my being a rising director," said Pendleton.

Pendleton was given an appointment to meet with Hellman in her Park Avenue apartment—the first time he had seen her since acting in the Mike Nichols *Little Foxes* thirteen years earlier. It was a Sunday. Five days before, Beatle John Lennon had been shot, and the singing from a memorial service in Central Park was drifting through Hellman's windows. With the music in his ears, Pendleton felt a distinct clash of cultures as "this tiny, nearly blind woman," a titan of another age, shuffled in and bade him: "Sit down!" The meeting went well, and Pendleton returned to *Borkman*: Critic Rich was coming to see it in two days. Before the play opened, however, Pendleton was called upon to visit Taylor in her rooms at the Waldorf-Astoria. Zev Bufman was at her side. Waving off talk of the play, she gossiped about a party she was supposed to attend that evening.

"She was trying to dissolve the tension of my proving I could direct the play," said Pendleton. "She said she didn't want to do matinees. And I said, 'Well, you have to.' She said, 'Why?' 'Because people are already looking to see if you're going to be a serious theater actress. And if you make the announcement that you're not going to do matinees, particularly in a production that so many people are going to want to see, they'll say, See, she's not serious. And that perception will affect the way they watch your performance.' So she said, 'Okay, I'll do matinees.'"

The following morning, Pendleton was offered the lead in Harvey Fierstein's new play, *Torch Song Trilogy*. He called up Julie Hughes, a casting director for *The Little Foxes*, and asked if he had the directing job. Yes, he did, she replied. To this day, however, Austin is still somewhat mystified how he, of all people, ended up directing Elizabeth Taylor in her stage debut. "There was a feeling around that Elizabeth would need a gentle soul, and I was perceived as that," he mused. "This is what people told me. I never really understood how I got it. I was perceived as being a hot director then." He paused and smiled. "*The Little Foxes* ended that."

Pendleton described the rehearsal period as "joyous." Taylor was eager and sweet-tempered. "She will do anything you ask her to," he recalled. "I think it's because she started at age twelve, and during the years she worked with a lot of great directors. And she learned that if you trust and follow a director who's good, then you're good."

The production opened out of town on February 27, 1981, at the Parker Playhouse in Ft. Lauderdale, Florida. The reviews were good, apart from the all-important *Variety*, which termed the production "diffuse and ambiguous," commenting that Taylor's search for vulnerability in the character of Regina was muddying the plot.

The production moved to the Kennedy Center, where Taylor's then-husband, Senator John Warner of Virginia, crowed over his celebrity wife and invited the Washington power elite to the production. Meanwhile, Pendleton was beginning to feel his power ebbing away. While getting his hair cut at a barbershop in the bowels of the Kennedy Center, the gentle snipping was interrupted by the barber's comment, "So, how do you feel about the fact that your producer is taking over the directing of your star?" he asked.

"Then this little tug of war started to happen," related Pendleton. "It never got out in the open, but I would see things I didn't like, and I would change them back to what I wanted or find something new. And then they would get undone again. I would see it in the performance. I would talk to her. I never said anything to Zev. She was very open, but he would give me notes. He would say, 'She's got to get good reviews in New York. It's our whole shot.'"

Both the Florida and Washington engagements sold out, and in New York tickets were selling briskly. The show landed at the Martin Beck Theatre. The first previews went well, the audiences ecstatic, the cast relieved. On the stage after one preview, Pendleton began to give the cast notes, and Zev "blew up": "There were several people on the stage. It was unprofessional. If you added up the things he objected to, it was maybe four little moments in the show. I was very calm. I wrote it off to pressure."

The next day, Taylor called in sick. The cast would rehearse without her during the remainder of the week preceding the opening. When Pendleton called the Carlyle Hotel where Taylor was staying, Bufman would pick up the phone. "It became a struggle to get her performance to go back to what he wanted, which was much broader than what I wanted. She was taken away from me during that critical period."

Meanwhile, there was Lillian Hellman, who, though seventy-five, had lost none of here infamous irascibility. Although Pendleton enjoyed working with her immensely, "she was not without opinions," as he put it. "I would get angry at her more than I have gotten angry professionally at anyone. She was outrageous. She and I got in a fight in the lobby once during previews in the intermission. I don't know why the audience went back for the third act, after they heard what we were saying to each other. I said, 'This is the worst night of my life,' in response to some new attack on the production, and she pounded her cane on the floor of the lobby and yelled back, 'Every time I see this production is the worst night of my life!'"

The Little Foxes finally opened, mercifully, on May 7. Most reviews were kind, if tempered; appraisals of Pendleton's work swung from "vulgar" to displaying "considerable finesse." Frank Rich's *Times* review, however, was a rave. "Pendleton . . . was clearly born to direct it. Using overlapping conversations and vibrant blocking, he gives Miss Hellman's artifice the relentless flow of real life. The old-style theatrical flair is often delicious." (Upon his retirement as a critic, Rich, in a *New York Times Magazine* article, would unfortunately retract the review as one of two he regretted having written.)

The reaction among the alternative press, however, was visceral. They were enraged by the production, which they considered crassly commercial and inept. They were further enraged by the critical press "non-reviews," which they felt dwelt less on theatrical standards than the matters of Taylor's appearance, weight, age, storied life, stage debut, recent birthday, and international celebrity. Richard Gilman, writing in *The Nation*, accused Taylor of "not even bare adequacy," and summed up the prevailing sentiment that the production "testified to the collapse of all our theatrical standards."

"*The Little Foxes* got people mad," admitted Pendleton. "I always thought that play did a lot of harm to my directing career."

It was, in many respects, a "Teflon" production. Crowds streamed in during much of its four-month New York run, and Taylor and Pendleton both received Tony nominations. The show, after moving to New Orleans and Los Angeles, eventually grossed $11 million, much of which was profit.

Finding His Voice While Pendleton was battling the daily problems of staging *The Little Foxes*, he successfully fought a war he had been engaged in for over thirty years. His stutter had improved in the days since *Oh Dad* through years of speech and acting classes and the disciplining effect of constant performance. But the fact was that the speech defect still remained.

One day soon after he had been hired to direct *The Little Foxes*, Pendleton was standing in the checkout line in a supermarket, flipping through a copy of *People* magazine. He paused at an article that mentioned the work of Ron Webster, the head of the speech department at Hollins College, in Roanoke, Virginia, who had experimented with a new treatment to combat speech problems. The program had made headlines by successfully treating Annie Glenn, the wife of astronaut and senator John Glenn. Annie had stuttered so badly that she was terrified to talk to the press the day of her husband's return from his first flight into space.

"At that time, I was completely cynical about all that," said Pendleton. "But after reading this article, I took down the information and I came home and called." Pendleton pointed out to the school that, because of his *Little Foxes* job, he was unable to go to Virginia. The school informed him that they had just opened a New York branch.

All through the weeks of casting, Pendleton attended the Hollins outpost, called the Communications Reconstruction Center (CRC) at Park Avenue and 57th Street, six days a week, eight hours a day, for three weeks. Webster contended that speech problems are primarily physical, but lead to complex psychological difficulties over the years. The program was intense. "You essentially learn how to talk all over again," explained Pendleton. "You learn how to form consonants, you learn how to form vowels. You sit in a cubicle for 20 minutes at a time and do these exercises with little machines. Then you go out and talk to the other people for 10 minutes. For the first two weeks, you have a stopwatch. Every syllable you say has to be two seconds long. In the final week, you get to reduce the syllables to one second each."

Pendleton practiced with workbooks for several months after the course ended. The eradication of his stutter was successful. A year later, he starred in a film for HBO about the CRC called *Talk to Me*, playing a man who cures his stutter.

Forging Ahead In the years following, Pendleton seldom worked in New York. Matters never became dire, financially; *The Little Foxes* had been a "financial bonanza," for all involved, according to *Variety*. The nest egg Pendleton secured from that assignment kept him solvent while he did most of his work in the '80s in regional theater and film.

At Williamstown, ever welcoming, Pendleton performed and directed often. His 1981 production of Gorky's *Summerfolk* was respectfully received, albeit with some grumbling over the play's mopey Russian aesthetic and nearly four-hour running time. He directed Gorky again in 1982, staging *Enemies*. The same year, Pendleton acted in Pinero's *Trelawny of the Wells* and in *Tennessee Williams: A Celebration*, a collection of scenes and monologues. The following year, he played Roland Maule to Richard Kneeland's Garry Essendine in Noel Coward's *Present Laughter*. The *Berkshire Eagle* praised his "stunning performance . . . a hilarious combination of the abject and the domineering."

In 1983, Pendleton played the first of his three Vanyas at Olympia Dukakis's Whole Theatre in Montclair, New Jersey. Edward Herrmann liked it so much he persuaded Psacharopoulos to stage *Uncle Vanya* the following summer in Williamstown with Austin repeating his role and Herrmann playing Astrov. Pendleton would play Vanya one more time, in 1987, at CSC Repertory in New York.

The actor has repeated several roles over his career: In addition to the three Vanyas, he had played Tartuffe three times; Trofimov in *The Cherry Orchard* twice; and the title role in Romulus Linney's *The Sorrows of Frederick* three times. "If the roles are that rich and complex, you could do it endlessly," he explained. "There is no performance you can give in any of those roles that begins to exhaust them. Also, in the meantime, *you've* changed, so you come back to the role from a different place. You live and learn and want to go back to these parts. There are certain roles you wouldn't want to do again, because there's nothing more you can do with that role. But these parts are so much larger than any one performance."

Additional financial stability came from a short run of film work which began in 1979 with *The Muppet Movie,* in which Pendleton played sidekick to Charles Durning's villain. Pendleton had known Durning from the days of *Fiddler on the Roof,* when Durning was in the road company until his part was cut. What one might expect to be an amusing and playful experience was not. Working with Muppets was "like working with pieces of cloth," said Pendleton. "It wasn't very interesting."

Durning went from *The Muppet Movie* to a role in Alan J. Pakula's film, *Starting Over,* and helped Pendleton get a supporting role in that film. Directly afterward, Pendleton shot what may be his longest film role, in Marshall Brickman's *Simon.* The spree of movies ended with a role as the romantic lead in Buck Henry's political satire, *The First Family,* starring Madeleine Kahn, Bob Newhart, and Gilda Radner. Everyone on the set had high hopes for the film, but it flopped with the critics and at the box office.

His few and far between New York jobs included a role in Martin Fox's *The Office Murders,* at the Quaigh Theatre, in 1979. Pendleton made no major New York acting appearance until David Wiltse's comedy *Doubles* returned him to the Broad-

way stage for the first time since Mike Nichols' production of *The Little Foxes*. The play concerned four tennis partners, each facing separate midlife crises. Pendleton played a philandering lawyer who had married young and was now sowing his wild oats. The other three men were played by John Cullum, Ron Leibman, and Tony Roberts. Most of the reviews were moderately respectful, offering faint praise, but Frank Rich dismissed it as a sitcom on stage, and thereby cut its run short. Still, *Doubles* represented a small return of reputation for Pendleton. His closet Lothario was reviewed favorably, even by Rich.

In 1986, he would act in New York again, at the Roundabout Theatre Company, in *Master Class* (not to be confused with the Terrence McNally play by the same name). It would be the events of the next three years, however, that would shape his future and presage his resurrection as an artist.

Three Years In 1985, Austin Pendleton was approached about directing a musical version of Mordecai Richler's 1959 comic novel *The Apprenticeship of Duddy Kravitz*, and agreed on the condition that he be allowed to write the book. Alan Menken, who then had *Little Shop of Horrors* to his credit, wrote the music, and David Spencer wrote the lyrics. Lonny Price—who had rescued the project after a version penned by Jerry Leiber and Mike Stoller had stalled a few years earlier—was playing the title role. Stewart Lane, a former acting student of Pendleton's, was the producer.

The team worked on the musical for two years in preparation for an opening, at the American Music Festival in Philadelphia, in the fall of 1987, and with the intention of moving it to Broadway. The raw material was surefire but problematic. All along, various forces, including Pendleton, endeavored to wrench permission from Richler to alter the ending of the book, in which the antihero, Kravitz, betrays his two closest friends. But the Canadian author insisted that his story's integrity be preserved. "The ending was not negotiable," said Pendleton. "It left a bad feeling. You're left as I imagine you'd be left after an affair that ends badly. You're emotionally invested in this person and then find that he's in fact the worst thing you thought he could be."

The work continued. Before the opening, *Duddy Kravitz* was workshopped in New York. In October, the musical premiered at Philadelphia's Zellerbach Theatre, in the Annenberg Center. The producers, who were hoping for a good review in *Variety* in order to take it to New York, got what they wished for. The *Variety* review praised the music, performances, and direction. The reviewer did, however, wag his finger at the vexing ending. "After spending almost two and a half hours building up a considerable reservoir of audience sympathy for young Duddy, a Canadian Sammy Glick using deplorable methods to acquire a parcel of land and his family's respect, the show switches abruptly from what seems a conventional upbeat ending to a depressingly sour one." Still, the review added, "Even with that problematic ending, Duddy is not a dud."

Pendleton had every reason to rejoice, but something told him all was not well. Sure enough, the next morning, Stewart Lane called the creative team to his hotel room and announced that they could not bring the musical, in its present form, to Broadway.

Lane tried to bring in new investors, while Pendleton tried to chip away at the rock of Richler's convictions. Richler wouldn't budge. "Then I was called in by Stewart and fired as the director," said Pendleton. "He said I could stay on as the writer. I said, 'Fine. My hands are tied in too many places.'"

Pendleton says he never became depressed over how Duddy turned out—he didn't have time to be. On the afternoon he was dismissed, Carole Rothman, co-artistic director of off-Broadway's Second Stage theater company, phoned. The theater was devoting a season to playwright Michael Weller—whom Pendleton had met when directing *Loose Ends* at Steppenwolf—and they wanted Pendleton to direct Weller's latest, *Spoils of War.*

"I was struck by the character of the mother, but I felt I didn't understand the play," remembered Pendleton. "So I had a meeting with Mike, and we began talking about places that the play could go." Weller, excited, went back to work on the script. Six weeks later, he showed Pendleton his new work. Pendleton began detailing still more suggestions. "Wait," Weller interrupted. "I'm not going to do any more based on our conversations unless you commit to directing it." Pendleton agreed.

The play, widely regarded as autobiographical, takes place in the 1950s. The story concerns Martin, who is sixteen, and his efforts to bring his divorced parents back together, but also touches on various themes of the era, including the McCarthy witch hunts and the extinction of Depression-era radicalism. Kate Nelligan was hired to play the role of Elise, Martin's beautiful, magnetic, promiscuous, capricious mother. Weller continued to scribble away during the play's tense rehearsal period, submitting new material daily, to the consternation of Nelligan. The play opened in May of 1988, and most notices, while positive, and admiring of Nelligan, suggested that further work was needed. The *New York Times*'s review, however, fairly glowed with adulation. Frank Rich called *Spoils of War* "the most intense and affecting work of [Weller's] admirable career."

As they often do following a good *Times* review, Broadway producers came calling. There was a hitch to their interest, though: They all wanted the package *sans* Pendleton. "So I called up Mike," recalled Pendleton, "and said, 'Don't prevent your show from going to Broadway just because of me. It's not going to make me feel good if this show does not have a future just because of me.' He said, 'No! I'm going to insist on you.'"

Finally, from the north came two Canadian producers, Edwin and David Mirvish, who said they would back the production, Pendleton and all. (Larry

Bryggman, who played the father, would, however, be replaced by Jeffrey DeMunn.) The show would have a tryout at the Mirvish-owned Royal Alexandra Theatre, in Toronto, and then move to Broadway. Weller produced an avalanche of revisions, working feverishly to develop the father's character and strengthen the parents' final confrontation. Pendleton arrived in Toronto in September with what he considered a better show, and received worse reviews.

Weller went back to his now-worn drawing board, where he spent much of October. "Meanwhile," said Pendleton, "the publicity mills were turning it into this great new American drama that was reviving the great tradition of drama on Broadway. And it was never that. It was this odd, colorful little play about three not particularly sympathetic characters. It wasn't a Broadway play. I knew that this just wasn't a show for the Broadway audience."

But to Broadway it went. Previews were rocky at the Music Box Theatre. Though industry professionals found much to admire, audiences didn't like it, and neither, it seems, did the critics. Rich, who had previously downplayed the work's flaws, now emphasized them. The "affecting" play was now "lumpen"; Pendleton's direction, once "sensitive," was now "erratic." Critics still adored Nelligan, but thought the new set ugly, and many contended the play had gotten worse. Audiences stopped coming, and *Spoils of War* soon closed.

Nikos Psacharopoulos, who had seen the premiere, afterwards strolled with Pendleton. The Greek director complained of pains. "Nikos," asked Pendleton, "do you have cancer?" Psacharopoulos replied, "No, they've looked for that." On January 12, 1989, the founder of the Williamstown Theatre Festival died of colon cancer on the island of St. John, at the age of sixty.

Since its beginnings in 1954, the festival had been associated with and autonomously governed by Psacharopoulos. In those years, its staff had grown to 150, its budget to $1.3 million, and its audience to 40,000 annually. It was, in the words of many a newspaper, America's greatest summer theater. Worried about preserving the numerous artistic and administrative relationships Psacharopoulos had fostered, the festival's board of trustees quickly appointed a triumvirate of artists meant to embody a continuum of Psacharopoulos' reign. Austin Pendleton, a long-standing artistic associate, was given the co-artistic directorship of the festival, to be shared with fellow Williamstown alum Peter Hunt. Actor George Morfogen, who had appeared in countless Williamstown productions, was made executive director.

Working out of Williamstown's garment-district New York offices, Pendleton, Hunt, and Morfogen mapped out the new season. It would open with Stephen Vincent Benét's Civil War saga *John Brown's Body*, directed by Hunt, and continue with *The Rose Tattoo*, starring Maria Tucci and James Naughton, Olympia Dukakis in *Mother Courage*, and Peter Nichols' *Passion*.

And a slot in the season was reserved for Pendleton. Psacharopoulos and he had been discussing, off and on for five years, an ambitious staging of Shakespeare's *Henry IV,* Parts I and II, but the timing had never been right. Pendleton wasn't at all sure this fragile season was the correct moment for such an undertaking either, but the others encouraged him to go ahead.

Meanwhile, the summer was fraught with politicking. All looked to the fall to whom would emerge as sole artistic director. In June, an article in the *New York Times* stated that Pendleton was the board's first choice for the position, but Pendleton wasn't so sure; nor was he certain he wanted the job. "All through that summer of 1989, I kept getting indications that the board was leaning toward Peter," he recalled. "People who thought I should take it over kept saying, 'You've got to fight for it.' I didn't want to fight for it. Peter would be awesome. I wasn't sure I wanted it, so why should I fight for it?"

If he ever did want the reins in Williamstown, he discovered after the opening of *Henry IV* that they were not to be his. The Shakespeare premiered to a public already sodden by the forbidding *John Brown's Body.* The show ran three hours and had a large cast. The reviews, including one from the *Boston Globe,* were negative.

"The board admired the ambition of it," Pendleton reflected, "but the show lost a lot of money. Nobody came to it, and there wasn't one good review. It was this huge fizzle, so . . . even though I had directed a number of very well-regarded productions there over the past twenty years, I could tell at the opening night: 'Goodbye.' I know it cost me the position."

Peter Hunt was appointed artistic and executive director in September. Pendleton, meanwhile, took stock: "That was three years in a row — *The Apprenticeship of Duddy Kravitz, Spoils of War,* and then Williamstown — where I was either directly fired, was threatened with being fired, or wasn't hired. In the job where I was threatened with being fired, but was kept on, the project failed, and in the press I was blamed for the failure.

"It was odd," he continued. "All three of these passed through my consciousness seamlessly. They didn't affect me at all. In each case, I kept waiting for the anxiety or depression to set in, and it didn't."

That autumn in New York, he sat sipping champagne at a table at Elaine's with Peter Hunt and George Morfogen, listening to the buoyant Hunt's proposal that Pendleton and Morfogen take subordinate positions at Williamstown and assist in the preparation of each season. Pendleton's thoughts drifted. That afternoon, a small off-off-Broadway company had offered Pendleton the role of Richard III. He recalled a favorable notice of his performance as Tartuffe at Stamford's Hartman Stage a decade earlier. "Where is the theater that will let Mr. Pendleton play Richard III?" the critic had asked. Here it was, he thought. It wasn't Broadway. The company wasn't revered or even known. But here it was.

Pendleton graciously declined Hunt's offer, drank his champagne, and went home. The next morning he called the off-off-Broadway company and accepted the role. "It was this great liberation. Now I was free to do what I wanted. It was around that time that I began to go underground as an actor."

Small Theaters, Big Roles

Pendleton's fortunes hadn't significantly rebounded since his repudiation by critics in 1978. Since *Doubles*, he had appeared in Steppenwolf's New York production of Willy Russell's *Educating Rita*, but not much else. There was little indication that New York's theater community was suddenly going to welcome him back into the fold.

Then one day in 1988, a tiny company on the Upper West Side, the Riverside Shakespeare Company, called and asked if Pendleton was interested in playing Hamlet. "What do you say to that question—*no*? I was way past the age you're supposed to play it. I would say it was the answer to a fantasy, but I hadn't even had that fantasy."

Soon after, another off-off-Broadway troupe, the Manticore Theatre, called and offered Pendleton the title role in Sophocles' *Philoctetes*. He accepted both roles. In July the Riverside group put on a staged reading of *Hamlet* in Riverside Park, then spent the fall rehearsing a workshop production, while Pendleton dashed back and forth from rehearsals of *Spoils of War*.

Meanwhile, Pendleton's relationship with the Ibsen Society of America began to blossom into something new. Since staging *John Gabriel Borkman* at Circle in the Square, in 1981, Pendleton had grown fond of that play's translator and president of the Ibsen Society, Rolf Fjelde. Austin was made an honorary member. Soon director Susan Flakes, referred by Fjelde, called Pendleton and asked him if he'd take part in a staged reading of Ibsen's *The Wild Duck* in 1984. The event, at the American Place Theatre, went well, scoring coverage in the *New York Times*, and Pendleton signed on for a series of subsequent readings.

Flakes began to branch out, doing Chekhov and Strindberg. The entire fall of 1986, Pendleton, Flakes, and Frank Geraci rehearsed for a reading of Eugene O'Neill's long one-act "Hughie," with Pendleton playing the part of gambler Erie Smith, who delivers a nearly unbroken monologue through the piece. The reading was a success, and Flakes began to prepare a theatrical evening of three one-acts, including Chekhov's "Swan Song," Strindberg's "The Stronger," and, as a finale, "Hughie."

It was soon after the new year in 1989 that Pendleton got the call from Williamstown and joined the triumvirate. But when he agreed, he told them of the roles he had lined up, and that he would not withdraw from any of them. He didn't think he'd to get the opportunity to do those roles again.

Philoctetes opened, in March of 1989, with little notice aside from a positive mention in the *Village Voice:* "Austin Pendleton brings a welcome comic edge to the title role." "Hughie," at Chelsea's Apple Corps Theatre, began performances not much more than a month later. Singled out among the three plays, Pendleton earned his best acting reviews since *Three Sisters*. *Show Business* said the play "succeeds completely. . . . Austin Pendleton is endearing. He has a nice sad, hangdog smile . . . and it's entertaining to watch him struggle with himself, talk to himself, and finally to the clerk." The *Chelsea Clinton News* said "Pendleton is fascinating as he shifts emotional gears and keeps reaching out."

Pendleton immediately jumped into *Hamlet*, which had resumed rehearsals all spring. It finally opened for a sixteen-performance showcase run in May, at the West Park Presbyterian Church, on West 86th Street. Only one reviewer, Wilborn Hampton, attended the actor's turn at the role of roles, but fortunately he was from the *Times*. While proffering reservations about Pendleton's age and reputation as a comic actor, he said, "Mr. Pendleton gives an intelligent, articulate, and reasoned reading of the title role. . . . [He] does not miss a line or nuance of Hamlet's sarcastic humor, and when the moment for passion comes, he summons a fury that is focused and gripping."

Thus, classical roles, for which he seemed unfit and which had nearly done him in at BAM, restored his acting reputation a decade later. The productions, undeniably small, would hardly have appeared on New York theater's radar screen if not for Pendleton's presence. But now they drew crowds, and people were turned away. "They just turned into shows everyone wanted to see. And they didn't have this insane pressure on them of being in the Shakespeare marathon or something. I had accidentally tripped into a good way of being in classics in New York. They were events that generated their own little heat. And they were very fulfilling. You worked as hard on them as you would in a full-scale production—even harder. But you weren't in a hostile environment."

The offers did not stop. Riverside Shakespeare, buoyed by the success of *Hamlet*, offered the actor *Richard III*. It opened in December, and while the reception did not meet that of *Hamlet*, the experience was another satisfying one. "It changed my whole perception of myself as an actor," said Pendleton. "I was almost fifty, and suddenly here I was doing these great Shakespearean roles. It was a kind of rebirth, like ten years before with Steppenwolf."

Though no year matched the intensity of 1989, Pendleton would never stop going underground. In 1991, he acted at the new Signature Theatre—which devoted each season to the works of one playwright—by reprising his title performance in Romulus Linney's *The Sorrows of Frederick*, to wide acclaim. The Malaparte Theatre, a company of youthful celebrities including Ethan Hawke and Robert Sean Leonard, had been impressed with Pendleton's performance in Yale Rep's *Ivanov*. As a result, they invited him to appear in their first venture, a production of Pirandello's *The Joke*. The following year, he appeared at the small Mint Theatre. In 1995, he performed, again to good notices, in J. Dakota Powell's *The Impostor*. In 1996, Pendleton was amazingly offered a second stab at *Richard III*. He took it, playing the king in a fourth-floor space off Eighth Avenue, near Times Square.

Photo by Richard Feldman.

Austin Pendleton in the title role in David A. Shepard's *Keats*, at the Williamstown Theatre Festival's Other Stage, in August of 1996.

Three months later, he played Iago on the Upper West Side in Centerfold Production's rendition of *Othello*.

"All of a sudden, there was this whole new lease on life," he observed.

Bread and Butter Off-off-Broadway work was amply rewarding in all but one way. Pendleton, reborn as an actor, was no longer making a living in the theater. In the early '90s, the rent came almost exclusively from Hollywood, where his most recent and longest run of film activity began in 1990 with *Mr. and Mrs. Bridge,* a Merchant–Ivory film based on novels by Evan S. Connell. He played an art teacher who falls on hard times and is forced to sell magazines door to door. Though he appeared in only a couple of scenes, he made a strong impression. The *New York Times* said that Pendleton "stood out," and Stanley Kaufmann, writing in *The New Republic,* termed it "a performance unusually close to the bone for Pendleton." Pendleton himself regards the performance as his favorite film work.

In the wake of that performance, Pendleton acted in more films in the '90s than he had in all the previous decades combined. That, however, had as much to do with the availability of jobs as it did with Pendleton's willingness to accept them.

"Because my daughter Audrey is going to college, I've decided to take virtually everything I'm offered," explained Pendleton. "I used to be much more picky about the movies I did. Years ago, I would have been insulted by the role offered to me in *Two Days in the Valley*"—his character is featured in a single, though vivid scene—"but it turned into a great little part," he said.

Among the films he acted in during the '90s were *The Mirror Has Two Faces*, *Guarding Tess*, *The Associate*, *The Proprietor*, *Amistad*, and *Home for the Holidays*. Many of these films made only a fleeting appearance in the movie houses before transferring to video, a situation that Pendleton claimed was good for his career, because it prevented overexposure in the industry.

Perhaps Pendleton's most high-profile film work during the decade was in the 1992 comedy *My Cousin Vinny*, in which he played a small-town public defender with a very specific problem. He had met that film's British director, Jonathan Lynn, twenty-five years earlier while traveling in London. Walking around the West End on a Wednesday afternoon, he passed the theater where the London production of *Fiddler on the Roof* was playing. Not knowing anyone in the city, he decided to introduce himself to whoever was playing his old role, Motel Kamzoil. He found the name in the program and later went backstage and asked for Jonathan Lynn. "Hi, I'm Austin Pendleton," he began, before Lynn stopped him. "I know who you are," Lynn said. "You must come back to my flat and have tea with me and my wife." After tea, Pendleton took in Lynn's evening performance, and then returned to his home, where they sat up talking until 5 A.M.

The two remained friends. Lynn went on to glory as one of the writers of the popular British sitcoms *Yes, Minister* and *Yes, Prime Minister*. In the early '90s, Lynn called his friend with an offer to work together: He had a terrific part for him in a movie he was directing, *My Cousin Vinny*.

"When the script came," said Pendleton, "I looked through it first to find my part—and the character stuttered all the time. I thought: Is this a sick joke?" He met Lynn at a Greek restaurant on the Upper East Side and said he couldn't take the part: "It will end my career." Lynn countered, "Look, you're the only actor in the world who can act and understand this from the inside. So you have to do it." Pendleton reluctantly agreed.

Though the film was well received and Pendleton garnered a lot of attention for his performance, he still believes his film career since then has flourished only in spite of *My Cousin Vinny*. He gained a loyal employer in Lynn, who would cast him in more films—including *Sgt. Bilko*, *Greedy*, and *Trial and Error*—than any other film director.

Booth Bounces Back Since its failure at Yale, Austin Pendleton had never separated himself, either mentally or emotionally, from his musical, *Booth Is Back in Town*. He never put the project to rest and was determined it should succeed.

After moving to New York following college, he contacted his composer, Jim Massingale, in St. Louis. In response, he received a terse letter from Massingale's parents informing him that Jim no longer wished to pursue such work. Pendleton turned to *Booth*'s musical director, Arthur Rubinstein (no relation to the famous pianist), who agreed to compose a new score, "as long as it doesn't turn into one of those things that drags on  for years." He, Rubinstein, and the original lyricist, Peter Bergman, wrote a new version, but Pendleton was not happy with the result, which was given a staged reading at Williamstown in 1963. "The version at Yale had been all over the place, but had a certain intensity to it. This was just a bland, standard-issue, incompetent kind of show."

Rubinstein and Bergman drifted apart, and, to replace the lyricist, Pendleton called upon Gretchen Cryer. Thereafter, *Booth*, constantly in chrysalis state, ran through its creators' lives like a running subtext. A workshop, directed by Peter Hunt, was given three performances at Lincoln Center in 1968. Williamstown held another reading in 1981. Time and again, the musical's imminent Broadway debut was announced in the press—once starring Jason Robards, once with Zero Mostel, once with Nicol Williamson.

By the early '80s, the rumors of *Booth*'s existence had become comic, along the lines of the decades-long reports which preceded the publication of Harold Brodkey's first novel, *The Runaway Soul*. Then, in 1983, a disastrous production at the Pepsico Summerfare, in Purchase, New York, seemed to seal the musical's fate. "It was an unalloyed disaster," remembered Pendleton. "I saw twenty-two years of my adult life lift off like a rocket and explode all over the place." Cryer suggested they junk the project, but Pendleton could not let go.

"For several years, people had been saying, 'Why don't you make it a play?'" Pendleton said. "I began to realize that I'd always just assumed it was a musical because it had started out as one. I thought about it. Several years went by, and I called up Gretchen and Arthur and said I wanted to write it as a play. Suddenly I began to write with such freedom. All of a sudden, it was easy. Or it was hard in the right way rather than the wrong way."

Pendleton followed the same basic plot as the musical, but created from scratch nearly all of the dialogue. He wrote in airports, trains, restaurants, dressing rooms. In 1991, the finished play was given a production on Williamstown's Other Stage as *Booth Is Back*. Williamstown veteran Frank Langella starred as Junius Booth, and Arvin Brown, artistic director of the Long Wharf Theatre, directed. The festival labeled it a work in progress and asked that it not be reviewed. One local critic, however, disobeyed the dictum, and, while he praised Langella's magnetic turn in the lead, found the play lacking in cohesion and too long at three hours.

Booth Is Back immediately traveled to the Long Wharf, where, once again revised, it opened that fall. The *New York Times* gave it a fairly good review, and the show was a popular success. Pendleton, Langella, and Brown expected producers to come in and bring the show to New York. The producers, however, stayed at home. "The day it closed in New Haven, we were very disappointed. There was just no interest in it."

Someone at Langella's agency had seen it, however, and had liked it so much he began to send the script to various New York theaters, while Pendleton reworked the play yet again. Finally, Janet Hayes Walker of the York Theatre Company responded. *Booth* (as it was now titled) opened at the York on January 22, 1994, under the direction of David Schweizer. The reviews were largely favorable, and sensational for Langella.

Booth was subsequently published by Samuel French, and while it never went as far as Pendleton would have liked, it was, after more than thirty years of effort, finally complete. That closure left him free to write other plays, which he promptly did. He got the idea for *Uncle Bob*, his second play, during the Long Wharf production of *Booth* and wrote it in his trailer while filming *Guarding Tess*.

As theatrical and vital as *Booth* was, nothing could have prepared anyone familiar with Pendleton for the change of pace of *Uncle Bob*. The play is an upsetting, visceral, and uncompromising look at the failure of the titular character's life. The story's two characters signify two distinct generations of existential despair. Bob, an aging baby boomer and former prodigy, is now a monumental, but philosophical failure, living on his brother's charity, who proudly views the AIDS he has contracted from a street hustler as the finale to the failure of his life. Nephew Josh is an empty, mocking, self-destructive Generation X-er who recognizes a kindred soul in his uncle. Caged together in Bob's Greenwich Village apartment for four scenes, they face off in a series of pungent no-exit discussions, bitingly funny, and almost Strindbergian in their intellectual heartlessness.

Pendleton wrote the part of Bob for his friend George Morfogen, who was overwhelmed and slightly disturbed by the material. He wasn't the only one. After several seemingly successful readings, Pendleton still had trouble finding someone to produce it. He finally found a benefactor in Kelly Morgan, who directed it at the Mint Theatre in early 1995. Some major reviewers came, drawn by Pendleton's name. Most showed a qualified respect for the work, some raved about it, but nearly all left the theater upset by the play. "There is nothing [here]," as Ben Brantley understated it in the *Times*, "that could be called calendar poetry."

"Clive Barnes's review," recalled Pendleton, "was savage, but I loved it, because he was so upset by it. But he wasn't upset the way you're supposed to be upset. He was enraged by it. He gave a description of the plot in its every particular, which he made sound riveting, and then he said, 'See, it's ludicrous.' He explicitly said, 'I'm probably not qualified to review this because it made me so angry.' See, I love that. I would love it if that had taken the form of a rave. But it was so honest. "

Uncle Bob became something of a *succés de scandale*. Unlike *Booth*, it had a life after its initial production, earning a production at Steppenwolf, Hartford Stage, and other theaters. "There are about three things I've done in my life that, if people didn't like them, I just thought they were wrong," said Pendleton. "*Uncle Bob* is one. I just think, 'Well, you missed it. It's there.'"

The Circle Game Off-Broadway's Circle Repertory Theatre was founded in 1969, and through its first fifteen years, it was about as vital as any American theater of its day. Home to such playwrights as Lanford Wilson, William Hoffman, and Craig Lucas, and breeding ground to a generation of famous actors, the Greenwich Village–based company had commanded admiration and excitement nearly from its inception. By the early, recessionary '90s, however, Circle Rep looked as bloated, dazed and inert as many another American success story let down by the go-go '80s. By 1994, the theater was $700,000 in debt and the philanthropic wells had suddenly gone dry.

Circle Rep co-founder Tanya Berezin, artistic director at that time, took such measures as moving the company from its longtime Sheridan Square location to a larger theater, Circle in the Square Downtown, on nearby Bleecker Street. But by December of 1994, she had resigned. In January, on the recommendation of Milan Stitt—who was by then the company's executive director—it was announced that Pendleton would take over as artistic director. It was the first time anyone outside the company had been chosen to lead the theater.

"The fact that I could get on the number 6 train and get right there had a lot to do with it," explained Pendleton. "The second thing was, it was put to me that if I didn't take the job, the place would surely fold. I don't know if that was true or not, but I bought it. Like so many people who work in the theater, for years I would sit around complaining about the state of the theater. And here I was being asked to do something about it. You can't keep going on about the state of the theater in New York when the one time you were asked to do something about it you refused. You say no, and then go back to complaining about it? That's kind of a negative reason for doing something, but it's a powerful reason."

Things went badly from the start. The hiring of Pendleton had angered many of the company's old guard, who were watching their home and legacy veer toward the brink. When Pendleton cancelled a planned production of William Hoffman's *Riga* because the production was deemed too costly, those feelings came to the fore. Wilson and Lucas had departed, and now co-founders Berezin and Marshall W. Mason resigned from the board. The Circle Rep of 1995 was no longer the theater which had previously borne that name.

"What you do is turn into the Lopakhin to their collective Ranevskaya and chop down the cherry trees to build what amounts to condos," explained Pendleton. "That's what it looked like. We were hopefully trying to create something new.

If we earned some money the next year, which would help us to raise more money—see, nobody wanted to give us any money because we couldn't earn any money—if we could do all that, then maybe, slowly, we could begin to build up the theater. I hoped in two or three years we could start to have a version of what they had had, because I liked what they had."

It was critical, then, that the 1995–96 season be successful, cost little, and earn a lot. Pendleton looked for economical, yet commercial plays: "Small-cast plays, with one set, with names in them," as he put it. The season would open with a three-character drama *Riff Raff,* by the actor Laurence Fishburne, in which he would also star along with the rap-music performer Heavy D. Kevin Heelan's *The Hope Zone,* with Olympia Dukakis, would follow, then Charles Evered's *The Size of the World,* with Frank Whaley and Rita Moreno. A planned-for Michael Weller production never materialized.

Pendleton hoped his selections would be inviting to audiences and increase the subscriber base. "The audience wants to see people they know. It's as simple as that," he argued. "It's a time-honored way. It goes back to Shakespeare's time. That's always been one of the reasons people go to the theater. Your only obligation is that they be good, not just well known for certain television appearances.

"I think theater's stopped being audience-friendly," he continued. "I never knew I felt that until I thought about it. You go see plays and the audience is just glazed; they feel like they haven't been invited. The play is about some obscure narcissistic trip that doesn't have anything to do with them. There are a lot of plays—and they have proliferated in the twenty-five-year reign of the nonprofit theater in America—that are interesting plays. But they are not designed to interest the audience. You can put yourself in a play objectively and say, 'Oh, yes, that's very interesting writing. He or she is doing something interesting there. This is a new voice—or whatever—but we've got so many 'new voices' now you could scream. Enough with this! The audience sits there looking like people who have been invited to a party and then sent to the corner with their punch. No one will talk to them."

The problems continued. In June, Pendleton's partner and associate director, Lynn Thigpen, backed out. Then, in the fall, there was a glimmer of light. *Riff Raff* was a hit. It was extended and stood to earn money for the theater. But then Heavy D fell ill, and Pendleton was forced to cancel several performances. The opportunity was lost.

Despite the presence of their star players, the next two productions were not commercially successful. By April of 1996, Circle Rep was forced to give up its Bleecker Street space and retreat into its small, sixth-floor laboratory space at its 632 Broadway offices. Pendleton struggled to operate the theater, but all efforts were becoming pointless. "You couldn't plan anything. You could offer people productions, but you'd say in the next breath, 'Of course, I'm not sure we'll still be open.' So how could you get actors and directors?"

The final straw came when *900 Oneonta*, the first production of the 1996–97 season, received poor reviews. Several more members of the board resigned. On October 7, it was announced that, after twenty-seven years, Circle Repertory Company was no more. Pendleton told the *New York Times* that if he had known of all the stress and hopelessness of the task up front, he would have done it all anyway.

An Actor's Philosophy

Austin Pendleton was now 58. He had been an actor for more than thirty-five years. He had also drawn upon and developed skills as a director and as a playwright, and had run or helped to run two theaters. *Uncle Bob* had not been a gigantic success as a play, and his reign at Circle Rep was not felicitous by any means. Still, his varied spectrum of accomplishments had returned him to the New York fold for the first time in many years.

His work during the 1997–98 season would bring him the closest he had been in some time to the kind of activity he'd enjoyed in the mid-1970s. In the fall, he opened on Broadway in a revival of *The Diary of Anne Frank*. The star attraction was budding actress Natalie Portman, but buttressing her were actors who, like Pendleton, had been around for years: George Hearn, Linda Lavin, Harris Yulin, Sophie Hayden. The press treated the ensemble with respect—they were "seasoned," "redoubtable"—the kinds of adjectives such performers earn after forty years of work. That spring, he also returned to directing for the first time since Circle Rep, mounting *The Seagull* for Greg Naughton and Joanne Woodward's Blue Light Theatre.

Is Pendleton content? Yes. Satisfied? Well, not quite, but he is philosophical about it: "There's a place I've always wanted to be that I've never been, a very specific place," he said. "I've wanted to be taken really seriously as an actor in the theater—wanted it more than anything, in terms of career. Somewhere in the '70s, whatever hope there had ever been for that ended. Since then it hasn't ever come back up again.

"I've long since not only made peace with it, but found another way to be there. You get beyond a certain age in this business, and I mean thirty-five, and you're surrounded by people eating themselves alive with disappointment. You have to not do that.

"The other thing you have got to do—and this is even more important—is take responsibility. To say, for example, that I lost some control of *The Little Foxes* to Zev Bufman is ridiculous. I was the *director*, for God's sake! This is clearly true when you're a director, but it's even true when you're an actor: If you're underrated, often it's because no matter how good you are, you're just not as good as you should be. You have to remember that. Otherwise, you sink into passivity, a 'victimhood.' And in this business, if that happens, you are finished."

Gloria Foster

To Seek and Not to Yield

YOUNG GLORIA FOSTER could consider herself lucky in 1962. In New York for less than a year, and a working actor for only a few years more, Foster was gainfully employed as an understudy in *Purlie Victorious*. Ossie Davis's comedy, in which he also starred, had been a hit for months, first at the Cort Theatre, then at the Longacre. One evening she had gone on, playing one of the few roles on Broadway available to an African-American actress. As Foster herself might have admitted, few black actors at the time could have hoped for more.

Still, she hated it. She hated studying another actor's performances. She hated working in another's shadow. It was not what she had been brought up to expect. It was not how she had been trained. At the Goodman School of Drama, in Chicago, students were cast according to ability, and Foster always had been given major roles: The title role in *Medea*; Sabina, in *The Skin of Our Teeth*; Jocasta, in *Oedipus Rex*. Her actor's appetite had been whetted with these big roles, and she had moved to New York to do them professionally. What most actors would consider presumptuous and unrealistic to expect, she regarded as natural and fair.

A post as an understudy was antithetical to her intentions. Her energy was geared toward being onstage, not backstage, not at home waiting by the phone. As she would later say, no one ever dreams of being a walk-on. You don't dream about it, and you certainly don't leave your home and roots for it. Foster vowed she would never be an understudy again. She never was.

Expectations Born on November 15, 1936, on the South Side of Depression-era Chicago, Gloria Foster never knew her father, and only formally met her mother when she was nineteen; her mother was hospitalized for mental illness not long after Gloria was born. Clyde and Elinor Sudds, Gloria's mother's parents, took over the care of Gloria and her older brother, George. Mental illness was not a topic of conversation in those days, so they told Gloria her mother was dead.

Chicago's South Side was then a friendly residential neighborhood. Gloria remembered dancing and playing in the street under the watchful eye of adults gazing out of their open windows. But the Suddses were older than most guardians. They took one look around, considered the complexity of the public school system, and decided the task of raising two small children in the city was too overwhelming. They then moved their belongings and their two new charges to the more bucolic surroundings of Janesville, the seat of Rock County, Wisconsin, about 15 miles north of the Illinois border. The Suddses kept pigs and chickens and a vegetable garden, and, as far as Gloria could remember, never locked the house. "I never had a key to her house in Wisconsin, because my grandmother was always there," Foster remembered. "I did not know what it was to come into that home without her presence. That was my standard."

Every day Foster would walk four miles to the local schoolhouse. That one-room institution was the locus of her childhood aspirations. "Everything centered around school," she recalled. "And I excelled. My grandparents expected it to be

my life. They were raising us. It was an expectation. That was what we were supposed to do. The thought of doing less, that just wasn't a part of the conversation."

Foster's tutelage was supplemented by the books that would regularly come in the mail—Nancy Drew mysteries and Zane Grey westerns, Jane Austen, and the Brontë sisters—from the book club in which Gloria's godmother had enrolled her. If the Suddeses represented, to Gloria, an even, wholesome upbringing in the country, Gloria Dunklin, her godmother and namesake, was Chicago's ambassador, the embodiment of all the excitement that city had to offer.

Gloria Dunklin was Gloria's mother's age. She had owned the South Side building in which the Fosters had lived. Nearly every new cultural influence Foster encountered in her formative years was introduced by Dunklin. She would take her godchild to the Art Institute of Chicago. They strolled through street fairs. She also took Gloria to the theater—on one memorable occasion to see a young Eartha Kitt purring "Monotonous," in *New Faces of 1952*. Dunklin was, as Foster would later say, "the model by which I was able to envision life outside of the home."

From Classroom to Classroom
The Suddeses later moved to South Beloit, Illinois, where Foster attended junior high and high school. She continued to relish learning and won a scholarship to Illinois State University, in Normal. Continuing on the path her grandparents had placed her on, she planned to become a teacher.

Her most obvious asset as an instructor soon became apparent: speech. Even then, Foster had a remarkable, sonorous voice, which she exercised through forensics. She enjoyed public speaking, and took classes in oratory and debate. She was fascinated by the dynamics of communication, the relationship between the orator and the audience, and even considered entering law as a way of exploring that symbiosis. "I wasn't thinking of law in terms of the legal sense," she remarked. "I was thinking of law in terms of defending someone's rights or pleading cases, the theatricality of it."

Foster met her future husband through her godmother. Dunklin knew him well; he was a part of that Chicago community from which she'd come, where everyone knew everyone else. He was a graduate student in business administration at Northwestern University, in Evanston. After he and Gloria married, she left Illinois State. "My grandparents did not object, they were so happy," said Foster. "They were of the period where women were protected. A career and life outside of the home was not the safest form of living, as far as they were concerned. I was safe—that was how my grandparents saw marriage—and I was not going to be involved in anything that was frightening to them: *life*. That was what the farm was about."

While her husband got his master's at Northwestern, Gloria shuffled papers at the University of Chicago's examiner's office, and later attended Chicago Teachers College. There, she finally decided that teaching was not for her. And while that may have been a relief, it did not help her discover what she did want to do with her life.

Gloria Foster has never been certain how she came to be enrolled at the Goodman School of Drama. As early as the 1960s, she is described in interviews as having "stumbled" upon the Goodman. The most likely connection, Foster mused, was, inevitably, her godmother, a woman "who knew everything," and frequently visited the Art Institute of Chicago, of which the Goodman was a part. Foster auditioned for the school which had produced Karl Malden and Geraldine Page, and was accepted, one of the few black students in her class.

Almost immediately, Foster realized that she had found her calling. "I loved everything that was going on there. In the summers I would work at the University of Chicago's Court Theatre. During the winter, I went to the Goodman. I would close the theater rehearsing: scene study, voice and diction, body movement. It was a conservatory, one of the few in the country at that time. I was consumed with that program. One says, 'You find your passion,' and that was it."

Foster attended the Evening School, which was chaired at that time by Bella Itkin, a former Goodman acting student who began teaching in the early '40s. Itkin considered her new student very advanced for her age, both vocally and emotionally, and immediately cast her in the title role in a production of Euripedes' *Medea*. "At that age," said Foster of the rage-filled role, "you don't have a grasp—thank God—on that kind of vengeance, that kind of hatred." The twenty-year-old Foster cried, protesting that she couldn't possibly play the part. Itkin looked at the sobbing student before her. "Save it for the role," was her only instruction.

Foster played *Medea* for three performances, in December of 1956, at the Goodman Memorial Theatre. The die was cast. She now hungered for other meaty dramatic roles, and she got them. During her three years at the Goodman, she would play Hecuba, in Euripedes' *The Trojan Women*, Sabina, in Thornton Wilder's *The Skin of Our Teeth*, Oparre, in Maxwell Anderson's *Wingless Victory*, and Volumnia, in Shakespeare's *Coriolanus*.

While her education at the Goodman, with its abundance of opportunity and affirmation, would make Foster the actor she became, it would also prove to be a professional handicap of sorts. She was now primed to become a serious dramatic actor, trained for leading roles in the classics—all in all, a tall order for a black woman in the American theater of the late 1950s. "How would I know?" she observed. "At the Goodman, you just got the parts before you knew it, because that was what you were supposed to do. Those were the roles that were offered to you. You never thought about it."

Leaving Home Now somewhat rudderless, Foster remained in Chicago for a couple of years after graduating from the Goodman, occasionally taking parts at the Court and elsewhere. In 1961, she received a call from Shauneille Perry, a friend

who had been in the directors' program at the Goodman. An Equity production of Lorraine Hansberry's *A Raisin in the Sun* was being mounted for a one-week stint in Syracuse, New York. "She arranged for me to play Ruth," said Foster. "She was playing Beneatha. That was the beginning of it. That was getting me away, getting me to make a commitment." The Syracuse job brought her to the attention of the producers of a ten-week tour of the same play, starring Claudia McNeill, Raymond St. Jacques, Ed Hall, Gail Fisher, and Al Freeman. Foster got the nod and was soon the beneficiary of a quick education on the road. Things happened fast; the rehearsal period was brief, and the cast traveled from city to city via train and plane. "It was wonderful exposure," recalled Foster. "We played every kind of stage. We did it in the round; we did it on thrust; we did in a proscenium; we did it in an amphitheater in Detroit. It played in Chicago, and all my friends came."

Though *A Raisin in the Sun* took Foster out of Chicago, she knew it would not keep her out. At the time, there was little indigenous theater in Chicago; most stage entertainment was imported from New York, and Foster knew it was there she must move if she wished to continue acting. But she was not altogether sold on the idea. A couple of her classmates had courageously made the journey to that theater mecca—and returned feeling beaten shortly thereafter. And there were other, more concrete, considerations. "I was married," said Foster matter-of-factly. "We had a life. What roots I had were there."

Her future, however, was not: In 1961, before *Raisin* went on tour, Foster—now no longer living with her husband—moved east, renting a garden apartment on West 55th Street. Later, she would move to a studio on West 74th Street, and, later still, settle into a tiny apartment at 26 King Street, in Greenwich Village.

She found work as a medical secretary for the Electrical Workers Union. Evening hours and a flexible employer made it possible for her to audition during the day. Many of these auditions did not carry her far from her King Street doorstep. The cultural environs below 14th Street were then thriving. Abstract expressionist painters could be found drinking and debating long into the night at the Cedar Tavern, on University Place; the world's greatest jazz artists played just a few feet from your table at the Five Spot, on St. Mark's Place; folk singers performed at Gerdes' Folk City, on West Fourth Street. And, just to pass the time, there were the White Horse Tavern, the San Remo, the Gaslight Poetry Cafe, Caffe Reggio, and countless other bars and cafes where newly inducted members of the writing, art, dancing, and critical communities could find kindred spirits with whom to exchange ideas between puffs and draughts.

The underground theater community had grown in equal measure. By the late '50s, in response to the growing cost and conventionality of the still-young off-Broadway scene, an off-off-Broadway had emerged. On Cornelia Street, just west of Sixth Avenue, Joseph Cino had opened his Café Cino; in a very small space he presented the work of aspiring playwrights such as Sam Shepard and Lanford Wilson, performed by struggling actors like Harvey Keitel and Bernadette Peters. A few blocks east, the Judson Poet's Theater, housed in Washington Square's Judson Memorial Church, and under the direction of Lawrence Kornfeld, staged low-budget productions of plays and musicals. And in the summer of 1962, Ellen Stewart, Jim Moore, and Paul Foster opened the part theater, part boutique on East Ninth Street that would eventually become Café La MaMa, a company dedicated to the work of new writers. In 1963, playwright Edward Albee, along with his producers Richard Barr and Clinton Wilder, formed the Playwrights Unit, which produced workshops of plays by young writers at the Village South Theater, on Vandam Street. The same year, Joseph Chaikin founded the Open Theatre, an avant-garde group of playwrights, directors, musicians, and critics.

It was there that Gloria Foster got one of her first acting jobs, cast in a workshop alongside Chaikin, who had been a member of the Living Theatre, another bastion of the off-off-Broadway scene. And though a lot of work was put in, the project never grew into a full production. But Foster began a lasting friendship with the Living Theatre's founders, Julian Beck and Judith Malina, and forged a tie with Chaikin that would last through several decades and productions.

A flurry of theatrical activity surrounded Foster, and she was determined to be a part of it. But, ironically, she would first make her mark in New York in another medium: film.

Underground and On Screen
In the '50s, independent filmmakers were just beginning to break away from Hollywood and the studio system, with its inflated budgets and mainstream tastes. Foster acted in two of these films in quick succession: Michael Roemer's *Nothing But a Man* and Shirley Clarke's *The Cool World*, two films which depicted life among African-Americans with more depth and subtlety than was usual.

"I had to beg for an audition for both *Nothing But a Man* and *Cool World*," said Foster. "It wasn't as rigid as it is now—now you can't get past the door. These were the early independent films. The casting directors were also actors."

Nothing But a Man was a quiet, dignified film which examined the trials of Duff Anderson, a young black man in the South trying to retain his dignity and self-respect while negotiating the prejudices and injustices of the culture. Abbey Lincoln had already been cast in the role of Duff's wife, Josie. That left Lee, the girlfriend of Duff's fallen father, as the only major role available to Foster. Lee, however, was in her 40s, a woman beaten down by life, and Roemer had difficulty seeing the stamp of harsh experiences in Foster's fresh face.

"When he first auditioned me, there wasn't a problem with the acting," explained Foster. "I was a very healthy young woman. The character was supposed to have lived a life of inner-city ghettos, single mothers. I was trying to arrive at an appreciation for a life I had not had." Still, Foster was certain she could bring something to the character of Lee. While in the waiting room, Foster had seen a thin, frail, worn-looking actress who was being considered for the part.  She went home, put on makeup, donned a dowdy house dress, and "tried to look like what I thought would be more representative of the life the character had lived." She got the part.

Shirley Clarke was a former dancer and choreographer who formed, with critic Jonas Mekas, a nonprofit company for the distribution of independent films, the Film-Makers Cooperative, in 1962. Soon after completing *Nothing But a Man,* Foster was cast in Clarke's latest picture, *The Cool World,* which was directed and co-scripted with Carl Lee, from a novel by Warren Miller. At the center of the film, which looks at life on the drug- and violence-infested streets of Harlem, is Duke (Hampton Clanton), a teenager who aspires to lead a local street gang, the Pythons. Foster, again playing against her age, was Duke's weary mother.

Both Roemer and Clarke worked in a *cinéma verité,* or quasi-documentary, style. *The Cool World*'s jump cuts and Mal Waldron jazz soundtrack lent a propulsive feel to the film, which was remarkable in several other respects: Clarke used a combination of professional actors, such as Foster, Lee, and Clarence Williams III (whom Gloria would meet on the set and later marry), and young nonperformers. Also, Clarke did no studio work, but shot entirely on the streets and in the buildings of Harlem. (Roemer had been similarly devoted to authenticity.)

"It was real," remarked Foster. "I hadn't done so much film work. I found it exciting mainly because of the material and being on location. You had so much to draw on. For example, the dwelling space that Lee and her boyfriend live in; the smells, the moldiness, the water-soaked walls—there's texture that cannot easily be created for the stage. There's an immediacy to it; you're in it. The building where we shot was one of these closed-up buildings—nobody lived there. You'd walk up these tenement stairs to get to where it was shot. There were rats."

Foster reached back to her childhood summers in Chicago to understand her characters' lives, and found that, despite her wholesome Wisconsin rearing, such urban despair was not beyond her grasp. "What exposure I had had in the city to a life you tried to prevent yourself from having—that was what I wanted to bring to these roles," said Foster. "When Lorraine Hansberry wrote about the kitchenette life in *A Raisin in the Sun,* I knew what that was. During my summers as a child in Chicago, I'd been in one of these buildings. A young girl I knew, her mother had lived in these kitchenette apartments, and I went over there to visit. These were apartments where you shared cooking facilities; bathroom down at the end of this long hall—everybody used it."

Foster spent several weeks on both films. The money wasn't much, but met the demands of the inexpensive life she had set up for herself. "That was never a consideration for me," she observed. "You're so young at the time. You're so daring. Your senses are just opening and you're there. It's all virgin."

She discovered one drawback about film; the lag time between the work and the finished product disturbed her. As a stage actor, she had grown accustomed to an almost instantaneous reception of her performances; she knew immediately whether she had failed or succeeded. She was not able to evaluate her work in her first two films until nearly two years later. *The Cool World* came out first, opening in New York on April 21, 1964. Judith Crist, of the *New York Times*, while calling the film "a forensic rather than an artistic triumph," praised Foster's performance. The *Daily News*, too, singled out her "stand-out sequence," a dramatic aria in which Foster, in stentorian tones, berates her own life, noting bitterly that "things always get too much for men."

Nothing But a Man was shown at the 1964 Venice Film Festival (where it won two awards) and at the New York Film Festival before it opened on December 28. Crist called it "the finest comment to date on the Negro revolution in the South . . . . Gloria Foster's is the most striking performance in her portrait of a woman who has cast her lot with Duff's father, who knows too much of men's harshness to one another." The film has since become a classic of its kind.

Setting the Standard By 1963, Martin B. Duberman, a history professor at Princeton, had completed research on his play *In White America*. The work—once called *Not in My History Book*—was a chronological patchwork of texts through which Duberman (who was white) hoped to relate the largely untold history of African-Americans in the United States. Included were not only the letters and writings of abolitionist John Brown, diarist Mary Chestnut, and black leaders Marcus Garvey, Booker T. Washington, and W.E.B. DuBois, but also the largely unknown racist sentiments of presidents Thomas Jefferson and Woodrow Wilson, and a remarkable passage from the 1907 Congressional Record in which a Senator Ben Tillman, of South Carolina, delivered an impassioned defense of lynching.

Plays written by, or depicting the lives of, or starring African-Americans had just begun to enter the American theater. Jean Genet's *The Blacks* began a long run at St. Mark's Playhouse in 1961. Among the cast were actors who would become the leading African-American talents of their generation, including Maya Angelou, Godfrey Cambridge, James Earl Jones, Charles Gordone, Cicely Tyson, Louis Gossett, Jr., Roscoe Lee Browne, and Billy Dee Williams. The next few years would see such landmark plays as *Blues for Mister Charlie* by James Baldwin, *Dutchman* by LeRoi Jones, and *Funnyhouse of a Negro* by Adrienne Kennedy.

Gloria Foster's agent, Ernestine McClendon, sent her on a cold reading for *In White America*. Gloria had been recommended to the producers by the play's stage manager, Charles Maryon, who had seen Foster perform at the Court Theatre. According to Foster, McClendon didn't think her client was right for any of the roles. It was a strange play, an odd format; each actor was called upon to play several parts. "It wasn't encouraging at all," remembered Foster.

Nevertheless, she landed a position in a cast of six; three white actors and

Gloria Foster and Michael O'Sullivan in Martin B. Duberman's *In White America*, at the Sheridan Square Playhouse, in the fall of 1963.

three black. Foster played several parts, including a woman whose husband had been lynched; a disciple of Reverend M.J. Divine, also known as Father Divine; Sojourner Truth; and an Arkansas girl, who, after the Supreme Court in 1954 declared segregation in public schools unconstitutional, tried to enter Central High School, in Little Rock.

This last sequence—in which the girl described being faced with a rabidly racist mob—ended the show on a harrowing note. The speech was, as were many in the play, addressed directly to the house, and Foster was invigorated by the energy she drew from her adjusted relationship to the audience. "It was a form that was new and exciting," she said. "It was dealing directly with the audience. I loved it. It was performance art before it was called that. It was living in the moment, but narrating it at the same time. It was painting images with words."

In White America opened at the Sheridan Square Playhouse on October 31,

1963. Except for the Open Theatre workshop performance alongside Chaikin, it was Foster's New York stage debut, and it would be one few would forget. "Most moving of all is Gloria Foster," wrote Howard Taubman in the *New York Times*, "a young actress with talent and intensity to burn. Three of her turns are in themselves justification for a visit. As a Negro woman who had thirteen children, all sold into slavery, but who never lost her zest for life, she delivers a speech defending women's rights with rich earthy gusto. She is ravaged by tightlipped furies as a woman telling of her husband's lynching and her own abuse by the Ku Klux Klan. And she is heart-breaking as the girl who first attempted to integrate Central High in Little Rock, Arkansas. Someone should write a play for Miss Foster."

The other reviews were equally laudatory, and even when critics faulted the work for being too much editorial and not enough drama, as did the *Village Voice*, they exalted Foster as "unforgettable," "faultless," and "magnificent."

As testimony to the power of the piece and of Foster's performance, *New York* magazine's usually unmoved John Simon related the following account: "Perhaps the most touching thing was to see Claudette Nevins, a white actress, watch Gloria Foster, her Negro colleague, act out the part of a fifteen-year-old Negro girl trying to go to an integrated school in Little Rock and nearly getting lynched. Miss Foster was magnificent, but no less so was the fact that there were tears in Miss Nevins' eyes. It must have been at least the sixtieth time that she was, from the sidelines, witnessing this scene, but the tears were brand new and absolutely real."

In future years, Foster would refrain from reading reviews until a production ended. But at age twenty-six, she didn't know any better. "I was shocked," recalled Foster. "I didn't know much about what reviews meant. I didn't know, at that time, that reviews can make you or break you; I didn't know the value that was placed on them. When people said, 'Did you hear?,' I don't know that I felt anything but grateful that I had made a contribution to the show. The play was what was valuable to me. At the Goodman, the play—and your relationship to it—was the thing."

Foster won a Vernon Rice–Drama Desk Award and an Obie Award for her performance in *In White America*. The Obie was presented to her by Colleen Dewhurst, who, along with her then-husband, George C. Scott, would become her friends.

Nobody followed critic Taubman's dictate by writing a vehicle especially for Foster, but the offers began to pour into her small apartment. (The move to King Street had been bankrolled by her $65 a week salary from *In White America*.) Among the plays seeking her talent were Alice Childress's *Wedding Band*, Kennedy's *Funnyhouse of a Negro*, and James Weldon Johnson's *Trumpets of the Lord*. "Once you were known back then, people came by and gave you plays—we were all living in the Village then. They'd leave plays at the theater. It was a wonderful time. The work didn't always come through agents. This was the playwright's time." But she felt she had stumbled into an artist's dream at the Sheridan Square Playhouse and was loath to wake from it. To a certain extent, naiveté ruled her rejection of these offers. "I thought you stayed with things," she explained. "My thinking was that some loyalty was involved. When you've been so unexpectedly and so richly noticed, you just don't leave. I didn't know that's what actors did; you know, they're in a play for two minutes, then they're gone and on to the next one."

But Foster wasn't staying simply out of a loyalty to the production. She had found a perfect instrument for her talents and intentions. In the simplest terms, she had something good: Why give it up? "I thought *In White America* was a valuable piece," she affirmed. "It was my first knowledgeable experience of being able to make a political and social statement that was so close to who I am and having it be, at the same time, a challenging acting experience. I hadn't known that all that could be combined. It wasn't like playing Ruth in *A Raisin in the Sun*; there, you're within it, as one person. *In White America* was so big, in the sense that you're reaching out in so many directions. It was instant characterization. For a while there, plays written in standard play format were not exciting to me.

"Young people today, I think, are thinking in terms of stepping stones. I don't know that I ever thought that way. It sounds ridiculous, but I was always thinking in terms of a more difficult role. I'm still in the process of investigating."

In many ways, Foster's experience in *In White America* would set the standard for all her future work. In the Princeton professor's earnest historical drama, she found everything she hoped to achieve in her craft and a few things for which she hadn't dared to hope. First and foremost was the towering, challenging dramatic role, a role of many dimensions and tremendous effect—a type of role she would continue to seek for the rest of her career. Such characters were typically years older than Foster—a trend in her casting which began at the Goodman and would find her played middle-aged women when in her thirties and forties, and a centenarian when not yet sixty. The ingenue never interested her.

Obviously, *In White America* also had a strong social message, a quality she would frequently demand in the projects she chose to do. Consequently, she would sometimes ignore more visible or lucrative jobs. Furthermore, Duberman's play also afforded Foster direct contact with the audience, and she would seize upon that relationship again and again in the years to come, in productions ranging from the Greeks to Brecht to Emily Mann's *Having Our Say*.

All in all, when Gloria Foster was cast in *In White America*, the stage was set for what basically could be called, and without snobbery, a principled career. Those principles would make her reputation as a leading dramatic actor. They would also make her, for many a month and sometimes many a year, an infrequently employed actor.

Early Successes Foster's reputation steadily grew over the next few years, Unemployment woes would come and go, but during the mid-1960s, a period of artistic experimentation and advancing opportunities for African-American actors, she would go from role to role.

Foster stayed with *In White America* through its entire fourteen-month run. While she was in the play, both *The Cool World* and *Nothing But a Man* came out, increasing her fame. The only time she was tempted to leave was in the summer of 1964, when a bigger, better role came along. She was offered Lady Macbeth in a production starring Moses Gunn (also from the cast of *In White America*), at the Antioch Shakespeare Festival, in Yellow Springs, Ohio. Foster took ill at the last moment, however, and was replaced by Pauline Flanagan.

She did her first role after *In White America* in Chicago. It was of appropriate size: Circle in the Square's production of *The Trojan Women*, performed at the Ravinia Festival Theatre. Foster played Andromache and was nominated for the Sarah Siddons Award, which commemorates the year's best performance by an actor in a Chicago theater.

Her next job, however, would test her mettle, as well as the public's willingness to accept the young African-American actor in any role. Every generation or so, there is a major production of *Medea* in New York. In the mid-1960s, the most recent had been Judith Anderson's widely acclaimed 1947 portrayal. (Future productions would feature Zoe Caldwell and Diana Rigg in the title role.) In 1965, Judith Rutherford Marechal, who had produced *In White America*, decided, along with producers Paul Libin and Jay Stanwyck and director Cyril Simon, that the current generation's Medea would be Gloria Foster, who was not yet thirty. This time Foster would play the vengeful heroine in the verse adaptation by Robinson Jeffers.

The announcement inspired great excitement, and not only because it would be the Obie Award–winner's next role. "There was no question who I was: an African-American actress," said Foster. "That was the only identity I had. I was always that. They had a very difficult time getting financial support, on one level because it was a classic and on another level, I'm sure, because [casting me] was a new idea. It wasn't until later that critics made arguments against casting in that way. It was a different climate. So much was changing. It was the '60s."

Medea opened at the Martinique Theatre, on West 32nd Street, on November 28, 1965. The reviews were not entirely sunny. Taubman wrote in the *Times* that Foster had not learned to master her emotions enough to become "the bitter, savage creature Medea must be." Most critics did not care for Cyril Simon's production, but some had kind words for Foster. The *New York Post* declared that Foster had "returned with a thunderclap." The *New York Herald-Tribune* called her "a majestic, full-voiced, statuesque and stunning actress."

No major reviewer mentioned Foster's color except Martin Gottfried of *Women's Wear Daily*. He observed a parallel between the plight of Medea—a foreigner transported to a foreign country and then abandoned—and the situation of blacks in America. "There is no implication in this that Ms. Foster's portrayal is in

Gloria Foster in the title role of Robinson Jeffers' *Medea*, at the Martinique Theatre, in the fall of 1965.

any sense 'Negro'," he continued. "It is simply an extremely effective performance by an enormously gifted actress who is bound to grow with experience."

Despite the mixed notices, *Medea*'s run was extended. To meet demand, the producers offered four matinees during the final week. All told, Foster played the role seventy-seven times. For her second New York stage role, she won her second Obie Award, as well as a *Theatre World* Award.

Once *Medea* ended, the waiting game began again. Being selective, in one instance she turned down a job with only $36 in her pocket. "Some of these roles were vulgar, just plain vulgar," she commented. "There was no real problem saying no." One she said yes to was a presentational evening of African-American poetry and folk music, conceived and directed by Roscoe Lee Browne, and presented by the Public Theater. The show, which featured selections by Gwendolyn Brooks, W.C. Handy, James Weldon Johnson, LeRoi Jones, Richard Wright, and others, was scheduled to play only a couple of nights, free of charge, at Central Park's Delacorte Theatre. But it transferred to Broadway's Longacre Theatre in September of 1966 with the new title, *A Hand Is on the Gate.*

Joining Foster in the cast were Moses Gunn, Cicely Tyson, Leon Bibb, James Earl Jones, and Browne himself. The women wore gowns, the men tuxedos. Foster, who recited several poems including Langston Hughes' "Bound No'th Blues" and Margaret Walker's "We Have Been Believers," was once again enjoying direct contact with the audience.

Critics, however, were not impressed with this first show of the new season. Composed of eighty different selections, the evening was too much, too long, and too static. "At its best," said Dan Sullivan of the *New York Times,* "the verse flames and the actors burst into eloquence. At its worst, the show looks and sounds like an elocution-school recital." The *Village Voice* even suggested that its "distressingly uncontroversial" nature constituted a "sell-out" on the part of its creators.

Two days after the reviews came out, the show was trimmed by 30 minutes. The production was budgeted at a mere $35,000, with a $13,000 weekly break-even point. Tickets were priced as low as $1.50 to attract audiences. Still, *Hand* took in only $10,000 the first week, and posted a closing notice for September 30. The black community quickly mobilized, forming "The Citizens Committee to Open the Gate." The group collected $7,000, which it handed over to the production on September 30. But nothing seemed to save the show, and *A Hand Is on the Gate* closed only eleven days into a scheduled four-week run.

Foster's next job later that same fall was the title role in Federico Garcia Lorca's 1934 tragedy *Yerma,* a production of the fledgling Lincoln Center Repertory Theatre, under its brief Herbert Blau–Jules Irving administration. The one gnawing desire of Yerma, the single-minded heroine, is to bear a child. When she discovers that her husband, Juan, has no desire for offspring and advises her to resign herself to a childless future, she kills him with her bare hands. The production was directed by John Hirsch, and Juan was played by another rising actor, Frank Langella.

While few of the reviewers thought *Yerma* a success, some granted it the qualified praise of being the troubled Lincoln Center's best effort to date. As usual, though, there were kudos for Foster. The *Village Voice* applauded her "quality of grandeur, her responsiveness to the scale of the tragedy, and her unmistakable understanding of Yerma." Comically, the *Times*'s Walter Kerr thought she had a "face straight out of Gauguin," while *Newsday* said she looked like something from a painting by Rivera. Her commanding locution was again noticed. One reviewer commented—perhaps not altogether charitably—that Foster added extra vowel sounds to her words.

Gloria Foster's first major Hollywood movie came in early 1967—*The Comedians,* a big-budget affair boasting the starry husband and wife duo, Richard Burton and Elizabeth Taylor. Graham Greene penned the screenplay from his own novel about a Caribbean dictatorship and the befuddled Caucasians who remain there, stupidly insistent on bearing their white man's burden. Burton played a dissipated, down-on-his-luck hotel owner infatuated with Taylor, the wife of the British ambassador, played by Peter Ustinov. The supporting cast, no less stellar, included Alec Guinness, Paul Ford, Lillian Gish, and Zakes Mokae. Foster played Madame Philpot, the wife of a murdered island leader. That she should find Roscoe Lee Browne, James Earl Jones, and Cicely Tyson working beside her was not a coincidence: Director Peter Glenville had selected many of the film's black actors from the cast of *A Hand Is on the Gate.* The movie was set in Haiti, but filmed in Dahomey (now Benin), West Africa. Though Foster had only one big scene, she remained on the set for some time.

On the long plane ride back from Africa to her next job—a production of Strindberg's surrealistic *A Dream Play* at the Goodman Theatre—Foster became ill. The cast of *The Comedians* had been warned against drinking the water in Africa, but somewhere along the way an ice cube had slipped into her Coca-Cola. The bacteria didn't strike until she landed at O'Hare. Two days into rehearsals, "my legs just collapsed under me," she remembered. She remained sick for ten days, oftentimes rehearsing from her bed, while doctors tried to discover the problem. Foster recovered in time for the first performance, on March 31, 1967.

Foster next appeared in *A Midsummer Night's Dream,* a Circle in the Square production presented at the Theater de Lys, in Greenwich Village. John Hancock, who had directed the play in San Francisco and Pittsburgh, considered his approach an "erotic black comedy" version of the classic. The set was based on drawings by artist Jim Dine; the show began with a vintage jukebox playing the famous incidental music by Felix Mendelssohn; a man played Helena; and all the performers wore costumes accented with iridescent paint.

Foster said she didn't contemplate the interpretation—she just accepted it. "It was an adventuresome time," she said. "You had no fears, you just did it. That was a period when you just accepted a director's vision. That was also a time when directors *had* visions and were able to communicate them to actors. I've met directors who have no dialogue that is valuable to the actor. They don't have communicative skills to express their point of view."

The critical judgments were predictably aligned with the prejudices of the publications doing the judging. "John Hancock's staging of *A Midsummer Night's Dream* sets a kind of high water mark for avant-garde productions of Shakespeare," remarked the *Times'* Dan Sullivan. "As the saying goes, it's magnificent—but it's not Shakespeare." *Variety* didn't care for the production or for Foster, who played both Titania and Hippolyta. The *Village Voice* liked both. "A tour de force of imagination," declared Michael Smith. "Gloria Foster is intense and statuesque as Titania and gives Hippolyta a wonderful roughness and burning sensuality."

By the summer, when she appeared in John Hancock's production of *A Midsummer Night's Dream*, Foster was a well-known and respected figure in the New York theater. A newspaper account of *A Dream Play* quoted director John Reich as saying many critics considered her "the greatest living Negro actress." Not all the plays she had appeared in had been universally acclaimed, but Foster usually emerged unscathed, and often with her stature heightened, as the critics observed that she had risen above the material or production.

In Tune with the Times Foster had come to New York in 1961 expecting, if not demanding, to do a certain level of work. The city's theatrical community had met her expectations, not only in quality but quantity. "It was a growing period," she recalled. "It was the beginning of African-American actors working in well-produced productions. . . . I came to the city with no other concept of theater but nontraditional. I was going to be a part of theater, as other people had prepared themselves to be a part of theater. That meant whatever was going on in the theater should be accessible to whoever was prepared to come in there, do their audition, and do the roles."

At that time, there was no such term as nontraditional casting. Joseph Papp, producer of the New York Shakespeare Festival, referred to it as interracial casting, and it was simply his policy. "He didn't explain his actions," Foster observed, "he just did it. I expected to be considered for whatever everybody else was being considered for. It just never entered my mind that I was not to aspire to that. And it never entered my mind that someone would say no.

"I was brought up in an interracial environment, and it never stopped me from doing anything. I didn't know any other way to think. I knew the way it had been, in terms of our history—that was all the more reason why I didn't know any other way to think than a positive, forward movement. If I had not had that expectation, I could not have stayed in this business."

California The years between *In White America* and *A Midsummer Night's Dream* had been productive and exhilarating ones for Foster. The next five would prove to be different, to say the least.

In 1967, Gloria Foster and Clarence Williams III got married. Soon after, Williams was cast in a lead role in the ABC television police drama *The Mod Squad*, and the couple moved to California. Since Foster had made her name in New York, she knew few people in Los Angeles. What's more, southern California had little theater to speak of, and the stage was Foster's medium of choice. From 1968 to 1973—the run of *The Mod Squad*—she would find much of her time and nearly all of her talent unused.

According to Foster, she was not overly frustrated; she had been prepared for

the change. "I was very much a housewife," she explained. "I went out there to be with my husband. This was before bicoastal living came about. Where I came from, when you got married it was to be together. There was a role to function in. Had I not been available, our marriage would have never survived."

Williams worked 14- to 18-hour days, eight months out of the year. To see her husband as much as possible, she drove him to the studio every morning, frequently joined him for lunch, and always picked him up at night. Once *The Mod Squad* completed filming each season, Clarence and Gloria set off immediately for their apartment on the Upper West Side. "We'd get off the plane and head straight to Harlem and bar hop and club hop," recalled Foster. "Clarence needed that energy. Those were his roots."

During her stay in California, to her great disappointment, Foster was never able to establish a relationship with any theater, not even the prestigious Mark Taper Forum. She did, however, occasionally land a guest spot on television. Many of these came through Bill Cosby. Cosby had been a rising comedian at the time Foster was taking nightly bows in *In White America*. One night the comic saw the show, and though he didn't introduce himself afterward, he did eventually.

Referring to Cosby's early TV series, Foster said, "Immediately upon his getting *I Spy*, he contacted me about doing a show with them. I was doing *Medea* at the time. I was told to return a call to Bill Cosby, and I said, 'Oh, yeah, right.' For whatever reason, I returned this call, and it was he." Foster couldn't leave *Medea*, but appeared on a later season of *I Spy*. She would eventually find a second family in the Cosby clan (she is godmother to Bill's middle child), and worked on all of Cosby's shows around that time, including *The Cosby Show* and some of his special programs. She also did two guest spots on her husband's show. Despite all the exposure to television, however, Foster would never be attracted to the series format, and has never seen it as a potential source of steady work.

"I've never done a series," she observed. "I don't know that I ever want to. I don't do pilots, because if the series is taken, then you have to do it. I don't know how to sign away for five years to so many people who control the thing. I cannot fathom it. I can sign away to a husband, to a relationship, to a friendship. I don't know how to sign away to entities.

"I've watched people do it; I've watched them go crazy, too. I've watched values change because of the money, the visibility."

There was also work to be had in the growing form of made-for-television movies, such as *The Outcasts*, in 1968. In *To All My Friends on Shore*, in 1972, she played—again opposite Bill Cosby—the mother of a boy afflicted with sickle-cell anemia.

The Mod Squad, meanwhile, was a resounding success, and Williams quickly surpassed his wife in terms of fame. There was, though, no rivalry between the two. As Foster saw it, they weren't traveling the same road, so there was no reason to feel competitive. He was in television; she was a stage actor. Still, she admits that the attention Williams was getting required a certain adjustment in perspective: "It was difficult to try to keep in mind a sense of your own interests and also be supportive of his interests," she remarked. "He was the recognizable one, and it was extraordinarily exciting to watch that development. I took great joy in that. But it also becomes harder to keep yourself focused and recognize that your work in the theater has as much value, though not as widely expressed."

Black Visions When Gloria Foster did *Black Visions* in April of 1972, it was her first stage role in New York in five years. The nation had gone through myriad political and social upheavals during those years, and in no area more than race relations. Hopeful prospects for peaceable living between blacks and whites had dimmed since the great years of the civil rights movement in the early '60s, for both Martin Luther King and Malcolm X had been assassinated. Now the voices of the Black Panthers and of black separatists had moved more to the fore. The change in the nation's attitudes could be spotted everywhere, even in the microcosm of the theater. At the time of King's historic 1963 march on the nation's capital, Foster had been about to join the interracial cast of *In White America*. In 1973, she found herself in a staging of Chekhov's *The Cherry Orchard* with an entirely African-American cast.

Black Visions was a quartet of one-act plays presented by the New York Shakespeare Festival. Of the four plays, only Foster's piece, a solo play by Sonia Sanchez called "Sister Son/ji," was even remotely well received, and it was Foster's return to the stage that the critics primarily noticed. Her performance was a *tour de force*. She played an elderly Mississippi woman who, first seen slumped over and barely audible, relates her history. Starting from a flashback to a journey north, then recounting her work in the civil rights movement and the loss of a son, Foster assumed the successive ages of the speaker as the monologue proceeded, her figure rising with the drama of the woman's story. The conclusion found her once again an abject heap.

"Gloria Foster brings clarity, dignity, power, as well as a handsome presence to the piece," wrote Harold Clurman in *The Nation*. Walter Kerr, in the *New York Times*, called her work "as breathtaking as anything the American theater can come up with just now. . . . [Her face is] ablaze with humiliation even as she is being tough, intimating the surrender inside a protest, catching the intolerable surprise of the most unexpected events."

Joseph Papp provided Foster with her next job as well. The idea of an all-black *Cherry Orchard* had been that of James Earl Jones, who was set to direct (Michael Schultz eventually took over directing duties). The script adaptation was by playwright Ed Bullins. Jones was to play Lopakhin, and Foster was cast in the central role of the self-centered, irresponsible Madame Ranevskaya. She was eager for her first stab at Chekhov.

"I absolutely loved it," she said. "I loved the way that production was cast. I loved the fact that our dialogue coach was a black woman who knew Russian backwards and forwards. I loved the fact that the music was being played by a young black violinist. I loved everything about that production."

Foster did admit, however, to some trepidation over the casting concept and its final reception: "I found it curious. I know, looking back on it, that it was a period when people were trying to find a way. Perhaps the thinking was that a Russian play could be done as long as all the characters looked somewhat alike. Maybe what was disconcerting was the contrast of white and black."

The Cherry Orchard opened in January of 1973, and the great debate began. In the sixth paragraph of his lukewarm review, the *New York Times*'s Clive Barnes remarked, "By the way, this is an all-black cast." He then went through a series of dutiful and respectful critical contortions to explain such a production to his reading public: "Mr. Papp felt the need to develop a concept of a classical theater for black actors," he reasoned. "At this stage in black nationalism in our political development, Mr. Papp believes less and less in integrated casts. . . . Therefore this *Cherry Orchard* is not to be regarded as a manifesto or issue. It is simply a special corner of the Afro-American cultural heritage that Mr. Jones and Mr. Papp wanted to explore."

Other critics were not so eager to excuse themselves from judgment, and the production, or the idea of the production, or both, became fiery topics of debate. The foundations of the critics' complaints were many, and seldom did two opinions match. Walter Kerr, also in the *Times*, thought the show "dull," and added, "The one thing we look for, I think, as Negro performers begin to tackle the major plays of the European tradition, is a freshness of eye and ear that will wake up that tradition, relieve it of its staleness, perhaps shatter its bad habits."

Martin Gottfried, of *Women's Wear Daily*, liked the show very much, but remarked that "the idea of using black bodies to make a point is backward not only in its liberalism, but also in its basic use of actors as racial figures." Another reviewer, Stephen Koch, argued the exact opposite, cheering Papp's and Jones's casting of the play while abhorring the production.

By March, the ever civically minded *Times* felt they should lend space to a printed symposium called "Should Black Actors Play Chekhov?" Among the contributing gadflies was poet Maya Angelou, who contended that *The Cherry Orchard*—which, in her opinion, "takes the cake" as the dullest of classics—"needs" the energy and talent of black performers. Among these suggested energizing contributions might be "improvisations" by Sammy Davis, Jr.

Many critics found fault with Foster's performance, judging her too strong and willful in her portrayal of the feckless Ranevskaya. But to Foster, the production represented a larger, more troubling defeat. Like so many racial issues in the country, nontraditional casting was no longer a simple one. And—at least for Foster—the critical gloves came off with *The Cherry Orchard*. "There were critics who could not see beyond our color to review the play," said Foster, "and could not see what we, as people of color, brought to the play, that might be different from somebody else. I find a lack of perspective in reviewing, when it comes to reviewing us." It was on such occasions, as she put it, that "all the anger of '*How dare you?*' came out."

The Long View In Gloria Foster's career, certain abiding features have made themselves apparent. Among them are the trail-blazing forays into the classics; the propensity for leading, almost exclusively dramatic roles; and the ongoing favor of critics. Another aspect of her career path, however, has been a lack of work. Foster has been regularly plagued by consecutive months—sometimes consecutive years—of unemployment. A case in point: After *The Cherry Orchard*, she would not take the New York stage in a major production until *Agamemnon*, four years later.

Foster seemed almost preternaturally prepared for this fate. As early as 1963, she told interviewers that, as an African-American, she did not expect her opportunities to be abundant. And, in a 1981 interview, she stated, "At a certain point, I faced a recognition that I was not going to work as much as I wanted to." Foster readily admits that this circumstance can be partially attributed to her aristocratic taste in roles. She was not interested in doing comedies or musicals, and her agents knew better than to bring her such jobs. "As long as my desires went toward major roles, and difficult roles," she said, "perhaps I thought I couldn't expect any more. I've always considered myself extremely fortunate if a challenging role came along every few years."

Still, she knew that her selectivity was aggravated by her race. The steady work that might be had by a white dramatic actor was not as easily accessible to a black actor. "When I first came here, this city was loaded with beautiful young African-American actors and actresses," she said. "It made such an impression on me, because I came from the Midwest. I saw all these off-off-Broadway productions with beautiful young people who should have been in the movies then. But that was not a possibility. Television and film was so far behind this enclave in the theater. Their beauty was being wasted, their youth was being wasted. They just dropped by the wayside."

The mid-70s found her with time at her disposal. Though there were lean periods, money was never much of a problem because of Williams's income. She spent some of her time renovating their apartment, putting in new walls, a new ceiling, and installing seventeenth-century stained-glass windows. Some nights, she would throw elaborate dinner parties. Later on in the decade, she set about completing her education, eventually securing a master's degree in speech at the University of Massachusetts in Elmhurst. Three times a week, she would board a northbound Trailways bus and attend classes.

So she never grew overly exasperated or branded herself a martyr. Asked what she did when unemployed, she replied, simply, "Live. I had a husband. I had a home. I had friends. I love New York. I've never been anxious about periods when I wasn't working, because I always felt I was going to bring more to it when a role did come up. I would have grown more.

"What probably saved me—in the sense of not going crazy—is that I've always felt it was important to live; to experience the day; to experience the hurt, the pain, the love; to experience the interaction. And come your next role, you're so much more vital. I wasn't going to be any younger. Once you pass that stage of the twenties, then it's about maturity.

"That's what's so fascinating about this form of communication for me," she continued. "It never stops. Every year, every day, hourly, you've got something else to give to it. And I don't want to sound silly, but that's all it is, having more to enrich a character. But that's also because that character is part of a bigger statement— it's part of a more valuable contribution to life or to the understanding of it. Day by day, you learn about acting. It's a part of living life."

Public Service In the spring of 1977, Joseph Papp, whose New York Shakespeare Festival was operating at Lincoln Center (as well as downtown), engaged the innovative director Andrei Serban to mount an ambitious production of Aeschylus's tragedy *Agamemnon,* at the Vivian Beaumont Theatre. Serban's vision could be seen in every aspect of the remarkable staging. Following the ancient Greek tradition, he had certain actors doubling up, playing several roles. Some audience members sat on bleachers at the rear of the stage. The playing area pierced the orchestra, and through a large triangular grid leapt the flames of torches held by a seemingly captive chorus of twenty-seven.

The lavish, primitive, and visceral production was actively disliked. Walter Kerr titled his review "Why? Why? Why? Why?"

Serban apparently reconsidered matters, because he staged the same play again that summer at the Delacorte Theatre, in Central Park, and drastically altered his approach. With an almost completely different cast, this new production was austere by comparison. Gone were the elaborate machinery and the double casting. Foster played the role of Clytemnestra in this second production.

The critics changed their tune. "Mr. Serban's new production . . . is in all senses restorative," wrote Mel Gussow, of the *New York Times.* "With it, the play regains its passion and terror, the director reaffirms his reputation as a theatrical innovator and respecter of text."

Agamemnon was Foster's first stab at the Greeks since *Medea.* She relished the experience. "I love the Greeks," she said, enthused. "I love the leanness and the specificity of the language. It fits with the passion, and it fits with the movement. You can move in the Greeks. They embrace a bigger passion—at least, in the way I like to do the Greeks."

"Gloria Foster, as a titanic Clytemnestra, makes us keenly regret her long absence from the classical theater," declared Gussow, in an appraisal that must have been particularly satisfying. "With her majestic presence, Miss Foster is naturally suited to play queens. . . . Her Clytemnestra is unmasked, but there is such intensity in Miss Foster's emotion that, speechless, her face is often like a mask—frozen in anguish, fixed for retribution."

For the next few years, Foster would not hurt for work, in classics British, German, and American—much of it at one address and because of one man, Joseph Papp. Years earlier, before even setting foot in Manhattan, Foster had been alerted to Papp. "My teacher had said, 'When you get to New York, try to audition for this new theater, the New York Shakespeare Festival.'"

Foster had met Papp in the early '60s when he was still a stage manager at

Gloria Foster as Clytemnestra in the 1977 New York Shakespeare Festival production of Aeschylus's *Agamemnon*.

CBS, and he cast her almost immediately in a television production called "Shakespeare's Women." Subsequently, Papp would use Foster often; his productions became the source of much of her New York stage work, as it was for many African-American actors plying their trade in the '60s and '70s.

Because Papp cast "according to what you had to bring to the role," the Shakespeare Festival came to match the meritocracy Foster encountered at the Goodman School of Drama. "I appreciated that. It was, for me, the most vital, consistent opportunity to work. Unless you were part of a repertory company, an actor had to work in order to grow. Joe offered that opportunity to many actors. I don't know where else one gets that kind of experience."

Papp—né Papirofsky—wanted his theater to represent the ethnic, many-cultured city that surrounded him during his youth on Manhattan's Lower East Side. He took a step in that direction by forming, in the late '70s, what came to be known as the Black and Hispanic Shakespeare Company. The troupe included such talented actors as Morgan Freeman, Earle Hyman, Michele Shay, Robert Christian, Mary Alice, and Samuel L. Jackson.

"Joe was looking for a way to give experience not only to white actors but to actors of all complexions, a way of presenting the classics, to be representative of this country," said Foster. "He had been doing that for his entire life at the Public. With this, he more aggressively pursued it."

The company's beginnings were not auspicious. In 1979, they launched productions of *Julius Caesar* and *Coriolanus*, running in repertory. Foster was cast as Volumnia, Coriolanus's ferocious mother. It was a role she knew well; she had played it in school and on television. Now, she would finally act it in her favorite forum, the stage. "I found it vital and exciting. I saw her as a political animal. Nobody speaks like she does in the whole play—her speech is different, her words are different; her rhythms are different. Particularly in those opening scenes, I found that she played like Greek drama."

Like Medea and Clytemnestra, Volumnia was a character far beyond Foster's years. Morgan Freeman, roughly her age, played her son in the production. Vanity might have driven many an actress from such casting. But Foster had rarely played anyone of her own age group.

"When I had the opportunity to do *A Raisin in the Sun*, I was Beneatha in real life, so I wanted to play Ruth," she recalled. "That was the role that interested me. As a young person, I was always moving toward something. I don't know how good that is, but I think as a younger person, I would have gotten fairly bored playing my own age. . . . I enjoyed playing Volumnia. I think I see the role differently, perhaps, from the way it has been played. It is a role that has normally gone to older actresses and I never understood that.

"That has been my life in theater. I was always reaching: older—meaning more mature—characters. Situations that I had not had an immediate exposure to. Variety. The difficult, dimensional characters that were beyond contemporary life. That was what I was always reaching for."

The critics hated *Julius Caesar,* but considered *Coriolanus* the redemption of the company. "Joe Papp's Black and Hispanic Company has taken a quantum leap forward," said the *Village Voice.* No one thought the production a triumph, but most found it skilled and engaging and praised the three central performance of Robert Christian (as Tullus Aufidius), Freeman, and Foster. The *Voice* said Foster "captures the brutality, authority, and intelligence of Coriolanus' mother." *Time* wrote, "Gloria Foster not only takes the stage, she rules it. . . . With her pleas, she saves Rome and delivers Coriolanus to his doom. The look of ashen grief frozen on Foster's face at the moment is desolating." *Coriolanus* was revived that summer at the Delacorte Theatre.

The public knew about Foster's next role at the New York Shakespeare Festival before she did. She remembered being at a press conference with several of her colleagues, including James Earl Jones and Roscoe Lee Browne, when Papp announced with great flourish that his next production would be Bertolt Brecht's *Mother Courage.* The star, he said, would be Gloria Foster. "He didn't ask me," she noted. "My mouth dropped open."

Foster had never thought about playing Mother Courage. Now she had to. At first, rehearsals were about as thought-out as Papp's press conference had been. Up until a week before rehearsals, the company studied the standard version of the play. Neither Papp nor the director, Wilford Leach, had mentioned anything about a new adaptation. Then, "three days before we went into rehearsal, I got this script," remembered Foster. "That shocked me to no end."

The new interpretation was by poet–playwright Ntozake Shange, and it was a doozy. Brecht's seventeenth-century Europe, during the Thirty Years War, was now the American frontier, directly following the Civil War, and Mother Courage was trailing after freed blacks who had been encouraged to join the armed forces during the last years of the Indian Wars (the famous Buffalo Soldiers). Thus, Brecht's unmistakable anti-war play became muddled by issues of race and oppression, and Mother Courage shifted from a montrous symbol of capitalism to a courageous survivor. Furthermore, William Elliot had composed a new score. Foster found the shift unsettling, particularly the new lyric of Mother Courage's opening song.

"As soon as the lyrics of one of the songs changed to 'And she's a light-skinned business woman,' the whole character of Mother Courage changed, in terms of our history. The song was her identity. And not only was she light-skinned, she was pretty. A 'light-skinned business woman' was no Mother Courage in the sense of that poor peasant that we'd seen her portrayed as. As soon as that description was provided, you've got a different Mother Courage."

The critics were confused. A few thought the new spin on the modern classic a master stroke. *Variety* found the production "powerful," noting that "Mother Courage thus becomes less a universal exploiter-victim of the insanity of war . . . than an object of racial hatred and injustice." That very switch, however, is what upset other viewers. "By having most of the characters black or Indians," wrote one critic, "Shange confuses things—she sets our liberal pieties in the way of Brecht's dark vision."

A young Frank Rich, newly with the *New York Times,* found enough provocation to write a 2,000-word think piece on the production. "What play are they doing?" he asked. "The text of Miss Shange's *Mother Courage* amounts to a whole new show, and it raises some troubling questions. . . . Is it right to call a play *Mother Courage* when it in many ways violates the spirit of the drama we associate with that title?"

The production was the most hotly debated show Foster had graced since *The Cherry Orchard,* and, as with that play, she was swept along in the wave of critical dissent. All bowed to her emotional honesty and regal presence—the traits they had always admired—while noting that such qualities were not at all suited to Brecht.

The next role offered to Foster also came as a surprise to her. It was one of the acting Everests of American drama, and not one she had ever considered scaling. Geraldine Fitzgerald had performed in Eugene O'Neill's *Long Day's Journey Into Night,* at the Promenade Theatre, in 1971. Now she wanted to direct it, and sought Foster to play the play's morphine-addicted mother, Mary Tyrone.

"That was a role I would not have thought would come to me," admitted Foster. "I'm saying that role is usually played as a victim. I asked Geraldine Fitzgerald about this. She had played it five different times, and even though she had apparently played it wonderfully well and was wonderfully received, she felt that Mary Tyrone was not a victim. She knew exactly what she was doing. That was her way of dealing with her life, her household."

Fitzgerald pointed out that O'Neill's real mother, Ella Quinlan, had kicked her drug habit as soon as her husband and Eugene's father, the actor James O'Neill, had been removed from the scene. That historical correlation provided Foster with the seed for a new interpretation of the character—one which intrigued her. "With that thinking in mind, I found it very interesting, because it made sense to me then," she explained. "If you've got an alcoholic husband, and an alcoholic son, and another son dying, why not get away from that? I'd take anything under the sun to get away from that kind of home."

Foster claimed she was given the authority to cast the production. Earle Hyman was selected to play James Tyrone, and Al Freeman, Jr. and Peter Francis-James were the sons, Jamie and Edmund. The actors, she said, giddy at finding themselves cast in a play they had never hoped to perform, were determined to do good work. The drama opened on March 3, 1981, at St. Peter's Church, in midtown, as a production of the Richard Allen Center for Culture and Art. The notices were good. Some reviewers thought the production worked because the cast ignored its ethnicity. Conversely, some said the show worked because the actors used their race to their advantage. Either way, most critics agreed it worked.

Critics struggled with Foster's strong performance, finding her more "substantial," "exquisite," and "imposing" than the Mary Tyrones they had seen. Some remained puzzled or displeased, while other fought to understand the performance. All, though, were impressed with her final mad scene. "Always an intelligent and commanding actress of star quality," wrote Douglas Watt in the *Daily News*, "she has never in my experience been this magical or gently compelling."

Foster, however, considered the press largely unreceptive, their minds set against her vision of Mary Tyrone. "When you get to the 'American classics,' something allows people to say things they wouldn't say to your face," said Foster. "Other voices thought that Mary should play the victim, so they said 'miscasting.' And that's not true—it's disrespecting the interpretation of that production. If you can see it is a deliberate reinterpretation, then that is what you should criticize; if it is obvious, then critique it, rather than say this part is miscast. Recognize that she is no longer a wispy victim."

The production was scheduled to play only nine performances, but the positive notices sent Fitzgerald dashing for the phone. The call she made was—naturally—to Joseph Papp, who suggested she take a look at the Public's Anspacher Theater. The production was transplanted on March 18, where it ran for twelve more weeks. Foster found the play particularly rewarding in its effect on the audience.

"It was a wonderful production, and there were people who came four or five times to see that show," she told. "I defy you to find people who have come four or five times to any other production that *Long Day's Journey into Night* has ever had. People who never in their life would have seen a production of it came to see that one."

A Dry Decade Gloria Foster's profession "was never about money," in her estimation, and during the 1980s, that definitely seemed to be the case. The decade would prove a dry one. Bill Cosby continued to lend aid. He used her on *The Cosby Show*, as the first woman president of the fictional Spellman College, and in his movie, *Leonard, Part 6*. And she landed a role in the high-profile mini-series, *The Atlanta Child Murders* and *Separate but Equal*. Stage roles, however, would be few. Even the dependable Public wouldn't come back into her life until 1989.

Joseph Chaikin had never forgotten Foster from their Living Theatre days—he had directed her in a production of Adrienne Kennedy's *A Movie Star Has to Star in Black and White*, in 1976; and in 1982, he cast her in one of his own works, *Trespassing*, a rumination on death and the emotions it evokes. Foster played "the Woman in the Bed," a victim of a stroke who examines her life as she sees it slipping from her grasp. The bed itself, constructed by Mark Frank, was an imposing set piece: a giant, wooden, wheeled object, featuring, on one side, a Picasso-like outline of a body.

The play, performed at La MaMa, provided her with her most unqualified success in years. "Miss Foster is the principal difference between *Trespassing* and other related Chaikin pieces," wrote Mel Gussow in the *New York Times*. "As a director, he has often worked with talented actors, but usually not with someone as emotionally charged as Ms. Foster."

There were few other jobs in the wake of *Trespassing*, however, and Foster spent three years during the 1980s on the opposite side of the footlights, working for the New York State Council for the Arts. Serving on the theater panel, she got a taste of the critic's life, attending one or two productions a week to help determine which theaters would receive grant money. Foster admits the experience was exhausting and somewhat discouraging; she wouldn't want to do it again. She didn't mind the classics, but found the contemporary works dispiriting.

"On some levels, I was disappointed with the nature of the material," she related. "Theater wasn't saying what I wanted to say. And I would have wanted to see a healthier level of integration. I got to be terribly aware that such was not the case. I would have wanted to see subject matter that engaged me more.

"I think it's got to be for more than just entertainment value," she continued, "even though it must necessarily entertain. That's where you start. You've got to know that is an important element of what you're doing. That's a given. But beyond that, I don't see how it cannot be used for a more important purpose, whether you're showing life as it is, or as it should be, or as it would be *if*."

Foster was delivered from administrative service to the theater on June 6, 1988, when playwright Bill Gunn said, "I have a gift for you," and handed her a script entitled *The Forbidden City*. They had met years before at a reading of *Blues for Mister Charlie*, at the Actors Studio, and Gunn had thought of Foster for the play after seeing her in a PBS production called *The File on Joe Hatch*. A reading was put together by Joseph Papp, and the play was soon scheduled for April of 1989.

The Forbidden City attracted interest from the day it was announced. Not only did it mark the return to the stage of Foster after a long absence, it was also staged by Joseph Papp, who rarely directed. Lending the production a bit of morbid notoriety, Bill Gunn died the day before the play opened. Finally, the play itself was unveiled, and people were appalled, amazed, astounded, and confused.

Critics thought the play overwritten, underwritten, and contradictory. As for Foster's character, a Philadelphian holy terror named Miss Molly Hoffenburg, they didn't quite know what to think. She was a "dragon," a "monster," a "the Wicked Witch of the West," a mother "out of *The Silver Cord* complicated by *Mommie Dearest*, Chekhov's Arkadina, and Cocteau's *Les parents terribles*." Foster's command of the role was admired, but her character was not. Critics had a difficult time accepting this regal wife who cheats on her husband with a white man in a cheap hotel, this mother determined to toughen up her bed-wetting poet son through beatings and a constant barrage of insults and embarrassments, until he finally cries out, "Ogress!"

Foster was not entirely surprised by the reaction. She thought she knew what escaped the average audience member about this frustrated grand matriarch. Molly, with her eye on Philadelphia's Main Line and envy of the life of Gloria Swanson, "was a fairly new character for our stage," she explained. "I don't know that she had been depicted in movies or onstage. She was a familiar character within the black communities but, I believe, unfamiliar to most of America and certainly the theatergoing audience. She's someone who sees things on a certain level. There's a no-nonsense about her, and yet she plays a game to survive.

"She wanted to be Gloria Swanson. She did not want to be Lena Horne. That tells you something. Miss Molly is the kind of person who would know that Lena Horne had the same problems she did, the same challenges, the same necessity to defend herself against racism. Gloria Swanson had it all. That was what Bill Gunn was saying: The adjustments and sacrifices that ambitious people have to make in order to receive any gratification out of life. Miss Molly was not intended to be representative of the best of us by any means. But then, that's what makes her an exciting character. If there was a pulling back from her, then what you're saying is you can't have exciting, multidimensional, less-than-perfect characters that are black."

Despite Miss Molly's personality, or perhaps because of it, the play was extended. And, befuddled or not, the Drama Desk critics' association nominated Foster for an award.

Having Her Say If Gloria Foster found one archetype of the black community in *The Forbidden City*'s Miss Molly, she found another, dearer one in *Having Our Say:* the 105-year-old Sadie Delaney. In 1995, when the show opened, Sadie was living in Mount Vernon, New York, with her sister Bessie, 103. Both African-American spinsters, they were living vessels of American history.

In 1993, *Having Our Say: The Delaney Sisters' First 100 Years,* an autobiography of their lives as told to journalist Amy Hill Hearth, had been published and surprised everyone by hitting the bestseller list. It remained there for a half a year, selling upwards of a half-million copies. A New York literary agent sent an advance copy of the book to her sister, Emily Mann, a director and dramatist who was also the artistic director of the McCarter Theatre, in Princeton, New Jersey. Mann was struck by the stories in it and mentioned the book to her friend Judith Rutherford James, a producer. James read the book and told Mann: "We've got to do this!"

In the fall of 1993, Mann, James, and James' sometime partner, Camille O. Cosby, approached Hearth. At first the trio had a movie adaptation in mind, or a television mini-series, but soon afterward all involved agreed upon the play format. Mann, who adapted the book, toyed with dramatizing the sisters' long lives, conjuring up a sweeping epic stage work with many set and costume changes. Eventually, though, she decided to mirror the book's storytelling approach with a minimalist, two-character conversational piece, the two sisters preparing a meal in their kitchen, while inviting the audience to pull up a chair and take in their tale.

There were two connections between the developers of *Having Our Say* and Gloria Foster. In the '80s, Mann and James had worked on an movie project about Winnie Mandela—an idea of Foster's. Also, Camille Cosby knew Foster through her husband, Bill. Before there was a script, Foster read the book. Though she couldn't imagine how the sisters' biography could work as a play, she was intrigued. She knew these women, had seen them before. "That's something that we in the black community have always known. People like the Delaneys were the important people in our community. There were thousands of Delaneys, by another name; hundreds of thousands, who surmounted their circumstances, who came out of slavery and just *did*." She added, "You always hear of those who did not survive that period."

Foster was asked to play the quieter, sweeter older sister, Sadie, who became the "first colored teacher in the New York City school system," and was the "molasses" to Bessie's "vinegar." "She had survived with such grace," observed Foster. "She had not been damaged. Bessie had been damaged. She had her anger until the day she died. Sadie was able to find a forgiveness. She had settled on who she is and her place in the world. She's solid. I admire that."

Mary Alice, who had won a Tony Award for her performance in August Wilson's *Fences*, in 1987, was cast as the feisty, opinionated Bessie. At first, Foster had difficulty in the rehearsals. Since much of the show was directed to the audience, the "guests," she felt she was rehearsing without the play's central character. It wasn't until the first preview that her performance fell into place. When it did, however, a remarkable symbiosis took place between her and her co-star. The two would perform the play together for the entire run at the McCarter, as well as its long stay on Broadway, and both would leave the production at the same time. There were no replacements, no use of understudies. Foster couldn't have imagined it otherwise.

"This is not a replacement show," she declared. "It's a play, to my mind, that cannot be done unless you've rehearsed it together. The two of you have to be like this"—she pressed her two forefingers together. "The worst thing in the world is to have a substitute come in. It does not work. The glance of an eye means something; the tone of a voice; the way in which Mary and I arrived at a physical relationship—certain things are done at certain times. There is a word cue, there is an arm cue, there is a body gesture. It's not just tossed out there. You're trapeze artists: When someone swings out and you're supposed to catch them, you don't miss that swing!

"When you're working with a replacement, you are no longer two people who have lived together a hundred years, no matter how good you are. A moment might be right with other people, but that doesn't compensate for the other [lost] moments. You have to start from scratch to breathe together."

During one rehearsal, when Alice and Foster had, unbeknownst to each other, both lost their place within the play's many stories and cues, they happened to pass one another onstage. Catching each other's eyes, they instantly realized their mutual dilemma. They didn't panic or stop the scene. Rather, they unthinkingly fell back on their maturing sisterly relationship and spontaneously burst into laughter at their shared folly, then went on. The moment was incorporated into the script.

Having Our Say opened in February of 1995. It was generously received. Audiences rose to their feet every night. It sold more tickets that any production in the McCarter's thirty-five-year history, with many of the performances playing to standing-room-only audiences. In April, it moved to the Booth Theatre, on Broadway. For further inspiration, just before beginning previews at the Booth, the two actors finally met with the Delaney sisters. (Bessie was recovering from an illness, which had prevented them from visiting beforehand.)

The Booth has only 785 seats. Producers pursue the house as the perfect home for a small-scale drama or one-man show. Foster, ever the idealist, would have preferred an even smaller space. The McCarter had been a cavern, true, but the Booth still wasn't cozy enough. To her, the immediacy of the art always took

Gloria Foster and Mary Alice (right) in Emily Mann's *Having Our Say*, at the Booth Theatre, in the spring of 1995.

Photo by T. Charles Erickson.

precedence over the size of the occasion. "I've always loved the intimacy of a small theater," she said. "I loved being at the Booth, because it is one of the small Broadway theaters. But my preference for theater, for drama, is a small house—always has been. If it's planned in a large house, unless I can have a seat in the orchestra, then I don't want to see it. I can't see the show, unless it's something that is so broad, like farce; it's not an experience that is satisfactory to me. Because of money, they put things in these barns that are just too big for drama. If I can't see the twinkle in your eye, I'm not interested."

The reviews were positive. Some wondered whether this historical, anecdotal talkfest was "drama," but no one could say a word against the two faultless central performances. The production, which ran through 1995 (Foster and Alice left in October, after six months), was a late-career triumph for Foster. She had not been on Broadway since the 1960s, and, as during so many other times in her career, the critics and audiences were rediscovering her once again. They recalled her "proven gift as an actress of high tragedy" and commented again on her "liquid voice . . . thicker than sugar."

"Always About the Parts"

Chances are, though, amnesia has since set in, and theatergoers will rediscover her once again. As of this writing, more than two years after her triumph in *Having Our Say,* Foster is still waiting on her next New York stage role.

Of course, Foster has not changed her ways. Striking while the iron was hot, "doing something for expediency," was never her style. The play must be good; it must present her with a challenge, a growth; and it must kindle a fire within her. Martha, in *Who's Afraid of Virginia Woolf?,* for instance, has been offered to her several times. But because it doesn't engage her on some basic level, she can't bring herself to play the role.

This is no doubt frustrating to her agents, her colleagues, and her fans. But she can't worry about their frowns. It is her affair, after all: Her art has always been about herself and nobody else—not in the manner of self-centered divas, but in knowing what to put first, the way a dedicated artist is always true not to her bank account or her career or her public, but to her art. Lucrative opportunities, high-profile jobs, expedient but regressive work, while understandable options, make no sense to her.

"Everything is an exploration, or building upon what you've learned," said Foster. "I'm not very good at the business of show business. It was an art form, as far as I was concerned, though I know it's a craft and I know it's a business. What has always interested me about it is the art—a theater of actors.

"It was always about the parts and the plays."

Lois Smith

Staying in the Game

I N 1981, LOIS SMITH WAS SITTING on a movie set in Chicago with four young actors. The film was *Four Friends,* and its creators were familiar to her. The director was Arthur Penn, whom Smith had known for many years through the Actors Studio; the year before, he had directed her in the play *Hillbilly Women.* And the screenwriter was Steve Tesich, whose play *Touching Bottom* she had recently performed in, at New York's American Place Theatre. They were friends, artists who, like Smith, had been in the game a long time.

To the young actors on the set—the four friends of the title—they were something else. Tesich had just won an Oscar for the screenplay to *Breaking Away,* and Penn was *the* Arthur Penn of *Bonnie and Clyde.* This was *the big time,* and the quartet of unknowns were already busy carving up their lives into sections: Before *Four Friends* and After *Four Friends.* Years later, Smith reflected, "I remember the young people in that film—one or two of them, especially—having this sense, clearly thought and expressed, of 'Here it is. This was the *difference:* Now I've got this job, I'm making this film. It comes out, and everything is *different!*' I was just horrified. It scared me, almost, that they felt this way. I thought it was a dangerous and false view."

Smith had had her share of pivotal moments in her, by then, three-decade-long career. *The Young and Beautiful* had put her at the center of a Broadway show at the age of twenty-five. Fifteen years later, *Five Easy Pieces* had won her acclaim and the National Society of Film Critics' Award. And life went on after both. A child was born and raised. Parts were won and lost. Her name was known, forgotten, and remembered again. Her life—that is, the actor's life—had not become different, but had been more of the same, only seasoned with experience. Smith had long since warned herself off great expectations.

As for the young actors; well, it was probably best to let them find out for themselves. They probably wouldn't have heeded her advice anyway. Observed Smith: "This is a very public and press-oriented profession, but there's also something else, where that is not the heart of it. And you'd better watch out about counting on fame."

From the Heartland Lois Arlene Humbert was born on November 3, 1930, in Topeka, Kansas, not far in time or distance from the Dust Bowl experience she would re-create onstage six decades later as Ma Joad, in Frank Galati's stage adaptation of John Steinbeck's *The Grapes of Wrath.* She was the youngest child of Carrie Davis Humbert and William Oren Humbert. On the surface, there seemed little chance that her devout family would raise a thespian. Her mother was descended from German Mennonites who fled to Pennsylvania to escape religious persecution and afterward moved to Kansas. The family became Nazarenes, a strict sect that forbade dancing, card playing, and movies. In Kansas, Carrie met and married William Oren Humbert. By the time Lois was born, however, her parents were members of the less extreme Evangelicals, which merged with the United Brethren when Lois was a young girl.

W. O. Humbert did not like the movies, but he had a weakness for the stage. Before Lois was born, he went to night school for acting and directing. He used his skills for the benefit of the church, directing biblical and moralistic plays in churches in Topeka, in St. Joseph, Missouri, and, later, in Seattle, Washington.

"Wherever he went, he slowly turned the church into something that could be a stage," recalled Smith. "I was part of that for as long as I can remember. That is clearly how acting began in my life. I was in the plays if there was anything for me to do. I was in rehearsals, I learned the lines." Moreover, her early association of the theater with the church perhaps enhanced the importance of the former in her young mind. "I realized that it probably had something to do with my taking it very seriously," said Smith.

After a couple of years in St. Joseph, the Humberts moved 2,000 miles northwest to Seattle, in 1941. The high school there had a drama department, and the young actress participated in many of the plays. She was a member of a circle of friends united in their fondness for a popular and influential English teacher named Elizabeth Graves. If her father was upset by her growing interest in theater and her declining attendance at church, he was further worried by this attachment to Graves.

"She was seen as *left*," said Smith. "She had a principal who appreciated her and stood behind her at that high school, but that was really a time when you were thought of as a Communist or called a Communist because of the literature you read." Or taught. And Graves was teaching her young acolytes such incendiary works as Frank Norris's *The Octopus*.

Neither of Smith's two older sisters had gone to college, or had wanted to go. Upon graduating from high school, she won, unsolicited, a one-year drama scholarship to the University of Washington, in Seattle. W. O. Humbert had hoped his daughter would attend a church-affiliated school, such as Seattle Pacific University, rather than a branch of the huge and godless University of Washington system. He was, perhaps, also aware that the University of Washington had a notable drama department. But he acquiesced; the scholarship was there, as was the theatrical seed he had inadvertently planted.

"He would not have wished it for me, I think—a life in the commercial theater," said Smith. "Yet, clearly he was at the beginning of what started it all, and you could see he was trying to guide it."

Early Journeys Lois Humbert had gone to high school with Wesley Dale Smith, though he was half a year ahead of her and she had barely known him then. They both happened to enroll in the University of Washington. He was studying Greek and Latin. They married on November 5, 1948, two days after Lois's eighteenth birthday.

Lois and Wesley moved into an apartment off campus. Her scholarship paid only for tuition, so she took a job at a delicatessen, later working in a butcher shop and as an usher in a movie house. Her heavy work schedule often kept her from participating in school productions, which demanded that she be available every evening. Smith managed to act in a number of plays during her time in college, however, the first being *The Joyous Season*, by Philip Barry.

Selected acting classes at the university were conducted by Donal Harrington. Harrington had been in New York when Stanislavsky's influence had taken root, and he'd transported those ideas to Seattle. "I became aware during those times that what I had done, just out of the pleasure of doing it, had a base that was serious in another way," recalled Smith. "When I started with Harrington and really studied acting—exercises from Stanislavsky—that was my first real training."

Smith was instructed in comedy, Shakespeare, Ibsen, and Chekhov. The effect was nothing less than exhilarating. "What fun to find out this was a true endeavor, that a lot of people had put a lot of work into it," marvelled Smith. "It felt just right. It felt serious and fun at the same time."

When Lois Smith married, she hadn't considered acting as a career. A year later, her future seemed clear. "I think it was about then I realized that I'd always done what was available to me in acting—in school, in church basements—and never really thought beyond that. I had always been as good as anybody. When I was at the University of Washington, that was the first time I thought, 'Oh, I do seem to rise to the top of where I am. Maybe I'm good at this.'"

At this time, her circle of friends, still in touch, were mulling over a group trip to India. One turned to Smith and said, "This decision is probably hardest for you, because you're the only one of us who knows what she wants to do."

After two years of school, things began to break up for Smith. Work was eating up more time, forcing her to take some incompletes in her last quarter. The uncertainty of her situation threw her unflagging interest in acting into sharp relief. Soon, her thoughts drifted a coast away.

In 1950, she left on a fact-finding mission to New York City. Wesley, in his fifth year of study, remained behind. Her stay didn't last long. She worked as a hat check girl in the Russian Tea Room, but homesickness took hold after two months, and she headed back to Seattle and husband.

Then Wesley applied and was accepted to graduate school at Harvard University. The couple decided to live in New York City until Wesley's first term began. With $350 and a used Ford to their names, Wesley and Lois Smith arrived in Manhattan in the middle of the summer of 1952. A close friend attending Barnard College helped them get a cheap apartment in Manhattan's Morningside Heights neighborhood, near the Cathedral of St. John the Divine. The flat was four flights up, the bathroom and kitchen down the hall.

As soon as she was settled, Smith tested her one connection to the awesome and unknown world of New York theater. A professor at the University of Washington had written a new play, and, before Smith departed, gave her the script, asking her to deliver it into the hands of his friend John Van Druten, the author of *Bell, Book and Candle* and *I Am a Camera* and director of Rodgers and Hammerstein's *The King and I.* On one ghastly hot Thursday afternoon, she called Van Druten. "Oh, yes," came the answer on the other end, "we've heard about you. Van Druten's away for a long weekend on Fire Island." She was informed that, during the time it took for the Smiths to cross the country in their Ford, the professor had written another draft of the play; the copy Smith carried was now obsolete and no longer needed. So much for connections.

"Then this amazing thing happened," recalled Smith. "Sometime the following week I got a telegram. Almost no one in the world knew where we were—we had no telephone. Van Druten had come back from his weekend, had heard that I had called, called the professor in Seattle who wrote the play, who didn't know where I was and called my mother, whom he didn't know. There were practically two people who could have told him where we were, and Van Druten sent a telegram saying 'Sorry.'"

Van Druten provided the young actress with the names of a few agents, which she dutifully called on. These were the days when actors made the rounds of talent agencies, à la Katherine Hepburn in *Morning Glory.* "You really could drop by. There would be gatherings of actors," she remembered. "Some agents would be more or less receptive—you certainly couldn't do that with all of them—but in general there was more contact."

When autumn came, Wesley departed for Cambridge to begin his graduate work at Harvard, and the two began a long period of commuting back and forth along the Eastern seaboard. Smith moved into what she would later term a "slum" in Hell's Kitchen. She roomed with another actress, Eulalie Noble. Wesley's scholarship barred him from taking an outside job, so it was incumbent upon Smith to bring in some money until an acting job presented itself. She found work sorting checks and fighting off sleep between midnight and dawn at a Wall Street bank. When daylight broke, Smith would then drowsily trudge off to whatever auditions she could line up.

One of Van Druten's contacts put her in touch with the agent Maynard Morris. One day, Smith delivered her best five-minute audition for Morris, while he busily jawed on the phone. Some of her talent must have reached him, because he called her back for a new play about a father and his three teenage daughters. "I think Maynard just called in all the young people," Smith remarked. "He just swept teenage girls into the office. I remember sitting in the waiting room, and an actress sat beside me, and we looked at each other. I remember thinking we looked alike. We were cast as sisters."

Smith went in to read for Morris and Shepard Traube, who was the play's producer and director. One of them scanned her Seattle headshots and resume of school roles. "And what have you done?" he asked. "Nothing," replied the twenty-two-year-old. "That's what's wrong with me."

"I think that amused them," said Smith. She got the part and was on Broadway by the end of the year.

On Broadway

Smith would remember for years to come the day she got the call telling her she was cast in a Broadway show. It was stupendous news, after all. Acting on Broadway—that was the dream, wasn't it? Still, Broadway was in New York; and her family was in Seattle, her friends were in Seattle, and her husband was in Cambridge.

"I was by myself during those days, and I remember thinking, 'Any day now, I really have to get a job. And then I got this call, and I had a job. I remember the sense very well. It was amazing news. I had this quite nice job in this Broadway play, and I didn't have anybody to tell. I remember that day in the city and that sense of this remarkable, wonderful news and being all by myself with it. It was thrilling and also lonesome. That combination of good news and lonesomeness is something that is common to my life and this profession. It is very hard to make schedules work, to make geography work, to be in the same place with one's loved ones."

The play was *Time Out for Ginger*, by Ronald Alexander, a comedy about a bank executive named Howard Carol, who has very definite ideas about how people should live, and his three young daughters, who have *their* ideas. The Ginger of the title dramatically bucks the status quo by going out for the high school football team. The middle sister, Jeannie (Smith's role), meanwhile, tries out for the school play.

The comedy—which was first tested in Texas and on the Eastern tryout circuit, before making it to Broadway—was primarily a vehicle for Melvyn Douglas, who played the patriarch. Douglas was easy to work with, and he and Smith became friends, the elder actor inviting Lois and Wesley to Thanksgiving dinner at his apartment between a matinee and evening performance in November.

Wesley Smith was, of course, still at Harvard when *Time Out for Ginger* first opened in Wilmington, Delaware. Though Smith's salary was little better than Equity minimum, there was enough for her to send money to Cambridge. Traveling to Boston, however, became more problematic. During rehearsals, she would take a slow train on Friday evening, returning late on Sunday. After the show opened, she would hop the train after the Saturday performance and return on Monday afternoon. Each option was equally taxing. "I remember thinking at one point, 'This is just too hard,'" she said.

On balance, though, "we were fine," she explained. "We both made the choice. He could have come to New York. He chose where he and his advisers felt was the best place to go and the best deal. He got some kind of scholarship pretty much everywhere, including Columbia. He chose Harvard. I don't think he was in a position to do too much complaining, and I was the one making money. I was making better money than either of us could have expected. I was successful. Those were pretty good times."

Soon into the run of *Ginger*, it began to dawn on Smith just how at odds her chosen profession was to the habits and timetables of the rest of the world. Acting, she realized, was the exception among occupations. Nobody played when she played; nobody worked when she worked. "When you are working, you are off the schedule of the world, because when they're at leisure and going out, that's when you're at work," she said. "And when you're at liberty, they're at work. It's not a tragic situation, but it takes its toll. I've felt in recent years that I am used to it, to the vagaries, to the insecurity, to the oppositeness of the life. But it takes a toll."

After Wilmington, the show moved to Philadelphia and then finally opened at Broadway's Lyceum Theatre, on November 26, 1952. Brooks Atkinson, of the *New York Times*, was pleased. He thought the play "fresh, warm-hearted, and funny," and Smith "bubbly and enchanting." Not everyone was as enthusiastic. Over at the *Herald-Tribune*, Walter Kerr thought *Time Out for Ginger* was "the sort of play that ought to go lie down someplace." Still, the production was a success and served Smith with gainful employment through June 27, 1953, when it finally closed. On that final night, Melvyn Douglas ad-libbed a line upon Smith's exit that she would always remember. "That kid," he said. "She's going to be a great actress."

Plays on the Air After *Time Out for Ginger*, Smith received further attention. She was interviewed. She went on radio programs. And she started working with agent Bill McCaffrey. McCaffrey's strong suit was the budding medium of television, which was almost exclusively centered in New York in the 1950s.

The jump from the stage to the small screen was, in that era, a relatively easy one. It was the Golden Age of television drama. Directors such as Sidney Lumet, George Roy Hill, and John Frankenheimer were directing the scripts of Paddy Chayefsky, Rod Serling, Tad Mosel, and Gore Vidal. The drama anthology programs then were run not unlike stage productions, only at an accelerated pace. "When I started out, there were six or eight weekly shows that were plays," recalled Smith, "and when you were in those shows, you rehearsed them like a play, and then you went into the studio during the last few days and did them on camera. So training as an actor in plays was the right thing for television. And the stage is where everyone came from."

Her first television job was for the dramatic anthology series *Kraft Television Theatre*, in an adaptation of a John Galsworthy story called "The Apple Tree." Fielder Cook, who would go on to direct the film version of Rod Serling's *Patterns*, was the director, and George Roy Hill was the artistic director of the program. As Smith tells it, the creators of these programs would routinely raid the literary canon for raw material. When Smith arrived, they had apparently gotten to the Gs on the library shelves. "They'd find an author, they'd find some stories, they'd quickly write an adaptation, and put it on the air."

In 1954, Smith herself acted in a television adaptation of William Dean Howells' *The Rise of Silas Lapham* called "The Laphams of Boston," which starred Paul Newman. In 1955, she appeared on a program designed to showcase young actors, *Star Tonight*, and followed it with another. In 1956 she was in "Bring Me a Dream" with John Cassavetes and George Grizzard, and an edition of the anthology series *The U.S. Steel Hour* called "Noon on Doomsday."

Smith didn't have a television, so she couldn't appreciate much of her handiwork (much of which was done live anyway). The steady stream of television jobs did, however, provide her with a crash course in acting, doubling and tripling her number of credits within a few years.

"It was terribly exciting," recalled Smith. "It wasn't this sense of 'Oh, my God, how can we do this?' You just did it. That was the only game in town. People were filled with enthusiasm. On a special, you'd have maybe four weeks in a rehearsal hall. In the last days, you'd move into a studio and have camera rehearsal, where everything would heat up. Suddenly, time is everything. You're on the clock.

"You would sometimes be changing your clothes on the run, running from one end of the studio to the other as the cameras, with their huge cables, made these flying trips across the floor while they tried not to run into each other's cables. And the director had to know everything that was going on."

Smith's career in television plays culminated in 1959 and 1960. In December of 1959, she appeared on *Ford Startime* in "Cindy's Fella," a Western adaptation of the fairy tale "Cinderella." Smith played the lead under the direction of Gower Champion (in his first foray into television). Playing the shy prairie prince was James Stewart. Early the next year, she appeared in two editions of the *The Play of the Week*, on the PBS station WNTA—once in the title role in Strindberg's *Miss Julie* and as Hilda Wangel in Ibsen's *The Master Builder*. She also acted that year in a teleplay of Joseph Conrad's *Victory* and a televised version of Sidney Kingsley's medical drama *Men in White*.

The end of the year, however, had her taping an episode of *The Loretta Young Show* in Los Angeles. The rest of the television industry would soon head west as well.

West to *Eden* In 1954, the eminent director Elia Kazan was in New York screen-testing actors for his upcoming movie version of John Steinbeck's *East of Eden*. He was seeing people for the lead female role, which would eventually go to Julie Harris. Smith met with Kazan and was later offered a smaller role in the film after she didn't get the Harris part. She had only one scene, but it was a good one. She played opposite James Dean, whom she rather sweetly described as "a nice young actor who was also making his film debut." Smith played a barmaid in the brothel owned by the mother (played by Jo Van Fleet) of Dean's character. The barmaid, in peril of losing her job, directs the young man to his own mother's office. Dean was a good acting partner, recalled Smith; off the set, he was "part farmboy, part cool character."

Kazan had his methods of extracting the performances he desired. Eschewing group notes, he would occasionally walk up to an actor and whisper an instruction in his or her ear, a direction unknown to the rest of the cast until the scene was reshot. Kazan, furthermore, wasn't the only one furnishing Smith with private ministrations. "There were so many people on the set doing so many things," she explained. "That was my first experience on a big movie set. It was very interesting and very seductive, because there were all these people doing things, and many of them had to do with me. When it came time to start to work, there would be people checking my clothes and my hair. I remember at the time just being available to everyone and how distracting it proved to be. Suddenly, we were ready to do it, and then everyone just sort of faded away, and there I was. And I was absolutely distracted. It was a lesson of how important it is to guard yourself in the movies. The conditions are so different for concentration. Everybody wants to be a part of the scene, but when the moment comes, they've backed out of the circle of light and it's just me—and I'd better have something going on."

Seeing herself on the CinemaScope tests months later was disconcerting. Dark-haired, big-eyed, and with the trademark quaver in her voice even then, she made quite an impression. Smith marvelled at the sheer size of what she had wrought. Her image was gigantic, endless, and alarming. "Look at that arm," she thought, gazing with disbelief at her larger-than-life cinema self. "It just goes on and on."

Soon after filming *East of Eden*, Smith signed a two-picture deal with Warner Bros. in order to appear in a western called *Strange Lady in Town*. The movie was a vehicle for Greer Garson, the popular wartime star. (Garson's career was fading by 1955, and she would retire from the movies soon after the film was completed.) Garson played a woman doctor and suffragette in 1880s Boston who goes west to Santa Fe to hang out her shingle. There, she finds a suitor and competitor in local doctor Dana Andrews. Cameron Mitchell provided drama as Garson's wayward brother, a former Cavalry officer turned bank robber, and Smith played a character named Spurs, who rides with and loves him.

The film had a number of things going for it, including a score by Dmitri Tiomkin and the able direction of Hollywood pro Mervyn LeRoy. Critics, however, gave the costume western little more than respectable marks. Smith got some attention, both good and bad. *Variety* wrote: "Miss Smith, who lifted a small spot in *East of Eden*, gives a virtually perfect portrayal of a young girl, emerging into womanhood." The *New York Times*, however, seemed to have viewed a different film.

"Lois Smith," wrote the paper, "plays her western tomboy daughter as though she were one of Chekhov's dames."

Smith's romance with Hollywood, while sudden, was brief. Soon after completing *Strange Lady in Town*, Smith asked to be excused from her contract to accept a role in *The Young and Beautiful*. "I think they rather quickly understood that I wasn't going to be likely to become a starlet," she said. She wouldn't make another major film for fifteen years.

Stardom Though Smith was not long on the Warner Bros. lot, she was present long enough to be discovered by producer Robert B. Radnitz, whose eye was caught by a distinctive straw hat the actress was wearing one day.

Radnitz was trying to bring to Broadway a play called *The Young and Beautiful*. The property had a troubled history which stretched back as far as Smith's youthful career. The play was the work of Sally Benson, whose "Junior Miss" stories in *The New Yorker* were later collected into a popular book, made into a film, and transformed into a long-running stage success. Her "5135 Kensington Avenue" series, in the same periodical, also found success in book and movie form as *Meet Me in St. Louis*.

The Young and Beautiful was based on F. Scott Fitzgerald's "Josephine and Basil" short stories, written in 1930 and 1931, inspired by a feckless young socialite Fitzgerald had unrequitedly loved at Princeton University. In fact, Benson's play began life as *Josephine*.

The selection of the lead actress had been a matter of some publicity; the original producer, Leonard Key, was quoted as wanting Julie Harris. The play opened in Wilmington, Delaware, on January 9, 1953, with Betsy Von Furstenberg in the title role. The show was beautifully timed to benefit from the recent resurgence of interest in Fitzgerald's work, but its journey to Broadway ended after the production played Chicago for only one of a planned two weeks. The production was then shelved, reportedly because of no appropriate Broadway theater was available. Backstage, however, director David Pressman was being replaced with Edmund Trzcinski.

Radnitz, production manager on *Josephine*, acquired the rights, and hired Marshall Jamison to direct. Then, once again, began a search for the perfect Fitzgeraldian flapper. The search ended on that Warners lot, where Radnitz was researching another project. Smith finally took part in a reading of the play, now renamed *The Young and Beautiful*, in April of 1955. The play was to try out in Boston, at the Wilbur Theatre, before hitting Broadway. Rehearsals began in August. "It was very exciting," said Smith. "It's a lot of fun if you have a good part and a lot of responsibility. I like to work hard. Sitting around can be a real drag. It's hard to keep the energy and flow."

At the same time, Smith and her husband were preparing to move to Princeton, where Wesley had secured a position as an instructor. The irony of this move

Lois Smith as Josephine, in Sally Benson's *The Young and Beautiful*, in the fall of 1955.

was compounded when they were housed in a three-story, university-owned build-ing which, they were told, had been Fitzgerald's residence during his school years. Legendary publicist Richard Maney, the model for the bull-headed press agent in Hecht and MacArthur's *Twentieth Century*, quickly seized on this tidbit and began spinning it to the papers. "That's the best present I ever got," he told Smith.

The show opened in Boston on September 14. The reception was mixed, and the box-office business lukewarm. A cast member was replaced, and rewrites were ordered. Smith, however, was roundly praised, with the *Boston Globe* calling her "an acting find." The opening at Broadway's Longacre Theatre, originally set for September 30, was pushed back to October 3, then moved up to October 1 to avoid coinciding with the premiere of another show. Ads featuring Smith in a low-cut formal gown and a wrist corsage began to appear in newspapers and periodicals.

The New York critical reception was also mixed. Some critics failed to find the play's callow youths of interest. "A chronicle about as self-centered and annoying a bunch of youthful pretenders as ever inhabited a stage," decreed one reviewer. *Variety* was more sanguine, particularly concerning Smith; Josephine was "a part fat enough to satisfy any ambitious ingenue. Miss Smith brings considerable precocious technique to the role, a fair amount of grace, and an impressive flow of energy."

Walter Kerr of the *New York Herald-Tribune* did something more than pay a compliment; he took the trouble to analyze Smith's performance: "Lois Smith plays her with enormous insight, tremendous technical virtuosity, and a strange candor that forbids affection. Miss Smith, youngster that she is, is quite above the old pro's habitual bid for sympathy. She is willing to tell the absolute truth. . . . She is often funny; she is sometimes faintly touching; but she is always grindingly actual. . . . When this mere slip of a girl suddenly stops in her frantic gaiety and says, with despair in her eyes, that she is terribly 'tired,' you believe in her absolutely."

Smith was now a star—not the biggest star on Broadway, but the star of a Broadway show, and thus an object for the idle interest of those journalists who are paid to be idly interested in such matters. Calls began to flow in. Profiles were written. Items were placed in gossip columns. "It was a lot of publicity," remarked Smith, rather matter-of-factly. Her head, however, was not necessarily turned.

"The press and the publicity is in some sense the least interesting aspect of it all," she commented. "Of course, it's easy to say that if you have some press attention. But I think there's a way in which I actually feel that way and have been able not to be so needy for it. I've been extremely fortunate to be able to get—not a huge amount, I'm not a household name—but from fairly early on I've had some press. It is heady, in a way; yet it's just not as interesting as rehearsing a play. I don't mean to sound lofty, because one does need [press attention]. You need it because if you get it you're much more likely to be visible, you're much more likely to be considered for good parts, you're much more likely to keep working."

Julie Harris continued to haunt the edges of Smith's career. The Longacre had to be vacated, for Harris was moving to that theater (in Anouilh's *The Lark,* as adapted by Lillian Hellman) on November 14. *The Young and Beautiful* moved to another theater, but closed soon after.

Smith repeated her performance as Josephine twice: Once in a 1956 summer stock production in Cincinnati; and later in the London production, which opened at the Arts Theater Club on August 16 the same year. Smith was the only American in a cast which featured, among others, "a newcomer from the provinces" named Brian Bedford.

New Jersey and Tennessee Princeton, New Jersey, lies
nearly 60 miles southwest of Times Square, but is easily acces-
sible by train; so, while the move made Smith's pursuit of acting jobs more difficult, it did not necessarily hinder her career.
Partly because she was involved in the opening of *The Young
and Beautiful* while Wesley was acclimating himself in Princeton, she was never completely integrated into the university's
academic circles.

"I remember going to a department tea," said Smith. "It was fascinating to
me. I was put at the foot of the table, because that was where my position was as
a faculty wife. It was amazing to me—like another world. I knew the people in the
department, but I didn't feel myself part of that hierarchy."

The Smiths were barely a few weeks in Princeton when Wesley—who, as a
student, had for years deferred service in the armed forces—received his draft
notice and was swept into the Navy, where he would spend much of the next two
years. Lois would visit him as often as possible in Virginia, where he was first stationed, and even more often when he was relocated to Brooklyn. On top of that,
the two-year period was among the most active and exciting of Smith's still-young
career, for it began with her sharing the stage with "the First Lady of the American Theater," Helen Hayes.

In late 1956, Smith was actually getting her second chance to work with
Hayes—in a City Center revival of *The Glass Menagerie*. She played Laura opposite
Hayes's Amanda. The great actress had undoubtedly remembered Smith from a
1955 production of *The Wisteria Trees*, which had opened at the Falmouth Playhouse, on Cape Cod, and then moved to New York's City Center. Hayes re-creat-
ed the role she had originally played in the 1950 Broadway production.

Until *The Wisteria Trees*, Joshua Logan's Americanization of Chekhov's *The
Cherry Orchard*, Smith hadn't done much summer stock. On Cape Cod, while cir-
culating among the tourists and watching them spend while she pinched pennies,
she once again experienced the sensation of being the other—an alien among her
own race. "There wasn't anything unpleasant about it," she recalled. "I had the
sense of being one who was brought out at night to be shown; that one was not
valuable in the daytime. It was something about being an actor. There was a sense
of being the entertainment, being the product."

At City Center, in midtown Manhattan, *The Wisteria Trees* cast included Walter Matthau, Cliff Robertson, Will Geer, Ossie Davis, and Frances Foster. Smith
was most struck by the talent of Hayes: "Near the end of the play, when the family is moving out," said Smith, recalling one memorable performance, "the Helen
Hayes character is calling, and then she comes in. Being onstage and having her
make this entrance, I experienced what must have been an electrical charge. If I
had been required to do something at that point, I don't think I could have. I just
stood there. It was an extraordinary moment. She had been famous from way back.

I remember thinking, 'This is what must have been going on with this young actress back then.'"

Hayes had played Amanda Wingfield in London, in 1948, under the direction of John Gielgud, but the City Center production was her first *Glass Menagerie* in the United States. The other members of the cast were in place by the time Smith's selection was announced in November of 1956: James Daly was to play Tom, and Lonny Chapman the Gentleman Caller. Alan Schneider, who would later become famous as Edward Albee's director of choice, guided the production.

During the first rehearsals of the Tennessee Williams classic, Smith had trouble. Whereas in *The Wisteria Trees* she had occasionally been dazzled by Hayes's work, now she was nearly paralyzed. "At the beginning of rehearsals, I didn't feel strong," Smith said. "perhaps because I was intimidated by Helen Hayes or the nature of her stardom. I was aware that I was creeping around the edges of the set, like I was hiding or skulking. I remember saying to myself, 'There's something wrong. I've played Laura's defeat and not her struggle.'" The revelation proved a turning point in rehearsals. "It was a conscious effort," said Smith.

The production was embraced by the critics, who declared that it affirmed the lasting power of the play. Hayes, while not surpassing Laurette Taylor, who originated the role of Amanda, was just as good, "more positive, direct, and quicker." Smith, too, was praised. *Variety* called her Laura "a stunning portrayal." Brooks Atkinson of the *New York Times* said she played the role "beautifully and poignantly." Walter Kerr, in more considered words, wrote, "Lois Smith stammers out her first blundering evasions, then slowly melts into a radiant lost princess, with a sure and moving grace." Finally, the *Morning Telegraph*'s Whitney Bolton, showing himself a close student of Smith's career, said, "Lois Smith continues to bring tones and shrill emotion to her work. . . . [She is] attractive, a good actress, young and sufficiently off-beat to be more interesting."

Tennessee Williams did not attend rehearsals of *The Glass Menagerie,* but Smith would meet him soon enough. Only weeks after the play closed its two-week run at City Center, she moved from playing one of Williams's most famous characters to originating a role in a new script—that of Carol Cutrere, in *Orpheus Descending*. It was another milestone for a young actress whose career had taken off from the start.

The new script was actually Williams's reworking of his first produced work, *Battle of Angels,* which had closed at the Wilbur Theatre, in Boston, in 1940. The playwright had never stopped working on it and, by his own admission, 75 percent of this 1957 version was new writing. The play tells the tale of Lady Torrance, a denizen of a small, hate-filled Southern hamlet and the wife of its most vicious resident, the drygoods store owner Jabe Torrance. Jabe once led a gang of locals in the killing of Lady's father, when it was discovered the old man had sold liquor to blacks. Into's Lady's stifling world drifts Val Xavier, an idealistic, handsome musician who takes a job in the store and eventually becomes Lady's lover. Carol

Photo courtesy of Photofest.

Lois Smith and Cliff Robertson in the Broadway premiere of Tennessee Williams's *Orpheus Descending*, in the spring of 1957.

Cutrere, a scion of a distinguished local family, is hellbent on tarnishing her good name through a life of decadence; her credo is "live, live, live, live, live!" She tries to get Val to run away with her. He hesitates and is destroyed, along with Lady Torrance, in ghastly fashion, by the town's death squad.

Orpheus Descending was directed by that grand master of the theater, Harold Clurman, who would become a lifelong friend of Smith. The play opened its pre-Broadway run at the Shubert Theatre, in Washington, D.C., on February 21, 1957. At that time, it was called *Something Wild in the Country*. Williams, displaying his grand ambitions for the play, had originally tried to get Marlon Brando and Anna Magnani for the leads. Brando played with the idea for a while, before finally declining the offer. Maureen Stapleton eventually topped the bill as Lady Torrance, and Robert Loggia was Val. Smith received third billing. Clurman had a rather macabre vision of Carol Cutrere. Smith's skin was painted ghostly white, her eyes outlined in black, and her dark hair swirled atop her head—all in all, a slightly Kabuki southern belle.

The D.C. reviewers panned the production. Whatever revisions Williams had made to the play had not worked, in their opinion. *Variety*, however, found Smith "brilliant," and the *Washington Post* called her "splendidly effective."

The production, trailing rewrites along the way, next travelled to Philadelphia's Walnut Street Theatre. In a move Smith remembered as painful to the cast,

Loggia was replaced by Cliff Robertson just weeks prior to the Broadway opening. The Philadelphia notices were slightly improved, with one review favorable, one negative, and one mixed.

Throughout this pre-Broadway turmoil, Smith found herself invigorated by the work, as she had been by *The Glass Menagerie.* "I certainly felt in *Orpheus Descending,* from the early days of rehearsal, that if I do my work, the play just lifts you up. With the hurriedness and quality of television writing, I was already getting used to the fact that much of the time you are trying to make something really good with material that is, perhaps, casual. I became aware, working on both of Tennessee Williams's plays, of how strong they were. I remember that image of being lifted by it. . . . The reward for doing the play was very great each day."

She also felt inspired by Clurman's passionate style of direction, which ended each day in a utilitarian ceremony cherished by Smith: the giving of notes. "It was a great way to learn," she said, "not only from one's personal notes for a scene, but because it was constantly building up the group's shared knowledge. Increasingly I notice—and this may be partly economic, because of the lack of time—that 'notes time' gets shortened, gets cut away. Time is taken away from group notes. It isn't as essential a part of rehearsal as when I grew up. Both as a student and a young professional, this was, for me, one of the strongest and happiest times. I really loved it."

Orpheus Descending opened at the Martin Beck Theatre on March 21. Rarely did one review of the show match the next in its appraisal; just as rarely was one wholly positive. Best, perhaps, was Brooks Atkinson, in the *Times.* Williams, he wrote, "is in a more humane state of mind than he has been in several years."

The reception of Smith's performance also varied. *Variety* wrote that "under Harold Clurman's strangely accented and slanted direction, the performances tend to be played with a sort of portentous casualness in the early scenes, and then become slightly overwrought in the final passages." Under this guidance, Smith "gives a curiously contorted portrayal." *Newsday,* meanwhile, called Carol Cutrere her "finest performance." The *Morning Telegraph*'s Whitney Bolton took a middle stance: "Miss Lois Smith again is assigned one of those offbeat odd roles she does so well," he observed. "Her tendency to move too much in quiet moments and to keep in motion no matter what the occasion or sense of the scene, still is on hand, but subdued."

Another play was scheduled to move into the Martin Beck on May 20, and the producers prepared to transplant the production to the Morosco. Business, however, did not support such a move, and *Orpheus Descending,* having made it to New York after eighteen years, finally lay down to rest on May 18.

Motherhood and Other Changes
Lois and Wesley Smith had often talked about having a baby. During the run of *Orpheus Descending,* with Wesley stationed at the Brooklyn Navy Yard, they often stayed at a friend's apartment near the theater. Soon afterward, the baby discussions were no longer just academic.

Wesley's tour of duty was cut short, and he returned to Princeton and his job in the fall of 1957. Smith continued to work during her pregnancy, filming two episodes of a Los Angeles television program called *Matinee Theatre*. The first job went smoothly. By the second one, however, she was four months along and beginning to show. "We began to think, 'Oh, maybe the apron has to be tied a little differently,'" recalled Smith. "When they started to put makeup on me, it would just be absorbed. Your body reacts differently when you're pregnant; it would just be gone. I remember thinking, 'Well, maybe there's going to be no more work for a little while.'"

Later on, Smith had an interview with film director Fred Zinnemann, who was casting for his new movie, *The Nun's Story*. She was quite pregnant by then, and the job fell just after her due date. "We both just sort of looked at each other," she recalled. "It seemed not possible. I think I was disappointed. It just seemed like bad timing." Wesley and Lois's daughter, Moon Elizabeth, was born on February 8, 1958.

Shortly thereafter, Clurman gave Smith a call. He was going to mount O'Neill's *Touch of a Poet*, with Robert Whitehead producing, and wanted her to come in for a reading. She participated in deed, though perhaps not in mind. "I remember that it seemed very strange to me," she observed. "The baby was two months old. I was still so involved in babyland. I felt no concentration at all. I almost felt as though I wasn't there."

Smith was more collected later in the year when she accepted the role of Mary Devlin in the Broadway-bound production of *Edwin Booth*, a biographical drama starring and directed by José Ferrer. The play rehearsed in California and, by Smith's own account, wasn't very good. She did her part to improve it, however. After a long discussion with a friend who had seen the production, she decided to approach Ferrer about a scene between them, in which a courtship of sorts is taking place while Booth and Devlin rehearse *Romeo and Juliet*.

"It was apparent that it was limp and not working well," said Smith. "This is the first time I had ever done something like this, or felt that I could or even should. I had had these feelings, but I thought it just wasn't my place. I talked about what I thought was wrong—partly drawing from what my friend thought—and the writer changed it! And Ferrer changed it! And the scene became really fun."

The play failed when it opened on Broadway that November, but the scene Smith had helped improve was eventually performed on *The Ed Sullivan Show*.

In 1959, Wesley Smith received a fellowship to study in Europe for six months. The family flew to Rome in February, where Wesley had space to work at the American Academy; Lois, however, felt somewhat conflicted about the trip. In the past four years, she had been in five high-profile New York stage productions, three of them on Broadway. She was reluctant to take herself thousands of miles away from her primary source of employment for half a year. She did her best to pursue her craft overseas and received nibbles here and there. The most interesting of these encounters, by far, was a meeting with Italian film director, Federico Fellini.

Fellini was casting for his upcoming film, *La Dolca Vita*. Smith and he met in the filmmaker's office at the famed studio complex Cinecittà and discussed the possibility of Smith's playing the role of the wife, while Fellini's attention strayed to one or another of the many pictures which covered the walls. Nothing came of the interview. Nor did anything come of Harold Clurman's rumblings about staging Shaw's *Heartbreak House* in New York with Smith in the cast. He later cast Diane Cilento. "During that time, I was edgy," admitted Smith. "I wanted to work."

A Growing Distance There would be more work when the Smiths returned to Princeton in the fall of 1959. (Lois's television performances in *Miss Julie* and *The Master Builder* were right around the corner). There would also be more frustration.

Wesley was now an assistant professor, but looking for a new position. In 1961, he found and accepted one, at the University of Pennsylvania, in Philadelphia. Smith balked upon hearing of the development. Princeton was one thing, but Philadelphia, 100 miles from New York, was another. Few people commuted from Philadelphia, and few working New Yorkers would consider it a place to make their home.

"I was rather entrenched as a New York actress by then," said Smith. "When we left Princeton, it was difficult. I guess it was at that time that I began to realize it was an issue. I think I always partly felt that he was saying to me, 'You've had your chance, and it hasn't worked out, and we have to go where my work is. I'm the one who's successful here.' And I thought, 'That's how we're acting, but that's not so.' I began to realize that he wouldn't compromise the quality of his career. We always went where his work was."

Smith reflected on the course of her marriage and began to resent the patterns which emerged. When Wesley was a student at Harvard, she had repeatedly made the journey north. While in graduate school, Wesley had received offers from Hunter College, in New York City, but not accepted them. When Wesley was teaching at Princeton, they lived right across the street from the campus, while she was an hour from New York. Now, in Philadelphia, they again found a place a few blocks from the university — and Smith was two hours from any stage or television job she might secure.

"When this was going on, I remember thinking, 'This is just not right. It's not fair.' I wasn't looking for an apartment, but it was in my mind that I should have an apartment in New York. I went back home and talked about that, and he was very angry at me. We weren't able to deal with it. We thought we dealt with it, but we didn't. It was always a sore, guilty point."

After a year or so in Philadelphia, the Smiths separated. Though they would later reconcile, the tensions created by the dual demands of Wesley's and Lois's professions would persist.

Because of her relocation and the time required to raise Moon, Smith did most of her work during these years in the more expedient medium of television. In 1961, she filmed her first episode of the road series, *Route 66*. She would film three more over the next three years, working on location. In 1962, she played opposite George C. Scott in an episode of the New York-based *The Naked City*, and, later that year, appeared on *The Defenders*.

In 1963, she went to Los Angeles for an episode of *Dr. Kildare*, and, later, *The Outer Limits*. The latter, however, was never actually shot. Traveling with both Wesley and Moon, she was met at the Los Angeles airport by an associate who handed her a $2,000 check and told her the episode had been cancelled. After standing dumbfounded in the terminal for a minute or two, the family took the money, booked a flight on a helicopter, and flew to nearby Riverside, where they spent the week vacationing with friends.

Smith managed to find her way back to Broadway in 1963, as part of an ill-starred play improbably titled *Bicycle Ride to Nevada*. Adapted by Robert Thom from Barnaby Conrad's novel *Dangerfield*, the drama told the thinly-veiled story of the tortured final days of writer Sinclair Lewis, whose secretary Conrad once was. Franchot Tone played the lead character, Winston Sawyer, a Pulitzer and Nobel Prize–winning author now sinking in a sea of drink and bile. Richard Jordan played his angry son, and Ron Leibman was an athletic instructor, getting Sawyer in shape for the titular race. Smith played the writer's mistress, Lucha Moreno.

The play was termed "good theater" by *Variety* during its New Haven run, but New York critics didn't agree. When it opened at the Cort Theatre, on September 24 (only the third production of the season), the press found it too strident and relentless. The closing notice was posted thirteen hours after the first performance. There wasn't a second performance.

Broadway called again the following July, when Smith was hired to succeed Ann Wedgeworth in the Actors Studio production of James Baldwin's *Blues for Mister Charlie*. That the play was still there to provide her with work was something of a miracle. *Blues*, an incendiary drama on race relations in the South, had aroused controversy when it opened at the ANTA Theatre. Reviews had been mixed, but support within artistic and politically liberal circles had been fierce. The show was scheduled to close after only six weeks of performances, due to tepid business. Four days before closing, two daughters of New York State's governor, Nelson Rockefeller, took in a performance. After the show, they went backstage and announced they were each contributing $1,500 to the production out of concern for the civil rights movement and the role the drama might play in furthering it.

Two days later, large ads appeared in the *New York Times* and the *Herald-Tribune*: "Once in a great while, a play transcends its form and becomes an experience

—as real, as imposing as experience itself." Among the signatures attached to the ad were those of George Plimpton, Geraldine Page, Lorraine Hansberry, Lena Horne, Sammy Davis, Jr., Harry Belafonte, Studs Terkel, Miles Davis, Lillian Hellman, and Sidney Poitier. Actors Studio stars stumped for the show on television, and in June a benefit—sponsored by Leonard Bernstein, Myrna Loy, and Jackie Robinson—was held for the three civil rights workers who were then missing in Mississippi.

The Rockefellers' money kept the show open until June 13, and the publicity kept it running through the summer. Smith came into the production on July 29, playing the wife of racist murderer Lyle Britten. Rip Torn played Lyle. "Even in New York, there were serious racial troubles during this period," remembered Smith, "so it felt very volatile. By the time I came into the play, they had succeeded in getting a big black audience. That was also exciting. There was this feeling that not only was there this play about racial trouble, but there was racial trouble in the streets and in the air. It was a very hot situation."

She shared a dressing room with actress Diana Sands. "She was a tough, lovely lady. This dressing room had no cot or bed, but there was a chaise. It wasn't very large. She looked at me and said, 'I take a nap on matinees.' I said, 'So do I.' We were looking at this one thing, and I said, 'I'll sleep on the floor on Wednesdays and you sleep on the floor on Saturdays.' So that's what we did."

Ensemble and Dissolution

Smith soon found a way to act without hopping a plane or train. The regional theater movement, a trend all across the country, had reached Philadelphia in the form of the Theatre of the Living Arts. The company was the invention of three men, Louis Silverman, Fred Goldman, and Anthony Checchia. The theater was to be a year-round subscription house with a five-show season. Its base would be a converted 500-seat former movie house on South Street. André Gregory, at age thirty the co-founder of Seattle Repertory Theatre and a force in regional theater, was hired for a three-year term as artistic director.

Gregory was enthusiastic about the Living Arts' prospects as an aesthetic forum. "The serious dramatic shows seldom get out of New York," he told a newspaper at the time. "The only chance for the country at large to see the classics and important new dramas lies in the regional theater groups." Gregory assembled a company of actors. He lured Ron Leibman, Sally Kirkland, and Smith, among others, into the fold.

It was an exciting, experimental time in the American theater. Company members were reading *The Theatre and Its Double*, by Antonin Artaud. Gregory, who had recently observed Brecht's Berliner Ensemble, dutifully opened the Living Arts's first season with that playwright's *Galileo*. He followed it with Giraudoux's *Tiger at the Gates* and Molière's *The Misanthrope*. Smith threw herself into the new venture, appearing in all of the first three plays. In *The Misanthrope*—her first stab at Molière—she played the lead, Célimène, in a modern-dress rendition of the play.

For her trouble, she received one of the most glowing notices of her career. "[Lois Smith] brings an erotic combination of ingenue pulchritude and feverishly impulsive passion to the role," wrote Henry Hewes in *The Saturday Review*. "With won-  derfully understated humor she responds to Alceste's enraged and rude statement of his feelings for her by puffing on a Tiparillo, reclining voluptuously on her sofa, and trying unavailingly to feel complimented as she says, 'I've never been so curiously wooed.'"

"It was very consuming, and hard work, and it was great," said Smith of her first experience as a member of an ensemble. "It was many things. We were almost always agitated and upset, and there was very little money." Indeed, she recalled becoming upset one day upon discovering a fellow actor couldn't scrape up enough cash to take the bus. "But we were also very excited about what we were doing and the progress we were making."

Smith's industriousness took her away from home and family more often. Since having the baby, she had worked only intermittently and primarily on television. Now she was performing in a full season of stage plays. Smith skipped the last two productions of the first season, (O'Neill's *Desire Under the Elms* and Beckett's *Endgame*), but in fall of 1965, the hectic schedule began anew. She was in Chekhov's *Uncle Vanya*, as Yelena, and then in Sheridan's *The Critic*, which was paired with Arnold Weinstein's *They*. Later in the season, she received the chance to play *Miss Julie* again, this time onstage.

"There was always a sense of upheaval," she remembered. "It was hard to make a new theater. It wasn't peaceful, it was intense, and people were extraordinarily involved in it. We really did feel like a company in a theater, and it was exciting to take things on."

After a while, the national press was beginning to take notice. "People began to come down and pay attention to it. The local press started out much more critical and sniffy. And as the company became more noticed, they sort of climbed on the bandwagon."

The progress of the Theatre of the Living Arts, however, was a little too progressive for some, particularly the company's board of directors. As Gregory pointed out, the company's distance from New York granted it the freedom to be adventurous in its programming; yet that liberality was not necessarily welcomed by the theater's more provincial audiences. Molière was fun and Brecht could be tolerated. But *Endgame* and William Carlos Williams's *A Dream of Love* did not pack them in. And one board member walked out of Saul Bellow's *The Last Analysis*, the final play of the second season.

As the *New York Times* diplomatically put it at the time, "The gravest of the growing pains afflicting the resident professional theaters that have mushroomed across the land in recent years is the failure of communication and comprehension between artistic directors and governing boards of lay, public-spirited citizens."

"During that last season," recalled Smith. "there was this constant sense of crisis. Every day, 'What's going on?' Everybody had the best will in the world, but the boards and artistic directors and the companies were all jockeying for position."

That same board member who walked out of *The Last Analysis* resigned after *Beclch*, the third play of what would be Living Arts' last season. *Beclch* was the work of Rochelle Owens, who would make her name the next year off-Broadway with *Futz*, the story of an affair between a farmer and a pig. The play centered on a middle-aged woman who asserts her individuality at every opportunity but only in the vilest ways. Over the course of the play she murders a child in front of its mother, pushes a man into a cock fight, and tricks her husband into contracting elephantiasis. Henry Hewes, somewhat impressed, called it "an uncharted excursion into violence and sensuality." The board had other words for it and for André Gregory, whom they promptly dismissed.

The company dissolved in the wake of his departure. "I don't think there was any sense of our company continuing as it had existed, or of wanting to stay, or of being wanted," Smith observed. "I think it was a kind of rout. It utterly fell apart, whatever it was we had made, and that was a great sadness."

Several months before the company's breakup, Lois and Moon moved out of the home they shared with Wesley and took an apartment. "My own life was very much a mess," said the actress. "The breakdowns in the theater and my life were simultaneous."

Looking back on the breakup of her marriage, Smith said, "I've had it both ways: I've been with an actor, and I've spent a long time with an academic. It's hard both ways—whether you are both in this profession, or whether one is and one isn't—in terms of the stress, the insecurity, and the notoriety that can come with the acting profession. There's just more jazz around acting. There are all kinds of ways to get attention, but somehow it's worse on the partner when your picture is in the newspapers and the magazines."

Beclch was the last Living Arts production in which Smith performed. After that, she flew out to California to film a *CBS Playhouse* called "Do Not Go Gently Into That Good Night." When she returned, the theater company, as she knew it, had been dismantled. There was no longer anything keeping Smith in Philadelphia.

The Lean Years Mother and daughter moved back to New York City in 1968. Smith bought an old boat of a car, filled it with her belongings, and drove into Manhattan to an apartment she rented at 86th Street and York Avenue. Soon after, she drove the vehicle back to Philadelphia and sold it for junk.

She had lived outside the city for over a decade now—ten years of marriage, motherhood, and regional work. Her life was markedly different from what it had been. But, then, so was the city. "When I moved back here, my life had changed, certainly," remarked Smith. "I was thinking about where to go and what to do. I needed to make a living, and I had a child to take care of. I had never wanted to move to L.A.; I had assumed I'd move back to New York, where my professional life was. But through these years, not only had I changed, in age and visibility, but the profession had changed. I was aware I had been away. By the end of the '60s, the situation as far as making a living as an actor was not what it had been when I'd started in the '50s."

Harold Stone, who had directed several plays at the Theatre of the Living Arts, had a wife named Antonia, who taught math at the Town School on 76th Street, near the East River. She tipped Smith off to a last-minute opening in that year's fourth-grade class. (Ironically, the exiting child's parents were moving to Philadelphia.) Moon took the spot and began classes.

Smith now had shelter and a school for her child. All that remained was to find a job. The agent she had secured through Van Druten began to look not-so-connected. His strong suit had been radio and television, which was now of little use. Furthermore, he had no clout in Los Angeles. She decided to break off the arrangement, and, though the matter was painful, the agent didn't stand in her way.

Her efforts did not result in much employment. In 1968, she participated in the National Playwrights Conference, in Waterford, Connecticut. Later she stood by for a major role in the soap opera *As the World Turns*. She never played the part, though, and was paid only $225. The soap money, along with unemployment and child support, constituted her entire income for that year.

"Looking back at the records, 1968 was pretty scary," she observed, somewhat startled by the stark figures. "I had always been rather prudent financially and had always saved money since I was a kid. I always had some money in the bank. At this point, I was lucky I was raised that way."

Picking Up the Pieces
Bob Rafelson had forged one of those odd, John Huston–like careers which made for movie legend. A rodeo hand at fifteen, in Europe at seventeen, playing jazz in Acapulco at eighteen, he eventually ended up, as many drifters do, in Hollywood. There he directed, co-produced, and co-wrote, with Jack Nicholson, the movie *Head*, a vehicle for the Monkees, a manufactured pop group he helped create. Still, by 1969, nothing on Rafelson's resume told the entertainment community that they should stand up and take notice—certainly not the sort of notice they would pay a year later to the director of *Five Easy Pieces*.

Smith had met Rafelson in 1960, when he was in the script department at PBS. She was in Los Angeles playing Sonya, in *Uncle Vanya*, when Rafelson told her he had her in mind for a part in a new movie. "They just gave me the part," she said. The film starred Nicholson, who, only months before, had broken through in an acclaimed supporting role as a dropout lawyer in Dennis Hopper's independent film *Easy Rider*. In *Five Easy Pieces*, he played Bobby Dupea, a disaffected itinerant construction worker and piano prodigy who returns to his idyllic Washington State home to reconcile with his estranged father, the dying patriarch of a family of musicians. Smith played his sister Partita, a neurotic, lonely concert pianist.

The movie industry had changed substantially since the days of Smith's brief participation in the studio system. In the wake of *Easy Rider*'s success, the studios were taking chances on independent, visionary filmmakers such as Robert Altman, Francis Ford Coppola, and Martin Scorsese. These directors were, in turn, giving work to young and unknown actors with faces, accents, and personalities more in tune with the times than with Hollywood tradition. In this brief era of originality and experimentation *Five Easy Pieces* was one of the first triumphs. "I had that sense of it being a new deal . . . a place these new filmmakers had within the studio system," remembered Smith.

Rafelson's approach was raw and edgy, his storytelling style less a linear narrative than an accumulation of mood and moments. He shot the script more or less sequentially, beginning in Bakersfield, California, and ending on Vancouver Island, in Canada, which doubled for the Pacific coast of Washington State. There, on one of the island's peninsulas, a standing house was transformed into the family home to which Nicholson returns. Rafelson's wife Toby was in charge of designing and furnishing the interior. Smith arrived on the set first, the other actors temporarily kept away by a storm. She passed the time watching the fictional home come alive. "There was this sense of moving into the house," she recalled. "It was very interesting and lovely. In the arc of the six or seven weeks we were there, it felt like we were moving in, and on the last day of shooting, as they were beginning to move the stuff, it felt like we were moving out."

There was an air of collaboration on the set. The company all roomed together in a nearby hotel, and they would gather for dinner each night and talk. The original screenplay had begun with a pan across a collection of family photos and playbills which wordlessly told the history of the protagonist's family. Rafelson later decided to place the photo sequence in the middle of the film, sweeping over them as Nicholson played a piece on the piano. When the time came to film the scene, however, there was a slight problem—there were no pictures.

Smith helped improvise a solution—photo mementos of Partita's concert career. "It was as if I directed it myself," said Smith. "I figured out what I needed. I had the driver go back to the hotel and get a black dress that I owned and some pearls. Then the still photographer shot me at the piano, dressed for a concert. And in Jack's scene those pictures appear on the wall. I had a real sense of being a collaborator in the making of the film."

Shooting began in November and lasted through the start of the new year; Smith was able to spend Christmas with her family in Seattle, and Moon was with her during the school holidays. *Five Easy Pieces* opened at the New York Film Festival on September 11, 1970. It was a critical and commercial success and went on to win a slew of honors. Jack Nicholson and Karen Black received Academy Award nominations. Smith won the National Society of Film Critics' Award. "It was one of those films that people really cared about," she said. "I remember people talking about how important it was to them, how much it touched them. That's so much more satisfying than 'Gee, you were great.'"

Five Easy Pieces put Lois Smith back in people's eyes and minds. In retrospect, it can't be said to have completely revived her career, for no important film roles followed in the next few years. Neither was she inundated with stage and television work. She admits that she wasn't prepared to capitalize on her success in *Five Easy Pieces*, either practically or temperamentally. But then, it was never her practice to think in those terms. This film was a success; the next might be a bomb, or might not be at all. Every job was work, and some jobs were more satisfying than others, but all were opportunities to advance her *craft. Five Easy Pieces*, in other words, was not a stepping stone.

"About this time, I expected just to figure out how to get along from year to year," she observed. "It's not that I don't know the difference or don't enjoy it when something is a success or a real boost. There is just another thing about me that is really different from a lot of people: I don't expect one thing to make the difference—as in 'Now it's all different. Now I'm a success.'

"I don't feel that way. I just don't feel that way."

Selling Soap, Making Soaps

Back in New York, the financial outlook hadn't improved much. In 1969, Smith benefitted from residuals from a Geritol commercial. The spot was a success and earned her nearly $2,000 over time. Smith had never done commercials before, but in the next few years she did them more and more often. Another spot for Scope mouthwash did not take off. But one for the headache powder Vanquish did, and paid out even more than the Geritol job (over $6,000 in 1974 alone).

Smith's other big source of income during this period was that one form of television which had not yet abandoned Gotham: the soap opera. "They kept me going," she said. "I was in New York, I had this child to raise. Making a good amount of money was not that easy. The soap operas were what there was."

In late 1970, she began to work here and there on *As the World Turns*. In 1972, she spent much of the summer as Mrs. Bendarik on *Love of Life*. In the fall of that year, she received her first contract part, in a soap called *Somerset*, which was filmed in Astoria, Queens. This helped substantially with paying bills and raising Moon, who had begun high school at the Dalton School. (They had by now moved to the Upper West Side.) The soap schedule also allowed her to lead some semblance of a normal life—that is, working during the day, being at home at night, resting on the weekends. The characters she played, of course, did not lead normal lives. On *Somerset*, she played Zoë Cannell, a wife and mother in a family that was new to the program. After six months, she was sent to jail for murdering an ingenue and her role came to an end. Or so she thought. In July of 1973, she was back on the set. Apparently her character had escaped and was at large. In months to come, *Somerset* could not build a prison strong enough to hold Zoë. Smith was called back for a few days at a time in August, September, and November. Each time, some actor would pay for the visit with his or her life. "I had become the company hit man," joked Smith, "because I would escape from jail, get out, and kill somebody. That meant somebody's contract was coming to an end. I joked that whenever I came on the show, all the actors would quake and wonder which of them was going to be out of a job."

Smith's second contract job was on *The Doctors*, where, from 1975 to 1977, she was the unfortunate Eleanor Conrad. Eleanor began as the mentally unstable wife of a philandering husband attempting to "gaslight" her into an institution. The characters were written out after a year. "Just at that time, they got a new head writer on the soap who didn't want to get rid of me," told Smith. "He thought I was wonderful. They called back and said, 'Wait a minute, will you stay?' I said yes."

The trouble was, Eleanor now knew nobody in the small world of *The Doctors* except the central character, Dr. Althea Davis, played by Elizabeth Hubbard. "So for the first few weeks of my new contract, I would have coffee with Althea every once in a while. That was all I could do." Eleanor would eventually take a young ne'er-do-well as a lover before being written out for good.

Smith would do soap stints now and then for years to come, though she never enjoyed the work half as much as her stage and film roles. "I definitely did not prefer it," she stated. "They were very helpful to my overall situation. It keeps you busy, it keeps you off the streets. But it's not satisfying."

The Seventies Smith's career during the 1970s continued to be a somewhat patchwork affair, in great contrast to the one she had had in the late '50s. It was now a time of extracting a living from a very different New York, in which off-off-Broadway, above all, lent a new energy to the theater, even if it did little to supplement the income she got from the occasional film, the odd television special, the soaps, and the commercials.

Smith's began the decade with *Sunday Dinner*, a Joyce Carol Oates play directed by Curt Dempster, at the American Place Theatre, in 1970. Oates, then just gaining fame as a novelist, had not written an easy play. Smith played Mary, member of a fatherless family who all visit the grave of their mother every week. One day a blind, ragged "Census Taker" pays a call, asks nonsensical questions and unearths dark family secrets. "It is as though," wrote the *Times* reviewer, "Miss Oates imagined that a third-rate thought—what beasts people are under the surface!—given a second-rate treatment—dramatic symbolic realism—might emerge as a first-rate play. It does not."

Sunday Dinner was, however, the occasion of a fortuitous meeting between Smith and Dempster, who was forever calling together friends and colleagues and notifying them of his intention to found a theater. In 1972, he made good on his word. He called his company the Ensemble Studio Theatre, or E.S.T. for short. Its first major production was an evening of Frank D. Gilroy one-acts entitled *Present Tense*. Dempster cast Smith and Biff McGuire as the two central players. Smith appeared in each play: in "Come Next Tuesday," as the wife of a philandering husband; "'Twas Bril-

lig," as another wife, this time to a neophyte screenwriter; "So Please Be Kind," as half of an adulterous couple comically trying to complete a tryst; and "Present Tense," as a mother with a son in Vietnam.

The production first opened at E.S.T., then reopened, on July 18, at the Sheridan Square Playhouse, in Greenwich Village. The critics found the plays variously amusing, terse, sketchy, and, most of all, inconsequential. But *Variety* commented on the "first rate" performances; and Jerry Talmer, writing in the *New York Post*, observed that he hadn't seen Smith in a while, adding wryly that her performances were "variously Amurrican and excellent, most excellent."

She reflected on doing off-off-Broadway: "It means that you perform a lot and do different roles, and they don't last very long. It's sort of like the early days of television, when it's a matter of three or four weeks. But in those days, you got paid some money." It seemed to her at times that she was working as hard as ever, but with less to show for it.

Smith had seen the original New York production of O'Neill's *Long Day's Journey into Night*, and remembered staggering up the aisle afterwards, struck by its power. "I had that sense of something life-changing," she recalled. In late 1973, cast as one of the deluded whores in Ted Mann's production of another late O'Neill work, *The Iceman Cometh*, at Circle in the Square, she had new reason to stagger. The show ran four and a half hours, and the cast played it eight times a week.

"By the end of the week, I was absolutely blotto with fatigue," related Smith. "By Sunday night, you really couldn't hardly stand up and think straight. Then you'd sort of recover, and by Tuesday you'd think, 'Oh, it's all right. I can do this.' My character didn't come on for the first hour, and then I was on for much of the time. But there were some people who were always on. There was a terrible problem of people going to sleep onstage, because a lot of their characters were sleeping on the tables for long periods, and you'd just get so tired."

In 1975, Corinne Jacker's play *Harry Outside* brought Smith back to Greenwich Village, where the Circle Repertory Company was in its sixth season and its first flush of success as an important new American theater. It had had triumphs with Lanford Wilson's *The Mound Builders*, Mark Medoff's *When You Comin' Back, Red Ryder?*, and Edward J. Moore's *The Sea Horse*. And *The Hot L Baltimore*, also by Wilson (one of the theater's founders), was playing at Circle in the Square Downtown, not far from Circle Rep's Sheridan Square headquarters.

Jacker's play concerns Harry Harrison, a once-esteemed, later institutionalized, architect who has detached himself from his former life and current wife to live entirely outdoors—and never again inhabit a dwelling. Of course, everyone finds Harry fascinating and won't leave him alone, including his wife, played by Smith. *Harry Outside* opened to the critics' slightly confused respect. Most were positive, all allowed that Jacker was a good writer, and many compared her style to Chekhov's.

During the run of the play, Smith was cast in the Paul Mazursky film *Next Stop, Greenwich Village*, which was being shot, appropriately, in the Village. Often, she would arrive home from an evening performance at 11:30 at night and then have to be on the movie set at 5 A.M. the next day. "That was exciting, but it was also very hard," said Smith. "Sometimes the days would overlap. I would shoot all day, and then do the play at night. That kind of schedule is just killing. You can do it for a while. I used to run from location and dash over to the office of Circle Rep and take a nap—just lie down and sleep—for whatever time I had."

Smith returned to the commercial Broadway stage in a brief venture which may rank as one of the strangest productions ever to flicker on the Great White Way. *Stages* was the first dramatic effort of Stuart Ostrow, the producer of musicals such as *1776* and *Pippin*. Though Ostrow produced commercial fare, *Stages* did not fall into that category. It was, or, at least, was intended to be, an avant-garde play. Its five sections—"Denial," "Anger," "Bargaining," "Depression," and "Acceptance"—were based on the five stages of death as outlined in Elisabeth Kübler-Ross's *On Death and Dying*. Only here, they were meant to represent the stages of an actor's life. Directing this singular production was (as Smith put it) "Richard Foreman—of all people." In an article, Foreman said he was attracted by the experimental quality of *Stages*, which he viewed as being in the Ionesco tradition. *Variety* wondered aloud if Foreman wasn't directing the play on a dare. The production closed the very night it opened, losing $250,000.

Smith found work again later that year, however, in Steve Tesich's *Touching Bottom*, a trio of one-acts. She acted opposite Harold Gould at the American Place Theatre. With the help of a long memory, Mel Gussow, of the *New York Times*, observed that she looked "as vivacious as she did years ago in *The Young and Beautiful.*"

The next year found Smith in a number of screen projects, beginning with the Daniel Petrie film *Resurrection*. She then did a PBS movie written by Corinne Jacker called *The Jilting of Granny Wetherall*, and, later, a PBS dramatization of Edith Wharton's *The House of Mirth*, which was filmed in Newport, Rhode Island. Most of the time, however, Smith remained rooted in New York. "There is something to be said for staying in one place," she observed. "It helps with a sense of community and a steadiness which is hard to find in this profession, which tends to be discontinuous, almost entirely. Having a sense of place has filled very real needs."

Curt Dempster's Ensemble Studio Theatre would provide Smith with many roles over the years in its popular annual marathon of one-act plays. In 1979, the theater called her at the last minute to play the central role in a Romulus Linney one-act called "Tennessee." The play took place in 1870 and concerned the mountain folk of North Carolina. Smith played an old woman who wanders onto a family's homestead, sits on the porch, and begins to tell her long and comical life story. Eventually, the family members take on the various roles of the people in her saga. As a girl, the  woman swore she would only marry a man who would take her to settle in the wilds of Tennessee, thinking such a demand would scare off all suitors. One takes the bait, however, and takes her on the journey west. Only after he dies does she realize he had only driven in circles in order to arrive at the Carolina plot of land he'd had in mind all along.

The *New York Times* said, "[Smith] never seems either 90 or 19—the range of her years—but a definite feeling of rejuvenation pervades the stage as Miss Smith removes her ragged jacket and adds an adolescent edge to her voice."

In exchange for short investments of time, E.S.T. would continue to give Smith satisfying material and artistic sustenance. "I've been fortunate to have E.S.T.," she said, "There are times where I haven't been doing anything onstage and will do something in the marathon. That's one little thing, but they all accumulate and add up to what a career in acting is in our time."

Rewarding Roles Smith would have another satisfying experience in the spring of 1982, when Harris Yulin asked her to play Molly Malloy in a production of *The Front Page* he was directing at the Long Wharf Theatre, in New Haven. She was not very often offered comedy, let alone out-and-out satire, and here she delivered some of her best work. "That was an absolutely wonderful time," she said. "There are times when you really know you're working well and you're really original. It was like that, I think, both for myself and for the collaboration."

Smith's next gift of a role came at another regional theater, thousands of miles away in Minnesota. The Guthrie Theatre, in Minneapolis, was doing Chekhov's *The Seagull,* and director Lucian Pintilie auditioned Smith for Masha. "I remember thinking I was a little long in the tooth for Masha." Still, she went in. Like the Guthrie's artistic director, Liviu Ciulei, Pintilie was Romanian and took a rigorous, hands-on approach to auditioning. Waiting her turn to audition, Smith would watch people stagger out, rumpled and wild-eyed. She went in. The Romanian worked with her; they went over several scenes. "I was good. I had fun and I was alive," she remembered. The next day, however, he had her read a few times as the self-centered actress Arkadina, and Smith's prospects began to change. "Now, do you really want to do this?" the director asked. Smith swore she did. He hesitated. The next day, however, he gave her the role, explaining, "It took me a while to get over your Masha."

Smith counts the experience as one of the most exciting of her life. She had always liked Chekhov, and for many years *The Seagull* had been her favorite of the author's works. She raced to rehearsal every day.

The next spring, she did another E.S.T. marathon, performing in a play called "Bite the Hand." A year later, she took the lead role in a reading of Darrah Cloud's *The Stick Wife* at Hartford Stage. "I was very interested in the play, but something was really wrong with the second act," said Smith. Then they offered her the role in a full production. "I remember thinking, 'Oh, I don't want to go to Hartford.' So I took the play home and sat down to read it, and thought, 'My goodness, they fixed it. I can't say no.'"

The play was inspired by an article about the wife of one of the men responsible for the bombing of a black church, in 1963, in Birmingham, Alabama. Four children died in the explosion. In the play, author Cloud examines the corrupted, narrow world of such women, living in the shadow of the Ku Klux Klan. Smith played Jessie Bliss, a woman lost in delusion, forever hanging out symbolic linen to dry (which turns into even more symbolic red dresses in the second act). Director Roberta Levitow, designer Michael H. Yeargan, and Cloud endeavored to achieve a brand of heightened realism for the production. The process by which this was achieved was a collaborative though not always a clear one.

"During tech and previews, there was something mysterious about what Darrah was asking for," Smith said. "She didn't quite know herself what it was. We just started to talk about it. We kept at it—author, director, designers. It was so exciting. We just kept figuring out what it was, and finding a way to realize it."

One effect came to be known as the "inviso-dog." It began with an indication by Cloud in the text of two unexplained yellow lights visible at the edge of the stage. Levitow had asked Cloud what the lights were supposed to be. "Well, it's a dog," she answered. The dog theme—a metaphor for the evil pervading the wives' lives—was developed: At times, the menacing animal would be heard; other times, it would throw itself against a fence. The designer even found a way to have it make paw tracks across the stage.

"What I find really satisfying is when something is nonliteral," said Smith, "when something is outside of normal experience and yet the piece is very rooted in experience. It's fun when you can make it work on both levels, and make it understandable to the audience. Somehow, this piece was like that. It was both stylized and natural."

The Stick Wife opened on April 3, 1987. The critics, on the whole, found the tale powerful and were willing to accept the drama's fantastical elements. Much credit was given to Smith's central performance. "Ms. Smith's performance is extraordinary," wrote Mel Gussow. "She is a member of the walking wounded, scarred by her husband's malevolence and withdrawn into a fantasy world." *Variety* concurred: "Lois Smith is extraordinary as the fantasy-indulging informant. Here's a woman who's let herself go entirely—physically and mentally—yet neither Cloud nor Smith allow her to become a caricature, despite her bizarre behavior."

Rediscovery Lois Smith had now been an actress for more than thirty-five years. She had become a "veteran." And, as any performer who has stayed with it long enough to become a veteran can tell you, there comes a time in one's career when the audience and the press slowly return their glance and gaze upon you quizzically, as if they've never seen you before. At such times, you are rediscovered for being and doing what you've been and done all along.

The seeds of such a turnaround were unknowingly being sewn in the mid-1980s. Smith began doing some well-watched television, a couple of episodes of *The Equalizer* and a *Spencer: For Hire.* There was a confluence of movies. Bob Rafelson's *Black Widow*, Adrian Lyne's *Fatal Attraction*, and Martin Brest's *Midnight Run* were all during this period. Granted, she had small parts in these films, but they were popular films. And Smith was working more steadily on New York stages. She did Roger Hedden's *Bodies, Rest, and Motion* at Lincoln Center, in 1986; Romulus Linney's "April Snow" at the E.S.T. marathon, in 1987 (which *The New Yorker*'s Mimi Kramer called "probably the best play I've seen in New York all year"); Albert Innaurato's *Gus and Al* at Playwrights Horizons, in 1988; and two other E.S.T. marathon plays that same year.

Smith's resurgence would begin in earnest, however, in late July of 1988, when her agent took a long-distance call from the Steppenwolf Theatre Company, in Chicago. Four years earlier, Frank Galati had proposed to the theater his long-time ambition to adapt and stage John Steinbeck's *The Grapes of Wrath.* Now Galati had Steppenwolf's permission, the Steinbeck estate's assent, support from AT&T, and a budget of a half a million. He had a Tom Joad in Gary Sinise and a Jim Casy in Terry Kinney. What he did not have was a Ma Joad.

Steppenwolf had no actresses of the appropriate age in its ensemble. Galati and company asked people to suggest someone to play the enduring, hardscrabble Ma Joad, someone who could work within an ensemble. The name that kept coming up was Smith's. Rehearsals were a few weeks away when Smith flew in to audition. Galati was there, along with artistic director Randall Arney, managing director Steve Eich, and Jim True, who was playing Tom Joad's younger brother, Al. Smith read with Al and an actress auditioning for the part of Rose of Sharon, and pretty much covered the entire play. The atmosphere, like Galati, was relaxed.

Afterwards, she went next door to a restaurant, hungry after the lengthy audition. "I was eating, and Randy came running over and offered me the part. I told him I had to call him. I was pretty sure I wanted it." The reason for Smith's hesitation lay in Pennsylvania, at the Pittsburgh Public Theatre, whose artistic director Bill Gardner, along with playwright Horton Foote, had offered her a part in Foote's new play. Earlier that year, she had acted in Foote's "The Man Who Climbed the Pecan Trees" at E.S.T. "After that, I was told that Horton said: 'After Geraldine Page was gone, I didn't think there was going to be anybody to do my plays, but now I think there's Lois.' I treasure the remark, even though I'm not sure he ever said it." Smith called them personally, declined the part, and set her sights on Chicago.

Galati's adaptation was quite faithful to the classic novel and eschewed the plot of the popular 1940 John Ford movie, which ended with Tom Joad leaving the family to go underground. The play followed Steinbeck's tale of the Joad family's remaining ordeals, including Rose of Sharon's stillborn child, and the family being flooded out of the boxcars, their temporary homes. The play ended with the striking image, full of tragedy and hope, of Rose of Sharon offering her swollen breast to a starving black man in a barn. Galati staged the show in the sparest fashion possible, the production's design evoking water, fire, earth, and air. Consequently, the show featured a rainstorm, pouring down from the fly gallery; various campfires, kept in traps in the floor; the inescapable Dust Bowl; and the uncluttered stage, backed by sky. The central set piece was the Joads' rambling old Hudson Super Six truck, piled high with people and possessions. Almost every location was evoked by lighting: flashlights, headlights, firelight, sunlight.

Adhering closely to the text of *The Grapes of Wrath* meant a long play. "At the beginning, it was *quite* long," recalled Smith. "Those were wild days. We were cutting it and working on it all the time, even after opening. But when we started performing, there just weren't enough hours in the day to do the work that had to be done. So we would do as much as we could. We would come in to humongous cuts and rearrangements that we would throw in that night. The first weekend of performance, it was still over four hours long. And our playing times were 5 P.M. and 9 P.M. on Saturday, and 3 P.M. and 7 P.M. on Sunday. So the performance wasn't finished before the second audience was ready to come in. The first weekend was absolute chaos."

Smith would often go on stage unsure as to whether, at this point, the truck would turn right or left, or in which camp the family was. During the two-show days, she and the cast were speedily fed—"like animals for slaughter"— between performances. On the afternoon of the fourth preview, Galati came in with 52 pages of cuts, what the director would later call the "Friday night massacre." The revisions all went in that evening. The next night, the show's duration dropped 36 minutes.

Still, despite the never-ending sense of crisis, Smith loved the charged atmosphere. "The rehearsal and performance period was probably the most collaborative I have ever known. Not that Frank isn't extremely strong and guiding, but he gave so much room, and there were lots of people eager to take it. After the show at night, we would go to the bar and just deal with it, just talk about what happened and what there was to do. It was work, but not drudgery. We were just processing what happened tonight, what to do. The concentration was there all the time."

The Chicago production of *The Grapes of Wrath* placed Smith in close proximity to her Kansas roots, and she felt the connection in a number of ways. Though

Photo by Michael Brosilow.

Lois Smith, as Ma Joad, with Christian Robinson (left) and Dana Lubotsky in the Steppenwolf Theatre Company production of Frank Galati's *The Grapes of Wrath*, in Chicago, in the fall of 1988.

she had never lived on a farm, she had had farming relatives, and she drew on them to complete her portrayal. "There was a great deal of those people in my performance," she said.

Moreover, she felt an instant connection with the Steppenwolf Theatre Company, the founders of which hailed from the Illinois heartland. Sinise, for instance, spoke—in the play and in everyday speech—with a Midwestern nasal twang, matching the folksy traces which yet lurked in Smith's voice. "I feel we were very well matched," she said. "I felt, right from the beginning, this homecoming to the Midwest—a real shared experience. I also felt very clearly that what I was experiencing was this familiarity with the people and the milieu in this company. They were the right people to be doing this play."

The Grapes of Wrath opened at Chicago's Royal-George Theater on September 17. The notices were filled with awe and praise. Still, there were gripes about the show's length and its ponderous, novelistic quality. Galati continued to improve the show until its last performance. Frank Rich, of the *New York Times*, was anxious to review the Chicago show, but the creators, wanting a future elsewhere for the production, and fearful of the power of Rich's opinion, put him off again and again. Rich finally did see the show, and his review was largely positive.

When the cast dispersed in October, the production's future was uncertain. Smith went home, and in December director Mark Lamos offered her the role of Mistress Overdone in his upcoming Lincoln Center mounting of Shakespeare's *Measure for Measure*. The run would last until April. She called Steppenwolf to ask about the status of *Grapes*; the theater didn't know. Smith accepted Lamos' offer. Soon after, Steppenwolf received an invitation from London's Royal National Theater for a two-week summer engagement. This would be preceded by a run at the La Jolla Playhouse, in California.

Measure for Measure, which opened March 9, 1989, didn't fare well. Rich said Lamos's high-concept production languished "in an antiseptic void: the standard-issue vacuum of Modern Dress Theater." It did well enough with audiences, however, to be extended past the scheduled closing date of April 9. Smith, due in Chicago on April 11 to begin *Grapes of Wrath* rehearsals, had to be replaced.

For this second round, Galati further refined the script. An opening song was eliminated, comic moments were inserted to relieve the story's dreariness, and the show's narration, originally spoken by two characters called Brother and Sister, was distributed among the cast. The show opened in La Jolla on May 14. Reviews were good, but the cast continued to go out after performances and discuss what needed work. One part which was proving particularly troublesome was the boxcar scene. The creative team would fiddle with lighting, but something seemed intrinsically wrong with the section.

"We'd been just fussing, fussing, fussing with it, trying to describe what was wrong, what didn't feel right," explained Smith. Then one night, someone's friend made a casual remark. "They didn't understand why it was so bad in the boxcars, because it looked pretty good. It was the clarifying moment for everything I'd been feeling and trying to say. We were always going back to the book. In the book, the boxcars are on the ground, and they flooded, and people are standing in water; it was really terrible. We didn't have that. Our boxcars were actually slightly elevated." Smith talked about what the friend had said later that night in a bar with Sinise. He jumped up and called Galati, who was asleep.

The next day, the crew went about rendering the boxcars repellent. Most of the furniture was removed, and, during a blackout when the boxcars flooded, Smith and Sally Murphy (who played Rose of Sharon) drenched themselves so that when the lights came up they were sopping wet. "Now, indeed, the boxcars were unlivable and we had to go," said Smith.

The La Jolla production closed on a Sunday. On Monday, the cast flew to London, arriving on a Tuesday morning. On Wednesday, the cast, exhausted and jetlagged, went to the National's Lyttelton Theatre to tech the show. They had only Wednesday to do so, and weren't finished by the end of the day. The job was completed on Thursday morning. That afternoon, Steppenwolf gave a show for an audience of National Theatre people; a few hours later, they gave their first regular performance.

The effort was worth it. The London reviews were rapturous—the best yet—and the audiences were enthusiastic. It all made for a very emotional and magical two weeks. On closing night, as the cast stepped forward, they were met by a shower of flowers, raining down from the rafters. "We were just absolutely staggered," recalled Smith. "It was so beautiful."

Broadway is the hoped-for end of any touring regional production. A Broadway run hadn't been a certainty until after the British success. Only then were Jujamcyn Theaters, who had shown interest in Chicago, joined by the Shuberts, and the Suntory International Corporation as co-producers.

Smith returned to New York in August of 1989. The show would not open on Broadway until March, which left another gap in her schedule. Fortunately, she had been talking to Circle Rep about doing the Joe Pintauro play *Beside Herself*. Rehearsals would begin on September 4. "I was so lucky," said Smith. "There was this period of over two years. We started rehearsing *Grapes* in August of 1988, and we closed, on Broadway, in September of 1990. So it was slightly over two years for this most interesting, happy, privileged journey. After the Chicago run, I came back and did *Measure for Measure*, and after the London run, I came back and did *Beside Herself*. It was a great piece of luck to have those plays dovetail into those slots."

It did not occur to Smith that the exposure she was getting through *The Grapes of Wrath* had, perhaps, helped her get those supplementary roles. After all, she had known Mark Lamos before she did *Measure*, and had worked at Circle Rep before. She admitted, however, that it may have played a role. "Whenever you're working in the theater, that's good; working helps you get work," she reasoned. "It's all cumulative, but it's often hard to tell if this led to this, or this led to that. Often you just don't know."

Beside Herself was a production of some interest. The theater had lured back movie star William Hurt, who had performed regularly at Circle Rep during the late '70s and early '80s. Hurt played against type in Pintauro's drama, taking the role of a dim, eccentric, blue-collar UPS deliveryman. Augie-Jake. Smith's character, Mary, is a single, about-to-retire teacher who spends most of her time in isolation going over the events and mistakes of her life, aided by three phantasmic former versions of herself, as preteen, teen, and young woman. Augie-Jake is a dead ringer for Mary's long-lost love Roger, and Mary sets her sights on the simple man as her last chance for love and a cure for old regrets.

It was a rocky road on the way to opening. The script was not fully drama-tized as rehearsals got under way, and there was a change of director just before opening. The play was not terribly well received, but the praise for Smith was near-ly uniform. The notices were almost too much, too complimentary; they were the reviews of critics rediscovering an artist. Suddenly Smith was "her usual, honest, peppery self," "a formidable veteran," an institution. "Lois Smith is an actress I always feel we can't get enough of," wrote Mimi Kramer in *The New Yorker.* "She has an otherworldly quality—a half-crazed desperation—which, combined with a great gift for the prosaic, enables her to play highly eccentric characters without making them the least bit affected or objectionable."

The *Village Voice*'s Michael Feingold, too, penned a tribute: "Very few actress-es can stand comparison with Lois Smith: No fuss, no bathos, no affectation—all you see is a person living out her life and doing the things she does. It's only after-ward that you realize what an illusion this was, and how much effort it must have taken to create. Baking a pie, in a nonnaturalistic play, is one of the most artificial things you can do onstage: When Smith takes the preset prop pie out of the non-working oven, you know exactly how it tastes, what it means to her, how long it baked, and how costly the ingredients were."

In March of 1990, Steppenwolf rehearsed for a week or so at the Manhattan Theatre Club's offices on West 16th Street, prior to the Broadway premiere. The play opened at the Cort Theatre on March 22. Frank Rich called it "an epic achievement for the director, Frank Galati, and the Chicago theater ensemble at his disposal. . . . When Ma Joad—in the transcendent form of the flinty, silver-haired Lois Smith—delivers her paean to the people's ability to 'go on,' it isn't the inspi-rational epilogue that won Jane Darwell an Oscar but a no-nonsense, conversa-tional reiteration of unshakable pragmatism." Two months later, the show won the Tony Award for best play.

There was also a Tony nomination for Smith—her first. She appreciated the gesture, but didn't care for the idea of being placed in competition with her fellow actors. "We do seem hooked on contests, and it's too bad," she stated. "The ones where they just award them and say, 'Here, you get this for good work,' that's so satisfying. Nobody loses. The whole thing of honoring and being honored is love-ly. Competitions, though, are just a national bad habit."

For six months, until *Grapes* closed in September, Smith journeyed from her Upper West Side apartment to the theater, on West 48th Street. It was her first Broadway job in over ten years, and it was the most acclaimed play in town. She was getting more recognition as a New York actress than at any time since the days of *The Young and Beautiful* and *Orpheus Descending.* For many critics and theatergo-ers, she had gone away and come back. But for Smith, *The Grapes of Wrath* was just her latest show.

"I live in New York," she explained, "and have all the time. There's a way in which this is my city. My first job was on Broadway. So, I suppose, I have mixed feelings. Yes, on one hand, it's terrific to be on Broadway. It's terrific working at what is supposed to be the top of the line in my own city, in my own profession. On the other hand, I certainly didn't feel as though I'd been sitting around waiting all these years that I hadn't been on Broadway.

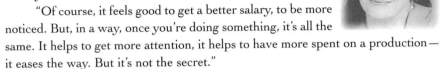

"Of course, it feels good to get a better salary, to be more noticed. But, in a way, once you're doing something, it's all the same. It helps to get more attention, it helps to have more spent on a production—it eases the way. But it's not the secret."

Whirlwind Years
Ma Joad has been, so far, Smith's best known role, her trademark, her most lasting creation. It was the role for which she became primarily known in New York, and—after *The Grapes of Wrath* was filmed for PBS's *American Playhouse*—the nation. It made and defined the latter part of her career. Not surprisingly, her pattern of employment altered dramatically after the show closed.

Some of it had to do with a change in agency. "I haven't changed a lot," said Smith. "I tend to stay where I am. I'm not crazy about the whole process of changing. I think it's fortunate to have a relationship that goes on." But Smith's dealings with her agency had, in her words, gone on too long. Her agent had no representative or office in Los Angeles. "So it meant having to go to somebody else with whom he would have a deal or something. It's not the same. I needed a strong agency."

Smith interviewed new agencies while performing *Grapes* at La Jolla. When she returned from London, she broke with her longtime agent. The scene was awkward; he was angry. "I do understand that it was harder for him than it was for me. I understand that it was hurtful. But it is a business relationship, and it was truly business I was talking about."

If it was better access to Hollywood work she wanted, she got it, though her first major, post-*Grapes* job may not have been what she'd bargained for. "I used to wonder, 'What would happen if I was confronted with a television pilot?—the kind where, before you do it, you have to agree that if it goes you'll do the series.' I never had been confronted with this before." In 1986 she had done a pilot called *Adam's Apple*, but nothing had come of it. Now, she had a chance at another, and there was no question as to its initial success. Called *Good Sports*, it starred Farrah Fawcett and Ryan O'Neal, and the series had already struck a network deal.

Smith tried out for the part of O'Neal's mother and then "went to network," as the phrase goes—auditioned for the network brass. Before being seen, though, she had to "sign away" for five years. Smith now found out what she would do in such a situation: "Partly because it was so different from what I was doing, I decided to do it," she said.

Series television is very different from theater or film, however, and Smith was soon unhappy. "There was an awful lot of tension on the set," she said. "I felt you could cut it with a knife, and I didn't know how you could be funny under those circumstances." Smith quickly found herself looking for a way out. Fortunately, the show's writers had created in Smith's part a character with little purpose and no place to go. They wrote the mother out of the series after two episodes. "I was delighted," said Smith. And her contract was paid off to boot. She rented a house in Silver Lake, California, for a month or so, while sweating out the *Good Sports* debacle, visited her family in Seattle for Thanksgiving, and finally returned to New York.

She didn't stay long. Her new representation began working for her assiduously. In 1991 she began several years of constant shuttling between the coasts. She began the year by filming a television movie called *White Hot: The Story of Thelma Todd*—her first non-series Los Angeles television work since she was a young actress. Immediately after, she did an episode of *Thirtysomething*, playing the mother of the character Ellen Warren. In June, she flew to stiflingly hot Atlanta to film a role in the movie *Fried Green Tomatoes*.

That fall, she inaugurated a habit of making stops in Chicago to catch the latest Steppenwolf production—in this case, Frank Galati's adaptation of Anne Tyler's *Earthly Possessions*. Smith finished off the year with two more television movies, a PBS documentary voiceover, and a stint on Garrison Keillor's radio show, "A Prairie Home Companion."

The pace did not let up. She began 1992 by recording a voiceover for the PBS documentary *The Donner Party*, and then spent a few weeks acting opposite Robert Duvall, as Michael Douglas's mother, in the movie *Falling Down*. The film deals with a man (Douglas), recently fired, who has a breakdown and suddenly lashes out at a desensitized, brutal society. Ironically, Smith's filming date coincided with the first day of the Los Angeles riots which occurred in the wake of the Rodney King verdict. She was met in L.A. not by the usual town car, but by two teamsters, who ushered her to her hotel; filming for the day had been cancelled.

She spent that summer in Toronto, filming a miniseries. She also appeared in *Skylark*, a sequel to Hallmark Hall of Fame's popular television movie *Sarah Plain and Tall*. On October 1, she went into rehearsal for *Dog Logic*, at the American Place Theatre, completing performances just before Thanksgiving. "These years I seemed to be traveling all the time," commented Smith. In 1993, more trips, new places. Smith began a relationship with Baltimore's Center Stage, where she would do Chekhov's *The Cherry Orchard*. Another television movie would introduce her to Great Falls, Montana. In late 1993, Steppenwolf asked her to join their company. She agreed.

Smith's first show as a Steppenwolf ensemble member, in early 1994, was Ara Watson's *The Mesmerist*, a work Smith had brought to the theater herself. The drama was an account of the life and downfall of the controversial Madame Helena Petrovna Blavatsky, a Russian-born American who co-founded the Theosophical Society, a spiritual group, in the nineteenth century. In the spring, Smith partici-

Photo by Richard Anderson.

Lois Smith and George Bartenieff in the Center Stage production of Chekhov's *The Cherry Orchard*, in Baltimore, in the fall of 1994.

pated in another E.S.T. marathon. Later that year, she was in Jocelyn Moorhouse's *How to Make an American Quilt*, a memory movie starring Winona Ryder and a cast of veteran actresses, including Ellen Burstyn, Anne Bancroft, and Kate Nelligan.

And More Whirlwinds After finishing *American Quilt*, in early 1995, Smith experienced a crisis of sorts. The early '90s had gone by in a blur. Several plays, half a dozen movies, countless television projects, and sundry readings and voiceovers — the sheer amount of her recent work, in all its bi-coastal breadth, finally hit her.

"I had been really suffering, and I didn't understand why," she attested. "Finally, all these things started to add up. I was away so much, and while I was doing things that I wanted to do, it really sort of didn't make sense. *The Cherry Orchard*, which was the thing I most wanted to do . . . and then this lovely part in this good movie — and yet I was feeling more adrift, and I didn't know what to do about it. I was troubled in a way. I thought, 'What am I going to do? This is what I do, but I can't stand it. I need to be home.'"

The New York actress, the Manhattan staple, the Lois Smith who had never considered living in California, was now a nomad. She didn't call up her agent and tell him to stop sending her all over the planet—after all, any day her dream role might surface. But she resolved to stay home more often, if at all possible.

"Geography has become a big deal. When my child was being raised, I rarely went away. I felt I couldn't, and I didn't want to. And now I'm on my own, and I can go anywhere I want to, and I do. But I also don't *want* to. I'm always balancing those needs. Those variables are always bouncing up and down, what one wants and needs. It comes with the terrain. And clearly one chooses that terrain. But it's wearying."

Smith couldn't relax just yet. She was about to enter the two most crowded months of her movie-making career. In April of 1995, as she was filming the HBO television movie *Truman,* in Kansas, playing mother-in-law to Gary Sinise's president, she flew to nearby St. Louis to meet the director of a Bill Murray vehicle about a circus, then called *Nickel and Dime.* She was offered the part of a tattooed lady. It was not the typical Smith role, which is precisely why she accepted it.

She then flew back to New York and met with Susan Sarandon and Tim Robbins about another movie, *Dead Man Walking.* Robbins would direct this drama of a nun (Sarandon) counseling a death row inmate (Sean Penn). Smith would play Sarandon's mother.

While negotiating the terms of the circus film, now called *Larger Than Life,* Smith got a call about *Twister,* an "event" picture with a summer release that would be seen by millions even if it somehow proved to be a box-office disappointment. Smith would play a sort of den mother to an excitable group of tornado-hunting pop scientists. The trouble was, the shooting schedule overlapped with *Larger Than Life.*

"Everybody said, *Twister* is the one to take," related Smith. "It's a bigger movie. Everyone will see it. It's a three-week guarantee. I tried very hard to get them both, because I saw that they almost worked together." She knew the casting director of the tornado film, and asked her to talk to the location person. The *Larger Than Life* people, meanwhile, had been quibbling about money, and when that movie's director found out that Smith might be lost to a better offer, he demanded they give her the amount she asked.

Finally, it came down to a matter of a 24-hour difference in the shooting schedules. Smith had to make a choice. Against all advice, she selected the tattooed lady. "I really wanted to do it, because it was funny, and it was an entirely different role."

Immediately after finishing work on *Truman,* Smith went to New Orleans, where *Dead Man Walking* was being filmed. She shot her few scenes and then reported to the *Larger Than Life* set, in Denver, on May 27. It took three people two full days to paint on all of Smith's tattoos, which were applied with a silk screen process and then colored by hand. Afterward, two people were in charge of maintaining the tattoos over Smith's fourteen-day assignment.

"At first it was fine," said Smith. "I showered and washed very carefully. The main thing that wore them off is that the skin starts to want to grow over them. At the beginning, we all thought, 'Oh, isn't it wonderful how well they all last.' At the end of the two weeks, every spare minute they were repainting."

Twister, in the meantime, ran behind schedule—predictably, since it was a special-effects movie. Smith was able to accept the offer when the film's casting people came around a second time. She did not battle invisible funnel clouds, as did stars Helen Hunt and Bill Paxton. Most of her scenes were in a large country house, where her character served the cast plates of steak and eggs, and which was subsequently destroyed to serve the movie's plot.

Of course, *Twister* became one of the highest-grossing films in history. It would end *Five Easy Pieces'* 26-year reign as Smith's best-known film role.

Mother and Child The release of *Twister* would coincide with Smith's return to Broadway. Gary Sinise, now nationally known after his roles in *Truman, Forrest Gump,* and *Apollo 13,* returned to his Steppenwolf roots to direct a revival of Sam Shepard's *Buried Child.* Sinise called on his one-time stage mother to play Halie, the matriarch of Shepard's twisted Illinois farm family with several skeletons in the closet and one more in the backyard.

Sinise had a history with Shepard. His 1982 production of Shepard's *True West* had salvaged that play's reputation while making Steppenwolf's name. Shepard took this opportunity to return to the drawing board, making many revisions to his Pulitzer Prize–winning play from 1979. Rehearsals began in August. The cast read the play for a few days, with Shepard listening intensely and making further changes.

Smith's main concern was the play's first several pages, during which Dodge (James Gammon) sits in the middle of the stage, planted on a moldering couch, while his wife, Halie, who is upstairs, yells down a barrage of questions and pronouncements. "I started reading the play, and I said, 'Oh, wait a minute. Twenty-two pages! It won't work," she said. It did work, though. In fact, Smith's first fifteen minutes of nonstop haranguing was among the most effective sequences in the production. It was hell on her vocal chords, however, since she was forced to project down Robert Brill's vertiginous staircase, which seemed to stretch up to the roof of the theater. "I had voice trouble in that play like I've never had," recalled Smith. "The whole company almost had voice trouble. Mine was bad. James Gammon's was bad."

In the first act, a white-haired Halie departs wearing a black dress, black gloves, black veil. In the third act, the stage directions had her returning in a yellow dress. Sinise had an additional idea. Smith said, "One day, Gary said, 'What do you think about dyeing your hair?'"—Sinise wanted Halie to return as a redhead. It would have meant stripping and dyeing Smith's hair to get the exact effect. "I finally said to Gary, 'I make my living with my hair.' I was not ready to make a permanent change." Sinise resorted to a wig. Many people would come to comment on the decision and ask how Halie's hair came to change color overnight. Smith developed a reply to bat off such inquiries: Halie dyed her hair in the sink, she would tell them, and leave it at that.

Sinise and producer Fred Zollo had always intended their production to move to New York. That cause was not greatly aided by the Chicago reviews, which were positive, but with reservations. In a replay of *The Grapes of Wrath* story, the *New York Times* came to the rescue, this time in the person of Ben Brantley. He wrote that, in its current rendering, *"Buried Child* emerged as a bonafide classic." Smith, he said, was "superb." Before the show's November 11 closing, the announcement of a Broadway transfer was made. Smith and Gammon would remain, as would cast members Leo Burmester, Jim Mohr, and Kellie Overbey. Ted Levine and Ethan Hawke (the show's movie-star draw), who played Tilden, Dodge's son, and Vincent, Tilden's boy, respectively, would be replaced by Terry Kinney and Jim True.

Buried Child's spring opening occasioned a collision between Smith's theater, film, and personal worlds. Moon, who was pregnant, was approaching her due date, and Smith was determined to be by her side when the baby came. *Twister* wanted to reshoot a scene in which Smith appeared, but she told them she couldn't go until Moon delivered. Smith and the film kept in touch every day. As soon as the baby was born, the crew would be ready to roll. Two weeks of daily communiqués later, there was no baby. Soon, Helen Hunt would have to report back to the set of her sitcom *Mad About You*. What's more, rehearsals for the Broadway *Buried Child* were about to begin.

Finally, the call came. Moon's water had broken. Smith rushed to her daughter's home in Philadelphia, where Moon had chosen to have the child. Sunday night, she went into a stalled labor. By Monday morning, nothing had changed, and Smith was due in New York. She went to rehearsal. Sinise was acting in the film *Ransom*, which was filming in New York and running behind schedule; he managed, nonetheless, to make the rehearsal. That first day, the production held a press day. Reporters flooded into the rehearsal hall. Pictures were taken; questions were asked; Smith ping-ponged from interview to interview.

Suddenly, she was informed that Moon's labor was under way. She dashed to Penn Station for a train. Lois and Moon were up all night; Moon finally gave birth at 7 A.M. on Tuesday. Mother and child were sent to the hospital for more oxygen, while Grandma, perhaps in need of oxygen herself, boarded the train for Manhattan and rehearsal day number two. "By now, I was so. . . ," said Smith, drifting off. "If you looked at me sideways, I burst into tears."

And she still hadn't reshot *Twister*. On Friday, after rehearsal, the last possible day Helen Hunt was available, the movie people picked Smith up at the theater and took her to the airport. She flew out to the film site, where everyone worked through the night. Filming finished Saturday morning. Her return flight took her to Philadelphia, where the *Buried Child* people picked her up and dropped her off at her daughter's house.

"I was so wonderful to get there after this wild week," she remembered. "It was just the family. The baby was home again. Everything was peaceful."

Ben Brantley liked Smith even better on Broadway than he had in Chicago. "Ms. Smith and Mr. Gammon are magnificent," he wrote in the *Times,* "giving comic gargoyles the stature of figures in Greek tragedy. They are obscenely funny, yet when their characters touch on their family's past, they exude a real, fathomless anguish. . . . Ms. Smith, a bizarre counterpoint of ladylike hand gestures and a lewd, wide legged, pelvis-forward walk, is stunning. She shifts unflinchingly from pious homilies about the decline of manners to raucous physical slapstick."

The show brought Shepard to Broadway for the first time in his decadeslong career. He did not stay long, however. Drama, particularly Shepard's gothic brand, was a hard sell on Broadway, and despite the reviews and the Tony Award nominations (including a nod for Smith, her second), the play closed at the end of June.

The Perspective That Matters
The February prior to *Buried Child*'s opening on Broadway, Smith was invited to a curious benefit evening at Steppenwolf. The entertainment was to be presided over by Gene Siskel and Roger Ebert, the Windy City–based movie critics, who were to interview a group of company members regarding not their stage but their film careers. The panel was to include John Malkovich, Joan Allen, John Mahoney, Austin Pendleton, Gary Sinise, and Laurie Metcalf. Artistic director Martha Lavey called Smith and asked her if she, too, would attend.

At the event, each actor was introduced by a montage of film clips. Smith was shown opposite James Dean in *East of Eden,* Jack Nicholson in *Five Easy Pieces,* and Robert Duvall in *Falling Down.* Siskel and Ebert had greeted Smith early in the evening and told her how much they enjoyed her particular selections. But then, during the discussion, Siskel turned to Smith and said, "Obviously, you can hold your own with the major actors on the screen. So how come you're not a movie star?"

Smith was startled by his perspective—she hadn't thought of her achievements that way. She looked at the audience, who were presumably theatergoers, and at the cameras which were filming the event, which would help support Chicago's most famous stage company. "I wasn't offended," recalled Smith. "I never thought he was trying to be anything more than complimentary. But still, it was an odd question to be asked.

"What went through my mind is: I thought I was doing all right!"

Ron Rifkin
Shifting Scenes

N LATE 1983, RON RIFKIN AND HIS WIFE Iva sat down to dinner at Le Dome, in Los Angeles, with his mother, Miriam, and father, Hy Rifkin, "the Fur King of Seventh Avenue." Ron's parents were visiting him in Los Angeles, Ron and Iva's home since 1966. Ron was forty-five and had been acting for more than twenty-five years. While not a star—like Jack Nicholson and Dennis Hopper, with whom he had socialized in bachelor days—he had done well enough in his trade. He'd appeared on Broadway a couple of times; been a regular on half a dozen television shows; worked regularly at the Mark Taper Forum; and starred in a few movies. Only recently, he'd appeared to acclaim in Tina Howe's *The Art of Dining*, at the Public Theater.

Not bad for little Saulie Rifkin, who grew up an Orthodox Jew in the Williamsburg section of Brooklyn.

Still, he felt he could have been doing better. And the insecurity that comes with acting had not abated over the years. And while he and Iva had neither children nor a plan to have any, the financial worries accumulated. How would he pay all the bills, the mortgage? What about old age? He had never handled finances well. He was tired, and Iva was worried.

As the waiters and busboys came and went, Hy Rifkin, owner of Ronlee coats and a rich man many times over, talked about his business. It was difficult selling his line to the West Coast stores while based in New York, he complained. He was thinking of opening a Los Angeles branch.

Ron Rifkin, actor of stage, screen, and television, opened his mouth. "Why don't we run it for you?" he heard himself say.

The elder Rifkin was surprised. He was guardedly supportive of his son's choice of profession, if not exactly enthusiastic, and, while he had often tried to get him to follow him into the garment industry, he had long since given up hope that he would. In response to his son's question, he asked him to think it over. His son did, and Ron Rifkin left acting.

Early Theaters In the urban shtetl of Williamsburg, leaving the acting profession was never an option for Saul Rifkin—because joining the acting profession was never an option. The insular world where Rifkin was born, on October 31, 1938, was unusually separate from the larger ethnic universe of New York City. His mother, the former Miriam Chumsky, was the thirteenth of fourteen children; her relatives lived in the buildings and blocks surrounding the Rifkins' apartment at 97 Taylor Street. Yiddish was spoken in the Rifkin home, and on the streets young Saul would hear Russian and German as often as English. On Friday nights, the Sabbath, Jewish liturgical music would pour out of the tenement windows, and the civic life in the neighborhood would come to a halt. Lee Street, the main shopping district, seemed to fall asleep, kitchens grew cold as food preparation ceased, and people traveled only on foot.

Saul Rifkin attended Tifereth Israel, the favored synagogue of his maternal grandfather. It was a shtibeleh, a small shul with a domed roof, accommodating maybe thirty people, and its rabbi was Grandpa Chumsky's best friend. It was considered an honor to be in the holy man's presence, and Saul would kiss the rabbi's ring upon meeting him.

Entertainment was not a part of Rifkin's childhood, and he remembers few theatrical experiences from that time. There was the occasional exposure to the arts. His mother sometimes took him to the cinema, once to a Betty Grable film where Saulie was stunned to see that the leggy star was wearing the same ankle-strapped, open-toed shoes his mother owned. Other times, on Saturday night, his father would rent a film and projector and set up a screen in the apartment. Once, he stopped the film right at the heroine's death scene. "Everybody was crying," Rifkin recalled. "I remember the power of the film. The actors were doing something for us, and it made us feel."

Other times, Hy Rifkin would come home with records, Yiddish tunes with titles like "Pinkus the Peddler" and "You've Got to Have a Little Mazel." "I'd shown talent for learning songs quickly," said Rifkin. "He would play a song twice, and I knew it. Then he took me over to the bubbe's house, and he'd say 'Saulie learned a song,' and I'd get up in front of everyone, stand on the table and sing, 'You've Got to Have a Little Mazel,'" his proud father standing by.

Still, these infrequent events did not plant the acting seed. Rifkin recalled that when he was three, he would visit his cousin Lola's bedroom, which was divided by a curtain. He would get behind the curtain and instruct Lola to announce him, after which he would burst out singing and dancing. "How did I know about a curtain?" he wondered fifty years later. "It's very odd about the theater and me. I don't understand why I was attracted to the theater. Nobody ever talked about the theater, or literature or music. When I try to fit myself into any molds, I don't fit. I never read Shakespeare. I didn't know anybody in the theater. My parents didn't go to the theater. I didn't know the theater."

There was, however, one highly theatrical institution which was a constant in his childhood: the synagogue. Tifereth Israel had a simple, square floor pattern. At one side of the hall stood the bimah, or platform, where the rabbi stood when he read the Torah. The congregation sat on three sides around the bimah, men downstairs, women upstairs. Behind the rabbi, hidden by blue curtains, was the ark where the Torahs were kept. When the curtains were drawn and the holy scriptures, capped by beautiful silver crowns, were revealed, the entire congregation stood. Rifkin loved the ritual of it, and through Tifereth Israel young Saul found the theater in Orthodox Williamsburg.

"I realized only recently: That synagogue was my theater," said Rifkin. "That was my first exposure to the beauty and power of that magic. It was God, and in my little child's head, which was an odd little head, I thought, 'Where do I belong, where do I fit in?' And it was only in the synagogue that I belonged."

Acting Out The Rifkins moved from Williamsburg to Forest Hills, Queens, after their son Arnold was born; Saul was seven. The surroundings were more suburban, less ethnic, but Rifkin still got his schooling at yeshiva, as he had in Brooklyn. The days were long. From 9 A.M. to 1 P.M., he would study Hebrew; after lunch, he would study secular subjects until 6 P.M.. He soon realized he was smart and didn't have to adhere to the rigorous study habits of his classmates. He skipped several grades and became valedictorian of his graduating class.

As valedictorian, Rifkin was allowed to speak to the class, and he wrote a speech. But the rabbi at the yeshiva didn't approve of it and instructedRifkin to read something he had prepared instead. The young student hated the new speech and seethed at the idea that his hard-earned privilege had been taken away from him.

"When it came time for me to say my speech," recalled Rifkin, "something twisted inside my head, and I got up and made a speech in Hebrew double talk. I just started talking gobbledy-gook with a Hebrew accent. And everyone in my class started to laugh, and it was awful, because the rabbi and the principal were getting so angry. It went on for about ten minutes, and none of the parents really understood Hebrew, so they couldn't tell the difference. I don't know how I got the nerve to do it. The rabbi came over to me and said, 'What do you think you're doing? How dare you!' and I just laughed and laughed."

Rifkin went to yeshiva high school in Washington Heights. Each morning, he would arise early in the morning for the long subway ride. He would catch the local GG train, taking it to the Roosevelt Avenue station, in Jackson Heights, where he would change for the E express; that would take him into Manhattan. At the Seventh Avenue stop, in midtown, he would change for the D, take it one stop to Columbus Circle, where he would change again, to the A train. He would ride that line north for nearly half an hour, through the Upper West Side, Harlem, and Washington Heights, until he reached the school at 186th Street. Often he would be suspended for being late.

He felt as out of place in Upper Manhattan as he had in Brooklyn. The school was populated by Europeans and athletes, and he was neither. When Rifkin was twelve, he took up smoking, lighting Chesterfields as he left the school by the back way. Skipping down the back stairs, he would conceal the lit cigarette in the cup of his hand until safely out of the building. One day, he and his friend Stanley Stern found the back door locked and were forced to pass through the main part of the school to reach the front entrance, the Chesterfield burning between Rifkin's fingers all the way. Once out, he flipped the cigarette out from its hiding place and took a puff. Stanley sniffed. "Saul," he said, "I smell something. Look at you. Your coat is on fire."

So were his mittens. Saul threw coat and mittens onto the ground and quickly stomped on the flames. He stared down at the smoldering outergarments, shivering in the winter air. It was a brand-new coat, an expensive mackinaw. "What am I going to do?" he cried out. "My parents just bought this coat." All during the long trip home, on the A, D, E, and GG trains, he anguished over the punishment which awaited him in Forest Hills.

"When my mother opened the door, I was crying, crying," said Rifkin. "She said, 'What's wrong?' I said, 'The gang, they came at us and called us 'dirty Jew,' and they threw lighted torches at us.' She said, 'Oh, my God! My poor son!' She was so upset, she didn't know what to do. She was beside herself. My father came home, and I told him the same story. I was crying and carrying on. He just looked at me and said, 'I am really sorry this happened to you,' and he didn't say anything more. I was walking around with this terrible lie for about a week. Finally, I told him. He knew it was a lie all along." The Rifkins bought their son a new coat.

After one year of yeshiva, Rifkin told his parents he wanted to go to a public school. He began at Forest Hills High School the next fall. His junior year he joined Play Pro, the school's theater program. There had been no theater at yeshiva, and it took Rifkin a year just to figure out there were such a thing as student productions. "It was as if I had finally landed in the right country," he remembered.

The plays were supervised by William Kerr, a legend at the place. Rifkin loved him and his work. But because of his chubby, ethnic looks, he got only tiny roles or worked backstage. Rifkin graduated from high school in 1955, at the early age of sixteen. By that time, he knew he "would never be a doctor, the way I said I would be."

"Your Religion Is the Theater" Because Saul Rifkin was Orthodox and still kept kosher, he applied to only two colleges, both in New York City and close to the Jewish community he knew. He settled upon New York University's now extinct all-male campus in the Bronx, lived in a dormitory for a year, and then joined the Zeta Beta Tau fraternity, his "last attempt at being conventional. " He also joined the Green Room Honor Society, a thespian club, and spent much of his time hanging around the drama department. With the Green Room, he performed in Clifford Odets's *Waiting for Lefty*, The Gershwins' *Girl Crazy*, and other shows. (The female roles were played by girls brought in from Hunter College.)

Rifkin's interest in theater grew stronger. In 1958, following his junior year (he was nineteen), he was hired, through a distant, forgotten connection, by the summer-stock Cecilwood Theatre, in Fishkill, New York. The company was populated by graduates of the Actors Studio, including Lonny Chapman, who ran the theater and with whom Rifkin began studying.

That summer he appeared in Ira Levin's *No Time for Sergeants*, Gore Vidal's *Visit to a Small Planet* and John Patrick's *Teahouse of the August Moon*. In the latter, he was made up to play a Japanese character, and he encountered the first clash between his future profession and current faith. During rehearsals, the director, Logan Ramsey, assigning various duties to the play's bit players, instructed Rifkin that he was to light candles onstage at a certain point in the play. A Jewish precept forbids the lighting of any flame in challenge of the candles traditionally lit at the advent of Shabbat. Rifkin paused, and replied, "Okay, but I can't do it on Friday night or Saturday matinee."

Ramsey stared at the pudgy teenager before him. "What do you mean you can't do it?" he asked. "I can't light candles on Shabbat. I'm an observing Jew," explained Rifkin. "What's that got to do with anything?" he demanded. "I can't do it on Friday and Saturday," repeated Rifkin. "It's my religion."

"What religion?" yelled Ramsey. "Your religion is the theater!"

Rifkin persisted, and Ramsey eventually got someone else to light the candles.

In the summer of 1959, after graduating from NYU, Rifkin made his first journey west of the Hudson River, performing in summer stock at the Red Barn Theatre, in Saugatuck, Michigan. Still hampered by his weight, he was relegated to old-man parts, such as the doctor in *Cat on a Hot Tin Roof*. However, they qualified him for membership in Actors' Equity.

Rifkin also went through the motions of applying to medical school to please his parents, but knew he wouldn't go. "I just knew I couldn't fit into the world of my father, which was a business world," he said. "I didn't belong to academia. I didn't fit into the professions—doctors, lawyers. I knew that the only way I'd get on with my life was to become involved in this world of the theater." He was now twenty-one. Before he climbed into his father's Oldsmobile to drive to Sagatuck, he worked up the courage to inform his parents. "They couldn't have been too horrified. I think they were just resigned to it."

During the summer of 1960, he returned to Fishkill to play the part of playboy Bobby Van Husen in the musical *The Boyfriend*, again directed by Ramsey. Also in the cast, playing Hortense, the French maid, was a nineteen-year-old Brooklynite named Barbra Streisand. Every day, when the cast would go out to talk and socialize, she would stay behind in the theater, practicing "A Sleepin' Bee," a number she would perform a year later on the *Tonight* show (then starring Jack Paar).

"I knew," Rifkin remarked, "the way she focused, the way she worked, and the way she didn't socialize with us, she had something I didn't have, and that was this *drive*. This killer drive that would speed her along her way in a way that I knew was impossible for me. I remember thinking that." Still, Rifkin didn't covet Streisand's will. "I didn't like it. Not that she was mean or anything; she was great. But I don't think I've ever felt a conscious desperation to succeed. I think that's what she had that I didn't have—and don't have. I knew it was not something I would want to incorporate in me, although I would like some of it."

That same year, Rifkin performed in *Take Me Along* at the Melody Tent, in North Tonawanda, outside Buffalo, where the producers took a dislike to the sound of Saul as an actor's name. Rifkin remembered a friend remarking that a relative, Ronnie Rifkin, had a great name. Ron Rifkin it was.

Dues Paying Rifkin's debut in the New York theater was as an understudy in the Broadway production of *Come Blow Your Horn*, the first play by a television writer named Neil Simon. Prior to that, he had found work, through a friend of a friend, in a series of soap opera spots, and in stock productions of musicals. Rifkin began work on *Come Blow Your Horn* in mid-December of 1961, as understudy to star Joel Grey, who was also enjoying his Broadway debut.

Still observant, and living in Great Neck, Ron E. Rifkin—as he was billed in the program—would pack a bag and stay at the Edison Hotel in Times Square on weekends in order to avoid traveling on the Sabbath. Between some Saturday matinees and evening shows, he and Carolyn Brenner, a fellow understudy who was also Orthodox, would walk up to the Brenner home in the West 70s to have dinner. As the son of Yiddish entertainer Mickey Katz, Grey was familiar with such rituals and wasn't above gently mocking Rifkin for his orthodoxy. Every time the two actors met, Grey would adopt a Yiddish accent and ask, "Did you have your tsiken, Rifkin?"

Hanukkah fell during those first few weeks of work, and, in another asser-tion of his religion, Rifkin lit candles in his dressing room; he invited anyone in the Broadway community so inclined to join him in the ceremony. One woman came — a blonde dancer in *Carnival* named Iva March. A few years later, they would marry.

In early February of 1962, Grey, stranded on a Wednesday afternoon, missed a performance. Rifkin, the beneficiary of only a few rehearsals, was informed he had to go on for the matinee. Rifkin did not, however, make a good first impression on his co-star, Hal March, who played the handsome older brother, Alan, opposite Rifkin's shy younger brother, Buddy. In one scene, Buddy was supposed to finish his brother's whiskey. Rifkin left a little liquid behind and as March turned the bot-tle over to inspect it the dregs splashed in his face. "Hal March hated me, because I wasn't Joel, and I wasn't doing it the way Joel did it," he recalled.

March complained, and Rifkin was promptly dismissed. "I don't understand why I was fired," he pleaded to his co-star Arlene Golonka. "I'm too good an actor to be fired." Golonka replied, "You were fired because that prick didn't like your performance." She added, "You should study with Lee Strasberg."

Rifkin did so, beginning his studies in early 1962. And as it happened, only a week after he had been dismissed from his Broadway job, *Come Blow Your Horn*'s producers, William Hammerstein and Michael Ellis, rehired him to star, opposite Dick Shawn, in the Coconut Grove Playhouse production of the play, in Miami. "I thought, this is very odd, firing me, hiring me," said Rifkin. "I learned very early that it's all so ephemeral."

Good Morning, Hollywood Soon after the booking in Coconut Grove, Rifkin moved into Manhattan, following fellow Actors Studio student Barbara Mostel (who was Zero Mostel's niece), into an apartment building in Hell's Kitchen, near the theater district.

When not working, Rifkin spent much of his time at the Studio. Lee Strasberg supported and encouraged him. There were, however, no "eurekas" for Rifkin among Strasberg's fabled Method-acting teachings. "What I learned at the Actors Studio is that I'm not one of those actors who can talk about technique," said Rifkin. "I never talk about acting. Strasberg would say to me, 'How do you act? What do you do? What's your technique?' I would say, 'I don't know. I don't know how I do it.' I don't take a play and break it down and have a history. I don't do that. I don't know why I don't do it—I just don't. For me, the role has always explained itself in rehearsal and the working on it."

Rather than fully adopting the Method exercises he learned at the Studio, he found himself incorporating them into an acting approach already in place. "I think I always had a system. Some actors act intuitively. I can't explain it, except to say my system absorbed all of that stuff and found a way to make it mine. So if I run into trouble as an actor, I find myself intuitively doing something that makes it easier for me to go on to the next stage.

"The thing that's so deceptive about acting classes and the whole process of art in general," he continued, "is that you go to a class, you sit there for three hours, you listen to people comment on what the teacher is saying. Then you go out afterward and have coffee, you listen to five people talk about it, and you have five different responses. Everybody processes what they see through their own system."

By 1964, with jobs becoming scarcer, New York was looking less and less like the land of opportunity. Rifkin, like many before him, cast his gaze westward. "I wanted to get away from New York," he related. "I wasn't happy there. I wasn't getting work." That year, he travelled cross-country with a friend and began bouncing back and forth between the coasts. When he and Iva married, they decided to start their new life in Los Angeles.

At first, his instincts seemed on target. Success came quickly. In 1965, Rifkin tested for a television series and won the lead. And not just any series. It was the latest project of Carl Reiner and Sheldon Leonard, the men behind what was then the most successful comedy on television, *The Dick Van Dyke Show*. That show had explored the world of television writing; the new series, *Good Morning, World*, would examine another niche of the entertainment world: the life of a disc jockey. Rifkin was now in his mid-twenties—yet, perhaps, he still sought parental approval, and after getting the good news, he asked Carl Reiner if he would telephone and break the news to his father, who was relaxing at that moment in the Beverly Hills Hotel. Reiner, no doubt amused, complied.

There would be no further good news for Hy Rifkin. After the pilot was shot, everything changed, and Rifkin was fired and replaced by Joby Baker. The reason was not given, but Rifkin sensed the source of the rejection. "They said, 'You're too Method, you're too Actors Studio.' And I realized what they meant was: I was too

Jewish. I soon found that I didn't fit into any category. I wasn't traditionally handsome enough to be a leading man, and I wasn't goofy-looking enough to be a second banana. It wasn't until Dustin Hoffman, in *The Graduate*, that that all changed."

By the actor's own admission, his fall from the heights of *Good Morning, World* devastated him. "That was a disaster for me," he said. "Iva once said, 'That really changed everything for you. You remain fragile about that.' When I think of the experience that actors go through, in terms of the kinds of rejection and disappointment we get, being fired and replaced by someone for no reason is a particularly damaging experience. Actors put themselves on the line in a particular kind of way. It's not a product they're selling, it's themselves — their faces, their bodies. That experience made me protect myself, made me put myself in a box so nobody would touch me or hurt me like that again. And it sort of set up a pattern for me which was not very good, because you really isolate yourself in a way that doesn't let people in."

The misfortune that began with *Good Morning, World* continued in the person of a Rifkin's new, overly selective, California agent. Explained Rifkin: "My agent advised me, very poorly, that because I had now done the lead in a pilot for a television series, I must be very careful about what I take. I listened because I was young and stupid. So she kept turning down work for me for about a year and a half or two years."

Fortunately, Rifkin did not suffer enormously, financially or artistically. He had received a large payday for *World*, which kept him and Iva solvent, and the Actors Studio — to which he was supposedly too adherent — had recently opened a West Coast branch. "I was very lucky because I continued to work there. I never really stopped working."

Blooming In 1969, roughly a decade after he began acting, Ron Rifkin made a new beginning in his career. The vehicle through which he achieved an artistic and professional jump-start was a pungent play by Harvey Perr called *Rosebloom*. Perr was a young writer in the Actors Studio's writing unit, and he and Rifkin — two transplanted Brooklynites — soon became great friends.

"Harvey had written this play," Rifkin said, "He gave it to me to read, and thought I'd be perfect for the part of the young man. We couldn't get it done anyplace. Neither of us had much money; Harvey had even less that I had. He had a friend who worked at the *Hollywood Reporter*, and since we needed to get copies of this play around so people could read it, we went to one of the places in the office where there was a copy machine. It was a day when no one was there. We put ink in the copy machine, and Harvey started it, and the ink spattered all over. It just got all over everything, and we both got so nervous that we left. We ran like a couple of scared kids."

Somehow, they managed to get a copy of *Rosebloom* to Gordon Davidson, the artistic director of the Mark Taper Forum. Davidson liked it and decided to present it at the Forum as part of its New Theatre for Now series, a workshop program as old as the theater itself—that is, three years.

Perr's current creation was not for the faint of heart. Its four-character family was an Albee-like, angst-ridden, self-lacerating quartet, living with and feeding off each other. Harry Rosebloom, the title character, has spent the past twenty-six years in jail for his complicity in a gang murder. His wife, Sylvie, sits at home regretting her wasted life of many husbands and more lovers. Their crippled son Mark—Rifkin's role—pities himself, bemoans his life, and reviles his manipulative, catty wife, Enola Gay.

"I identify with that role as much as I identify with the role in *The Substance of Fire*," said Rifkin, invoking the Jon Robin Baitz play which would revive his career a second time, in 1991. "It's almost as if the role had been written for me. That role was so much a part of my life, and I understood that character so well. My rhythms and my inner sounds were so much Mark Rosebloom's. And I understood Harvey, and that role was really an extension of Harvey. There was no point in getting anyone else for the role."

In the early days of August 1969, after a mere two weeks of rehearsal, the play was presented in four workshop performances. By the time it closed, people were already clamoring for it to reopen. In the history of the New Theatre for Now series, *Rosebloom* got press notices that were unmatched in enthusiasm. The *Los Angeles Herald-Examiner* held back nothing, exclaiming in its opening line, "New Theatre for Now has come up with a genuinely brilliant play." It continued: "Surely it is as strong a play as the series has found in its three-year history. It is well worth a major production somewhere, including the Forum."

The other notices were equally effusive. And when the play, on the strength of those four performances, amazingly won the Los Angeles Drama Critics Circle Award for playwriting, it became almost incumbent upon the Mark Taper Forum to remount the play. *Rosebloom* was duly scheduled for the 1970 season, although with almost completely different personnel. Gordon Davidson took the reins from director Jered Barclay, and Rachel Roberts, Mike Kellin, and Rosemary Forsyth replaced Jan Sterling, Bert Freed, and Sally Kellerman in the roles of the mother, father, and wife, respectively. Rifkin was the only cast member to be retained. The play was due to open on the Mark Taper Forum's mainstage on June 18.

Almost immediately, the production was thrown into turmoil. The union, Actors' Equity, refused to allow Roberts, who is British, permission to perform; she did not have a green card from the U.S. Bureau of Immigration. Roberts applied for the card, but still Equity objected, despite in-person pleas before the union's council by Davidson, Peer, and Roberts. Davidson, claiming it was impossible to recast at such short notice, rescheduled *Rosebloom* for the fall, bumping Howard Sackler's *The Pastime of Monsieur Robert*.

At the end of this year or so of publicity—the accolades, the award, the Equi-

Ron Rifkin onstage with Sheree North (left) and Carrie Snodgress in Harvey Perr's *Rosebloom*, at the Mark Taper Forum in the fall of 1970.

ty fight—the buzz surrounding the mysterious work had become cacophonous. It was "that Great American Drama everyone admires but virtually no one has seen," remarked one tart-tongued writer.

The delay cost the production its second cast—again, with the exception of Rifkin. By the time it opened, the cast was Nehemiah Persoff as Rosebloom, Sheree North as Sylvie, and, as Rifkin's wife, Carrie Snodgress, who had recently attracted notice in the film *Diary of a Mad Housewife*.

When rehearsing and performing *Rosebloom*, Rifkin was bound to a customized one-arm-drive wheelchair, which, over time, he grew quite adept at manipulating. "The wheelchair was arranged so that the outside wheel on the right side was for the front wheels and the inside wheel was for the back wheels," he explained. Though his character was disabled, Rifkin was rarely immobile during the play. He would drive crazily about, his chair going click click click as he spun back and forth, around and around the set, now pinning other characters in a corner with the contraption, now wheeling rapidly away from them. As *Cash Box* would put it, Rifkin, "circling the stage in his wheelchair, [was] much like a caged panther, ringmaster for the rituals which reveal the relationship between each of the characters."

His hell-on-wheels portrayal was not without its physical cost. Opening night of the play was attended by an orthopedist. When Rifkin, his right arm swollen from the nightly strain, eventually paid the doctor a call, the man eyed him and said, "I knew I was going to see you sooner or later." Still, while his arm bothered him, the actor didn't mind much. "I was young and happy to be working," he said.

Rosebloom finally opened on the mainstage on November 4. By that time, the critics had predictably, and perhaps understandably, grown a bit cool and skeptical. Many found Davidson's full-fledged production inferior to Jed Barclay's earlier workshop. They preferred Jan Sterling to Sheree North, Sally Kellerman to Carrie Snodgress. Others—illustrating that in 1970, shock was still a possibility—were absolutely appalled at Perr's subject matter and use of language. A staffer at the *Costa Mesa Daily Pilot* said, "*Rosebloom* is a sickening, sordid and seedily succinct commentary on the dirty lives of a dirty group of people and this pathetic play wafts across the footlights of the Mark Taper Forum replete with four-letter filth and the visual impact of an unflushed toilet." Even the worldly *Variety* found the drama "an insult to [those] who still think there may be some entertainment left in the legit theater despite the avalanche of filth that characterizes so many of the new crop."

This sort of reaction became so common that the *Los Angeles Times*'s wry critic Dan Sullivan revisited the play in order to write about the topic, in an article titled, "Let's Go, Henry, They're Starting to Talk Smutty." On his first trip, however, Sullivan had liked *Rosebloom,* writing, "If one of the traditional functions of art is to sit you down and show you the incredible richness of even the most humdrum human moment, Harvey Perr's *Rosebloom* is a thoroughly traditional play."

But, like it or hate it, *Rosebloom* undeniably became, as one headline put it, the "season's conversation piece." And the most praised aspect of the theatrical event was Ron Rifkin's performance. The *Los Angeles Times* called him "absolutely first-rate." The *Herald-Examiner* said he gave the performance of the show, adding, "Rifkin's work was at once flamboyantly theatrical and unusually observant of the psychological complexities." Another reviewer exclaimed, "Rifkin is scarcely less than superb. Nothing in the role seems to elude him, and his cadenzas of self-hate—matched by a sense of Mark's capacity for love—add up to a truly remarkable performance. Rifkin represents the only member of *Rosebloom*'s cast who is not only comfortable with the monologues but who actually exults in them."

"It was a triumph for me," concurred Rifkin, "because I'd never really had a part like that before. It was my first really great part. It was the first time people wrote about me, and in such ways. Suddenly I found my voice. It was language. I discovered language."

It took another year for the play to travel to New York, where it opened at the Eastside Playhouse, on East 74th Street, in January 1972. Barclay was back as director, and, aside from Rifkin, the cast was again a new one. The East Coast reception for Perr's play wasn't nearly as warm. The *New York Times*'s Clive Barnes warily adjudged that "cripples, prisons and violence are rather ordinary imagistic metaphors, and that beyond their metaphorical function, the people are not quite interesting enough." The *Los Angeles Times*, sneaking yet another peek, allowed that "time has rubbed most of the bloom off *Rosebloom*." No reversal of fortune for the play, though, could have an effect on Rifkin. His role had opened up a new phase in a decade-old acting career.

Thirteen Weeks To say whether Ron Rifkin has had a successful career in television is a difficult proposition. For while it is true that, since the early 1970s, he has never had any trouble finding work in the medium, he was never a regular in a steadily running series, until his stint as Dr. Vucelich on *ER*. Prior to that, he was perhaps best known as one of Bonnie Franklin's beaus, on the long-running *One Day at a Time*. His status there, however, was as a recurring character. Of the series in which he has been a regular from the first show, few have lasted past their original order of thirteen episodes.

Rifkin's first series as a regular was *Adam's Rib*, an ABC romantic comedy based on the Katherine Hepburn–Spencer Tracy film. It premiered in the fall of the 1973–74 season. Playing the married, dueling lawyers, Adam and Amanda Bonner, were Ken Howard and Blythe Danner. The young stars had both recently made their names on Broadway: Howard in the musical *1776*, in which he played Thomas Jefferson; and Danner in *Butterflies Are Free*, for which she won a Tony Award. (Both are in the 1972 movie of *1776*, as Mr. and Mrs. Jefferson.) Rifkin played Adam Bonner's friend, assistant district attorney Roy Mendelsohn. He remembers it as a good experience, though he didn't have that much to do. The show was cancelled after thirteen episodes.

Two seasons later, Rifkin was cast in ABC's *When Things Were Rotten*, a situation comedy created by Mel Brooks, who was basking in the successes of his movies *Blazing Saddles* and *Young Frankenstein*. The series was a satire on the adventures of Robin Hood and his Merry Men, with Dick Gautier as Robin and Dick Van Patten as Friar Tuck. Rifkin got his hair permed for the part of an infantilized Prince John. The title of the sitcom was unfortunately evocative of his experience on it. Just before Rifkin was to begin shooting, he found out that a close friend of his had been randomly murdered, which left him in a fragile state. In addition, his relationship with Brooks was not a good one. "That was a horrible experience," he recalled. "Mel Brooks was not nice to me. He would come in once a week and bully me. I think, in retrospect, that if he had been in it, mine was the part he would have played. He just didn't like the way I was playing it."

Critics praised the series. "It was definitely very good and definitely before its time," agreed Rifkin. However, ratings were low, and the show was cancelled in December.

Rifkin's next project was an unusual one for network television: an hour-long situation comedy. The series, called *Husbands, Wives, and Lovers*, was created by comedienne Joan Rivers and debuted on CBS in March, 1978. The show concerned the travails of five couples living in the San Fernando Valley. Rifkin played Ron Willis, a dentist who is separated from his wife, Helene; representing Helene in the divorce is Willis's best friend, attorney Dixon Carter Fielding.

"That project had great, great potential," said Rifkin. "The pilot was hysterical. Hopes were very high. Then Joan Rivers left the show. It wasn't really a sitcom because we didn't shoot it in front of an audience." This attempt at a series didn't work any better than those before it. Again, it was thirteen weeks and out.

Next came *One Day at a Time*, for which Rifkin would be remembered — sometimes to his chagrin — for years to come. The series star, Bonnie Franklin, played Ann Romano, the divorced mother of two, who had several boyfriends throughout the series. Rifkin was Nick Handris, her man for the 1980–81 season. Handris was the divorced father of a son, Alex. Rifkin soon felt an uneasiness in the socially conscious sitcom format, of which *One Day* was one of the most prominent examples of the time.

"I knew that something inside of me wasn't fitting in right," explained Rifkin. "Somebody told me that they looked at old reruns of *One Day at a Time* and found that I didn't fit in because I was in another genre, or I was sort of ahead of myself in terms of my reality level. I was almost too real for the other people.

"I think what happened was, I took great responsibility in playing a divorced father, and I said to the writers, 'You have all these funny people, and it's not that I can't be funny, but I'm not good at being funny the way the other actors' parts let them be funny. So just don't give me gags to do. If I am playing a single father, and you write your jokes, I'll do them, but I can't do ba-dum-dum. It's not what I do. There are people who do it better.' They said that that was fine, but they wrote ba-dum-dum anyway."

Rifkin was told that he and his son were being written out at the top of the next season. It wasn't until after he had finished filming the television miniseries *The Winds of War*, however, that he discovered the entire truth. "I was on the subway," recalled Rifkin, "and some guy came up to me and said, 'You're supposed to be dead.' I said, 'What do you mean?' 'You died in a car crash, and Bonnie Franklin adopted your son.'" The network had not told him how he would be written out, and the boy had not vanished from the series at all. It was, he said, "another wound."

Photo courtesy of Photofest.

In 1980, Ron Rifkin joined the cast of the CBS television sitcom *One Day at a Time*, as the love interest of star Bonnie Franklin.

"So many actors have dreams which get lost or destroyed or squelched or cruelly rejected, and so they have to find other things to do," said Rifkin. "The nature of our work is so ephemeral. You can't hold on to it, because you're at somebody else's whim."

An Artistic Home During these years, Rifkin was working consistently at the Mark Taper Forum. "Everything I do there I love. It was sort of my artistic home when I was in L.A.," he affirmed. Harvey Perr stood by his friend and collaborator, and in 1973 he presented Rifkin with *Afternoon Tea,* a play written specifically for him and actress Barbara Colby. Rifkin would remember it as one of the greatest events of his life. Los Angeles theatergoers would, to say the least, likewise remember it, though for a wide variety of reasons.

Afternoon Tea was one of a group of plays presented under the canopy of Taper's New Theatre for Now "In the Works" series. The play was done at Stage B at the 20th Century Fox studios, where bleachers were set up surrounding the playing area. The play had only the two characters, Aaron and Rachel, lovers who convened regularly at a country house on Sunday afternoons and whiled away the time with ritualistic activities. These pastimes were very much Perr's point. Before the actors pursued any activity, they announced their intentions: "This is the small-talk ceremony," "the welcoming ceremony," "the music-listening ceremony," and so on. Then they would do just that, often with little or no traditionally "dramatic" action or dialogue. As one astounded critic exclaimed: "Rifkin picked up a copy of Lillian Hellman's *An Unfinished Woman,* and began reading the chapter on Dashiell Hammett out loud. He read for 25 minutes!"

"The play was a kind of a meditation," said Rifkin. "It required a certain kind of steeliness from us, a certain kind of concentration." But concentration is often a thing in rare supply among average viewers. Critics and audience members alike were stupefied as *Afternoon Tea* unfolded before their eyes. Gordon Davidson had said that he hoped the "In the Works" series would give playwrights the benefit of audience feedback. He got his wish in spades.

"We proceeded to do this play," said Rifkin, "and all at once the audience hated what they were seeing [or] became thrilled at what they were seeing. They would boo and hiss us, say 'This is a piece of shit!' The other part of the people would say 'Sit down! Shut up! This is art!'"

On Thursday, September 27, Perr made the unusual move of taking the stage prior to performance to explain the *raison d'être* for "In the Works." He was "experimenting with time." The *Hollywood Reporter* drolly observed: "This was most likely prompted by the fact that a number of people walked out of the Tuesday and Wednesday performances."

If Perr thought he would reason the audience into a respectful suspension of judgment, he was gravely mistaken. At a performance soon after, during the notorious "reading ceremony," a man—perhaps inspired, perhaps incensed, by the play—rose from his seat, strode onto the set, grasped an apple from the prop fruit bowl, and began to eat it. A little while later, another customer helped himself to a slice of teacake.

"I didn't handle it very well, I must say," recalled Rifkin. "At one point, where the guy started eating the apple, I could feel the heat in my eyes—that moment before you start to cry and you can feel your eyes get really hot and tears just about to spring out. I remember looking at Barbara and she looked at me with such incredible love that I smiled at her, and we waited until the guy left the stage and we continued."

Most critics considered the play a joke or an insult, but a few applauded its audacity. Dan Sullivan, of the *Los Angeles Times,* commented whimsically, "Since they were reading from Lillian Hellman's memoirs and playing Mahler I didn't mind one bit." As for the audience rebellion: "A most appropriate gesture for an experimental theater festival. Perhaps 'In the Works' will be remembered in the future as the opening shot of Audience Lib."

Many an actor might have run from *Afternoon Tea* straight to therapy, career counseling, or the playwright's throat. Rifkin cherishes it still today. "Think about all the emotions of having people boo you and hiss you, and cheer you and applaud you, yet want to stay and watch what this play was about."

Rifkin received his first major film role, in *Silent Running*, as a result of his performance in *Rosebloom*. Prior to that, his opportunities had been scant. In 1969, the action film *The Devil's 8*, starring a well-past-his-moment Fabian, had given Rifkin his first film role, as an FBI agent. "I had no idea what I was doing," said Rifkin, whose main memory of the shoot was of losing his contact lenses every day in dust storms. His next movie starred the more-of-the-moment Rachel Welch. That movie, shot in Las Vegas, was a murder thriller called *Flareup*.

Silent Running was in another league. It was an "ecological science-fiction" story in the good hands of Douglas Trumbull, a first-time director who had been an assistant on Stanley Kubrick's sci-fi classic, *2001: A Space Odyssey*. In the movie, which was shot on the abandoned aircraft carrier *U.S.S. Valley Forge*, moored off Long Island, the Earth is a uniform 75 degrees and barren of foliage. Four men have been sent into space with every species of plant native to Earth, charged with protecting them until further notice. When headquarters cancels the experiment, Freeman Lowell (played by Bruce Dern), the most avid of the mission's conservationists, kills the other three men. Supporting Dern were Cliff Potts, Jesse Vint, and Rifkin, who said he was hired as the cast's representative New York actor's actor. All three were dead 30 minutes into the film.

The film was released in April of 1972 to largely good notices and has been something of a cult classic since then. "I thought it was the beginning of a really nice career in film," said Rifkin, "which it turned out not to be."

At the Taper, in 1976, Gordon Davidson staged a season in repertory. It consisted of two new American plays, one new British play, and Chekhov's *The Three Sisters*. Rifkin appeared as Andrei in the latter—his first role in a Chekhov play. In *Cross Country*, Susan Miller's autobiographical play about a woman's journey from New York to Los Angeles, from marriage to independence, and from confusion to self-realization, Rifkin played the husband whom the protagonist leaves.

He was generally praised in both, but neither play matched his reception that fall in *Ice*, by Michael Cristofer, who had received acclaim for *The Shadow Box*. This stark new play examined issues of despair, regeneration, and hope. Murph is a former model whose youthful spirit has turned to disillusionment. He leaves Los Angeles for a cabin in Alaska, but, unable to stand the isolation, he drafts a wino, Ray, from a nearby tavern for companionship; then Sunshine, a sexual life force who upsets the balance between the two men. The talkative Murph turns to drink and slowly degenerates, while Ray gives up booze and reclaims his life.

Rifkin landed the part of Ray only after two other actors hadn't worked out.

Onstage, he was nearly unrecognizable, dressed in layers of tatters, his face masked by a mangy beard and a wool cap. Murph was played by Cliff DeYoung and Britt Swanson was Sunshine. The play left people hot or cold. *Variety* stated flatly, "In all, it's not a good play," while the *Los Angeles Free Press* issued a near manifesto of a review comparing Cristofer to Williams, Miller, Beckett, and Pinter. The ever-reasonable Sullivan of the *Los Angeles Times* struck a middle ground: "It's not the easiest evening you'll ever spend in the theater. Not even the most rewarding. But it's one that lingers like the pain from a bad tooth and demands exorcism."

As with *Rosebloom*, *Ice* divided the critics' opinion on everything except Rifkin's performance. The *Los Angeles Herald-Examiner* said, "Rifkin is the most sure of the actors, at ease with the coarse wit and the torrent of words and so unafraid of the sentiment." Another reviewer called his Ray "a thoroughly satisfying performance that fills all the corners of the character."

The performance would seem to be another career landmark, if Rifkin were the type of actor who thought in those terms. "I never think about my career," he offered. "I'm not one of those people who can say, 'Oh, my career is going well. Oh, my career is going terribly.' I wish I *could* think of it as a career, and say, 'This is where I am now, and this is where I was then, and look how far I've come.'

"But it embarrasses me. I think about my life and my work—if I were to sit here and talk to myself about my career, I'd start laughing. I'd get giddy."

The Goodbye Actor By the end of the 1970s, Rifkin wasn't feeling very giddy. Now into his third decade as an actor, he felt beset by the same uncertainty he had experienced in the previous two. Furthermore, that anxiety was now heightened by the prospect of advancing age—he turned forty in 1978—and the often declining prospects that go with it. "I was feeling sort of melancholy about my work and what I was doing and what I wasn't doing," he said.

But work continued to stream in from every medium. He got cast in the role of an EST trainer in the 1978 Richard Dreyfuss vehicle, *The Big Fix*. In 1982, he had a part in *The Sting II*, the late-in-coming sequel to the 1973 hit. Neither film was a success. "None of the films were any better or worse than the others," observed Rifkin. "I never really played a part long enough or big enough to feel I'd really accomplished something."

In the late 1970s, Rifkin worked on several episodes of the television satire *Soap*, playing a mad brain surgeon. On the prime-time soap opera *Falcon Crest*, he appeared as a doctor who is blackmailed by Jane Wyman into murder. Neither job lasted more than a season.

In 1979, Rifkin had been hired for *The Mary Tyler Moore Comedy Hour*, a show-within-a-show in which he played the star's director, but his character was eliminated after six episodes. The same year he returned to the Broadway stage. The play was Herb Gardner's sentimental comedy, *The Goodbye People*, about three "different drummer" types: A spirited Jewish octogenarian who is determined to reopen a hot

dog stand in Coney Island in the middle of winter, his therapy-addled daughter, and a banjo-carrying, sunrise-watching, dissatisfied businessman (Rifkin). The play had first premiered at the Ethel Barrymore Theatre starring Milton Berle, Brenda Vaccaro, and Bob Dishy. It ran only seven performances before closing. Gardner had never given up on it, however. A decade and several productions later, it was back on Broadway, this time at the Belasco, with Herschel Bernardi, Melanie Mayron, and Rifkin.

Rifkin remembered it as a great experience. Broadway remembered it as a short one. Critics carped that it was the same clichéd tripe they had dismissed ten years before. The morning after it opened, producer Joseph Kipness called Gardner, the director, and the cast to a restaurant. He left the room and came back with a huge fish. "See this fish?" he said. "It's dead, just like this fuckin' play."

A more lively affair was Tina Howe's *The Art of Dining*, which opened at Joseph Papp's Public Theater in December of 1979. In Howe's satire on the American way of eating, Rifkin played Cal, who owns and operates, with his wife Ellen, a gourmet restaurant, the Golden Carousel. Ellen cooks, while Cal, as the headwaiter, tries with little success not to devour the meals before they are served to the customers.

Some critics found the play slight; others, delightful and witty. Most of the acting laurels went to a young Dianne Wiest, who played a nearsighted, food-phobic young author who nearly singlehandedly destroys the restaurant. Once done with Wiest, though, the reviewers usually fell to praising Rifkin.

Still, there was no security. There was certainly no stardom, and there were no savings. There were, however, bills and a mortgage. In 1983, there was a forty-fifth birthday. "I had reached a certain time in my life," said Rifkin. "I had been acting for more than twenty years, and I looked at my wife and said 'What are you going to do if I die tomorrow? There's no life insurance. This is crazy.'

"I'm a bit of dreamer, and I'm not very good with money. I always spend whatever I make. I don't have any savings."

Shortly before their momentous dinner conversation at Le Dome, Hy Rifkin took his son along on a trip to meet the company's Korean partners. "I realized one of the reasons he took me to Korea, in retrospect, is that he wanted me to see how big the business was and how interesting it was, because he knew I would be interested in all this." And Rifkin was paying attention.

Leaving the Business
The West Coast Ronlee offices were in the Merchandise Mart, a monolithic, windowless building in downtown Los Angeles. Every day, representatives of the major stores would come to the office, where Rifkin dutifully showed them the line of ladies' coats. The utterly mercantile, workaday nature of the job quickly got to the recent ex-actor. Frustrated, he would retreat into the office and punch holes in the thin cardboard walls.

"The first year was horrible," he recalled. "I was doing something I really did not want to do; I was selling coats. I didn't know anything about that world. It didn't interest me. Every day I'd go to work, I would sit on my bed and tie my shoelaces, and I'd start crying and my chest would get all matted with tears."

Still he reported for work. His discomfort and unhappiness did not lessen. He felt no connection to the Merchandise Mart, to the line of clothes he had had no hand in creating, and to the role of salesman. Unaccustomed to the tricks of the trade, he would fret over how to attract customers. Flipping through the Yellow Pages, he would stop at a likely name, and pick up the phone with shaking hand. His attempts, through choked-back tears, to apply his acting skills to salesmanship failed utterly.

He grew a ponytail, and, for his first business trip to Korea, where the coats were made, he had a barber color it with a streak of green. "I just needed something to make me feel *me*—a little off."

By his own account, his neighbors and clients at the Mart were not completely comfortable with their oddly groomed colleague, either. A look of confusion often came over a buyer's face as he listened to Rifkin's pitch. Where had they seen him before? On television? No, it couldn't be. A coat salesman?

After a while, Rifkin told his wife, "Look, this is not working out. I can't sell these fur coats. I just can't do it. It's not for me. I have to do something else." The two put their heads together, and, drawing on their shared love of beautiful things and strong sense of taste, they decided to design a line of fur coats manufactured specifically for the working woman. Rifkin had noticed that Yves Saint-Laurent was selling rabbit coats for $5,000. What if they could sell furs for $1,000? They studied other collections, and Rifkin flew to Korea and instructed his partners to buy sheared French rabbit fur—a softer, more pliable pelt, less stiff than the Chinese animal.

Back in Los Angeles, Ron and Iva, concluding that the name Ronlee meant nothing to the fashion world, decided to hire a name designer to create the line. They settled on Carole Little, who recognized Rifkin from *One Day at a Time*. Why was he in the garment business? "Why not?" he replied.

Rifkin returned to Korea with Little's sketches. Unschooled in the ways of the industry, he developed his own business habits. Where others would commonly drop off their patterns and fly back to the United States, only to be unhappy with the samples they received afterwards, Rifkin decided to wait out the creative process. He booked a hotel and never left town until he saw the first samples and tried out every coat. Then, drawing on his experience in the theater, he would type out notes like a director after a run-through, advising the Koreans on what needed correction. "All my discipline in working in the theater suddenly started to work," said Rifkin. "Because I put in so much effort, they put in twice the effort. For me, it was a time of great creativity, once I stopped feeling sorry for myself. I got over the initial trauma of not being an actor."

He taught himself about profits and sales projections and constructed lists and tables, aiming at a higher-than-usual 40-percent profit margin. Finally, he unveiled his line of coats. They sold well. The best stores bought them: Henri Bendel, Saks Fifth Avenue, Bergdorf Goodman. His father was pleased. And, for once, so was the son. He began to enjoy showing the line and pleased his client audience with the the-  atricality of his presentation. "I was a total oddity in the business," he commented. "I was not of the garment trade. I was someone whose sensibility was quite different. People used to look forward to my showing a line because I did it in such a different way. I was very into it: I would describe it, talk about this particular style and how we made it."

Rifkin also began to relish his twice-yearly visits to Korea. Instead of booking the local Hilton, he would check into an Asian hotel for a month at a time and immerse himself in the culture. He would socialize with his partners, eat at Korean restaurants, speak Korean, sing Korean songs.

"You adjust to tragedy because you have to," offered Rifkin. "So if somebody dies, or somebody hurts you or betrays you, or if you think your life is over because you can't do this anymore, you find a way to go to the next point. Look at me. I'm attractive, healthy, intelligent; I have a great relationship with my wife; I have great friends who love me. So big deal, you're not acting anymore. I loved being in the coat business. I love designing coats. I loved going to Asia two months a year. It was thrilling to me."

The Kid Not that he didn't think about acting. He would go to great lengths to avoid the theater in order not to dwell on it. In one telling episode, a visiting friend cajoled the Rifkins into catching Mandy Patinkin's one-man show on Broadway. "We'll go backstage afterward," said the friend. Rifkin thought about his years-long absence from acting. He had known Patinkin somewhat, but after his disappearance and Mandy's continued ascent, who knew if Patinkin would remember? Why risk it?

"I don't want to go backstage," protested Rifkin. The friend persisted. "No," said Rifkin. "He won't know who I am, and I'll be embarrassed and have to explain what I've been doing. *You* go." Finally, Iva charged, "Why don't you just grow up and be a mensch and go backstage?"

Rifkin took his seat in second-row center and began counting the minutes until the concert would be over. "Mandy was singing," related Rifkin, "and he looks right out at me in the theater. And he says, 'Ron? Ron Rifkin? Is that you? How are you?' He stopped the show. I said, 'I'm fine.' Everyone was looking; who's that man in the second row? I felt all these eyes boring into me. And he said, 'I haven't seen you in so long! *Where have you been, man?*'"

For the most part, Rifkin didn't attend the theater, and during this period the only person he went to shows with was Jane Hoffman, his co-star in *The Art of Dining*. Hoffman was a founding member of the Actors Studio and veteran of many Broadway and off-Broadway productions. When the Rifkins moved their business from Los Angeles to New York, Hoffman rented them the ground floor of her brownstone on St. Luke's Place, in Greenwich Village. Hoffman had been concerned when Rifkin gave up acting, and she now made occasional attempts to reintroduce him to the industry. She would take him to the Ensemble Studio Theatre and introduce him to everyone. Once, she asked to hold a party in his apartment because "his floor was bigger" than hers. He agreed and soon found his living room full of actors and casting directors.

In late 1987, Rifkin accompanied Hoffman to London for a visit to Sam Wanamaker, whose longtime project and obsession was the reconstruction of Shakespeare's Globe Theatre on the South Bank of the Thames. The site had been a grim, gray neighborhood with no remnant of its legendary theatrical past save a plaque. Now, Wanamaker had raised enough funds to begin construction of the Globe's replica. Rifkin, who has, as yet, never performed Shakespeare professionally, looked about the area, a piece of ground sacred to his former profession.

"Something happened to me," he remembered. "I suddenly felt like I was going to start crying. I didn't understand why. So I went outside, and I remember leaning on an iron railing, looking at the water. I looked around, and I thought, this is the Globe where Shakespeare was done. And I'm not an Anglophile at all. I couldn't believe I was standing in the place where people used to do what I used to do. I was suddenly overwhelmed by the idea of being an actor, belonging to something that went back centuries and made people understand themselves a little better. It was an epiphany; it was like an earthquake inside me. That's when I started to feel anguish about not acting."

Soon after, Rifkin received a call from his friend Ethan Silverman. He was directing a play called *Temple* at off-Broadway's American Jewish Theatre. The script by Robert Greenfield, based on his novel of the same name, told the story of Paulie Bindel, a Harvard student in the 1960s who both drops out of school and leaves the counterculture to rediscover his Brooklyn Jewish roots and restore his faith. The "brat-pack" film actor Judd Nelson was signed to play Paulie, but Silverman was having trouble casting the role of his father, a divorced, disaffected postal worker.

Rifkin said no. Silverman called again. He even called Rifkin in Korea, pleading and saying how thrilled Judd was at the prospect of working with him. "First of all," Rifkin told him, "I'm not going to play it. And second, you're full of shit; Judd Nelson doesn't know who the hell I am."

Eventually, Silverman wore him down, and Rifkin agreed. Then there was the matter of informing his boss, who was also his father. It was not an easy exchange. As Rifkin recalled, his father said, "You're going to do some shit-ass play in some shit-ass theater?"

"We were tough on each other. He didn't like me stepping on him, and I didn't like him stepping on me. He wanted to stop worrying about me, to have me support myself."

Temple, which opened March 17, 1988, reaped Rifkin no immediate benefits. The reviews were tepid, and Rifkin was barely mentioned. In the audience one night, however, was a woman named Bonnie Monte, who was casting for that summer's Williamstown Theatre Festival. Austin Pendleton was set to direct a new version of Arthur Miller's *The American Clock,* and he needed an actor for the central role of Moe Baum. Monte suggested Rifkin. Pendleton agreed.

Meanwhile, Rifkin went about the business of selling coats. When summer came, he told his father he was taking time off again to do a play. Rifkin now straddled two worlds: He took his work with him to the Berkshires, and every day of his four-week stay there, he called into the office.

The American Clock had failed on Broadway in 1980, but never completely dropped from sight. It had since been restaged in London and Los Angeles. Miller had conceived it as a Depression-era mural, its more than fifty characters presenting a pageant of that period's songs and social themes. Rifkin played an unemployed father desperately trying to hold on to his family and dignity.

The reviews were respectful, and the audience reception tremendous. The *Berkshire Eagle* said that Rifkin was "touching as Moe . . . One of the production's more affecting moments comes when he asks his son to lend him a quarter so he can have lunch downtown." The *Union-News,* too, applauded his empathetic acting.

Again, Rifkin saw no immediate reward from his temporary return to acting. But, as in the case of *Temple,* he had an impact on somebody in the audience—a kid, tall, awkwardly handsome, with pale skin, a prominent nose, and tousled, jet-black hair. The kid introduced himself: Jon Robin Baitz. The exchange which followed has, in Baitz's words, become as mythologized an event as the discovery of Lana Turner in Schwab's Drugstore. "I saw you in *The American Clock,*" said Baitz. "My hair stood up on the back of my neck."

Rifkin looked at the stranger. "Why?" he asked.

"Because I knew I was seeing a man who was hiding his connection to a particular kind of melancholy."

"Then he said he was going to write a play for me," said Rifkin, still amused at the recollection. "I said, 'Whatever.'" After *American Clock* closed, Rifkin put on his other hat and flew to Korea. A month later, at the end of September, 1988, he saw Baitz's *The Film Society* at Second Stage, the play that put Baitz on the map at the age of 26. At the curtain, Rifkin thought in wonder, "That kid wrote this play?"

Death of a Coat Salesman Baitz originally had Rifkin in mind for his new play, *Dutch Landscape,* which Gordon Davidson was set to direct at the Mark Taper Forum in 1989. Davidson, however, wanted Rifkin to audition. "Robby said, 'Oh, just audition. Don't worry about it,'" related Rifkin. He dutifully went in and read his scene. He informed Davidson that he had to fly to Korea immediately; he could return in time to do the play, but needed to know before he left if he had the part. As he prepared to leave the country, no word came from the Mark Taper. "I called his assistant and Davidson had left for Poland without telling me," said Rifkin. "I called Robby, who said Gordon was supposed to call and say he didn't want me to do the play. I felt bad for Robby."

Rifkin told Baitz—with whom he was becoming fast friends—that he need-ed some distance between them to avoid any bad feelings arising from the incident. Rifkin flew to Korea and immersed himself once again in the garment business.

When he returned a month later, Fisher Stevens, a lodger in Rifkin's house in Los Angeles, told him, "Robby's having a terrible time. The play's a disaster." ("It was the *Heaven's Gate* of the theater," Baitz would later say.) And as Stevens was leaving, he said, "Oh, by the way, I'm going to meet Robby at the farmer's market."

"I thought, why did he tell me that?" Rifkin recalled. "I didn't want to see Robby. I didn't want to be reminded of what had happened; I didn't want to know about the play. But then a little voice said to me, 'You're a grown, mature man; he's a kid. He's having a rough time. His play is getting decimated. Why don't you just go?' So I went to the farmer's market, and when Robby saw me, he started to cry. He said, 'You came!' And I knew then that we were going to be great friends."

Baitz made good on his impulsive promise at Williamstown. Soon after see-ing Rifkin again, he returned to Rifkin's house and, in one night of coffee and cig-arettes, wrote what would become the first act of *The Substance of Fire*. It was the story of Isaac Geldhart, the imposing, cosmopolitan head of a small publishing house known for its literary pedigree and its sluggish sales. Rifkin had flown to New York, and Baitz read him bits of dialogue over the phone. The first act traces Isaac's downfall. Rather than compromise his exacting literary standards, Geld-hart—a guilt-ridden survivor of the Nazi death camps and self-appointed torch-bearer for a bygone European culture—has driven his family-owned firm to the brink of bankruptcy. While dismissing the suggestion of his son Aaron to publish a slick new novel sure to make a profit, he insists on going ahead with a six-volume scholarly tome on Nazi medical experiments. His children eventually rise with their combined interests in the business and force Isaac out.

There was much in the role of Isaac to which Rifkin could relate: the Jewish background, and Isaac's paternal power, in which Rifkin could see aspects of his own father. (The actor had told the playwright of the confrontation which took place when he told his father he was taking a role in *Temple*; Baitz took Hy's epi-thet "shit-ass" and put it in Isaac's mouth.) Rifkin also gravitated toward Isaac's aura of melancholy and his exquisite tastes.

When *The Substance of Fire* eventually opened, in New York, many an observ-er would comment on how well Rifkin inhabited Isaac's beautifully tailored suits. "I have a very strong aesthetic," said Rifkin. "Both Iva and I love beautiful things.

It's so interesting the way people live: the things they like to have around them; the way they arrange their things; what gives them comfort and solace. The thing about all the clothing, the accoutrements, what I take to my dressing room—this stuff is part of what makes me the actor I am, what I am about."

Baitz's first act was tried out at Naked Angels, a theater troupe founded by a group of artists including Fisher Stevens, Rob Morrow, and Baitz himself. Rifkin was now a member. It was well received. Soon after, Rifkin performed in Paddy Chayevsky's *The Tenth Man*, at Lincoln Center. Despite his growing success and steady work as an actor, he nonetheless refused to let go of the workaday world of his father. Associates would visit him in his dressing room to consult on coat linings. And Rifkin would spy his merchandise draped over the seats at the Vivian Beaumont Theatre and report his findings to Iva.

In the spring of 1990, Rifkin traveled with *The Substance of Fire* to the Long Wharf Theatre. It now had a second act, in which Isaac, bereft and dejected, is visited by a social worker three-and-a-half years after his forced retirement. David Warren directed. The cast included Rob Morrow and Gina Gershon. André Bishop of Playwrights Horizons came to see it and decided to bring it to New York, but with a different director, Dan Sullivan.

"I think the hardest thing for directors and actors is language," Rifkin reflected. "Because if a director says red to me, in my head red may be this, but in his head red may be that. Maybe his red is my blue. For me, the hardest thing has always been communication. That's why finding a director whose red is the same as your red is such a blessing. Dan Sullivan is one."

The cast and director readied the play for the March 17, 1991, opening. Though he knew the role was special and the play a good one, Rifkin—perhaps still chastened and weighed down by the trials of the last several years—did not realize the importance of the occasion. Others did. During a dress rehearsal, the lighting designer Arden Fingerhut came up to Rifkin and said, "I don't think you understand how important this play is, how important this character is." Rifkin stared at her and replied, "I don't."

Two weeks later, he took the stage on opening night—supported by Sarah Jessica Parker, Jon Tenney, Patrick Breen, and Maria Tucci—in a sharply pressed, double-breasted charcoal suit and a neatly trimmed beard, and delivered as precise and fiery a performance as he had ever given. He then retired with the cast to Naked Angels' headquarters, on West 17th Street, which had been rented for the occasion. After a while, Baitz's agent, George Lane, appeared, *New York Times* in hand. "Here, read Frank Rich's review," he said, eagerly. "I don't read reviews, George," said Rifkin. "I think you should read this one. It makes up for anything you've ever read," Lane advised.

"Career-transforming performance" were the words Rich used, words that would live up to their promise. Other critics expressed qualms about the play, but expressed none about Rifkin, who seemed an actor unknown to them. "Rifkin seizes on [Isaac's] every nuance with a burning fervor that gives meaning to the title," said the *Village Voice*. "His smiles cut, his epigrams sting, and his talk about old books has the weirdly erotic tone real collectors use." *Variety* called him "letter perfect. . . . He makes Isaac a compelling, almost tragic figure, and . . . demands that attention be paid to Isaac until his final moment has passed." *New York* wrote: "Ron Rifkin is a tightly wound, stinging, often devastating, yet never less than human Isaac."

"Everything really did seem to be different after that," mused Rifkin six years after those reviews rang in his ears, his voice more tinged with melancholy than swollen with pride. "When I think about that time now—which really wasn't that long ago—it seems as if I was existing on some other level, because none of it seemed important to me. It just seemed like another version of doing another play. So I got the reviews, and they just kept coming and coming. And then one day André Bishop called my house—I was taking a nap and was somewhere between sleeping and not sleeping—and he said, 'I just wanted to tell you, you won the Drama Desk Award.' 'Oh, good, that's good.' I had no idea what the Drama Desk was. My heart didn't pound. None of that.

"I think at my age, life teaches you that nothing is that important. Ultimately, the kind of thing you get excited about when you're young—'My God, I got nominated for a Drama Desk Award, I'm so excited!'—that goes, and it gets replaced by much better things. I still have enthusiasm for life, and I still get passionate about it—I can laugh—that's my nature. But I think I'm past getting overwhelmed and excited by those things. Too much has happened. Too many deaths. Too many sadnesses.

"I remember thinking, when *Substance* opened and Frank Rich said what he said: 'Okay, last year I was showing coats at Saks Fifth Avenue. And now Frank Rich is saying this, and now I win an award, and now I win another award. What's going on here?'"

Over the previous seven years, Rifkin could scarcely have covered more ground, emotionally or professionally. Yet, instead of robbing him of something—his spirit or will—those seven years had enriched him instead. He admits to being a much better actor now, one with more insight into himself and the world around him. The sadness and surprise, bitterness and regeneration of the coat-trade years fed Rifkin's soul, which, in turn, informed his subsequent portrayals. The fire and despair Baitz saw in Rifkin's defeated businessman in *The American Clock* might not have emanated from an actor who hadn't suffered defeats so recently, and who's to say Isaac could have come from a more contented, successful performer?

Perhaps most importantly, Rifkin's abandonment of his acting career also buoyed his flagging self-confidence: "I think having spent those years with coats gave me a strength of belief in myself—a sense that there was a lot I could do. You know, when I'd go to show a line to a CEO of a store, I was never frightened of that. But if I would meet a casting director, I would fall apart."

In early 1997, Rifkin was asked at the last moment to replace John Guare at a benefit reading of the love letters of Agnes de Mille and her husband. Looking out at the $1,000-a-plate gathering, he saw Mrs. Vincent Astor, Mike Nichols and his wife Diane Sawyer, Morley Safer, Bill Blass, and other luminaries. "In the old days, if I'd known Mike Nichols was out there. . . ," said Rifkin, trailing off. "I've been through so much, and felt torn down, ripped apart, and bloodied by this business, that no matter who I meet now, I don't care."

Plateaus—Perhaps After *The Substance of Fire,* and a regular role on the CBS series, *The Trials of Rosie O'Neill,* Rifkin returned to acting full time. His transformation, in the eyes of critics, casting directors, and the public, was nearly complete. His performance as Isaac Geldhart had won him the Drama Desk, Obie, and Lucile Lortel awards. In 1992 the production followed André Bishop, as he left Playwrights Horizons to become artistic director of Lincoln Center, and ran at the Mitzi E. Newhouse Theatre for 174 performances. Rifkin would reprise the role again, in early 1993, at the Mark Taper Forum, adding a Drama-Logue Award to his collection.

And he moved from casting directors' "C" lists to their "A" lists—a respected and sought-after artist. He had become, as one friend jokingly termed it, "Sir Ron."

Rosie O'Neill, which starred Sharon Gless in the title role of an attorney, was particularly satisfying for the actor. He played Gless's boss, an Orthodox Jew—a character Rifkin knew something about. "It was an enormous responsibility to play a character who had never been on prime-time before. For the country to see an Orthodox Jew every week who was not stereotypical—he had an important position, he didn't look a certain way people think Orthodox Jews look—it was a great opportunity to see an aspect of society they don't normally get to see."

One episode had O'Neill visit the character's home on a Friday night, the Jewish Sabbath. The writers, however, were unfamiliar with the rituals of the occasion. "I said, 'Guys, this is what happens on Friday night, and I know the prayer by heart. It's in Hebrew.' They said, 'Why don't you just do it?' To make kiddush in Hebrew with a yarmulke on my head for the whole world to see, to have an opportunity to do it really right—people don't get to see that. It's such a private ritual." The show fostered a great deal of positive feedback. People wrote to the show's producers and sent Rifkin handmade yarmulkes.

Rifkin's first major, post-"rebirth" stage role was in Baitz's *Three Hotels,* proving that neither his work in *Substance of Fire* nor his artistic communion with the playwright had been a fluke. Adapted from earlier work of his, written for PBS's

American Playhouse, Baitz's play comprises three monologues delivered in three far-flung hotel rooms. The first and third are delivered by Kenneth Hoyle (né Hersh-kovitz), a sour, corrupted businessman who has strayed so far afield from his left-ist, Peace-Corps roots that he finds himself peddling a mega-corporation's suspect baby formula in Africa. The second is delivered by his embittered wife Barbara, who unwittingly becomes the instrument of Kenneth's undoing and, perhaps, redemption.

Three Hotels was first staged on Long Island, in the summer of 1992, as part of the Bay Street Theatre Festival, in Sag Harbor. Rifkin co-starred with Maria Tucci, under the direction of Joe Mantello. It was then mounted at Manhattan's Circle Repertory Company, with Christine Lahti—and, later, Debra Monk—in Tucci's place. Opening April 6, 1993, it ran 252 performances, setting a record for the theater at its Seventh Avenue South location. Rifkin would win a second Lucille Lortel Award and another Drama Desk nomination.

"The extraordinary symbiosis between Mr. Rifkin and Mr. Baitz turns out not to be a one-play affair, but an actor–playwright collaboration built for the long haul," wrote Frank Rich in the *New York Times.* "For all the similarities between Ken Hoyle and the publisher in *The Substance of Fire,* the new character is a distinct cre-ation, imbued with his own brash comic voice and his own sad nocturnal shadows. Once again, Mr. Rifkin is indelible." *Variety* added, "Baitz has been blessed with an incomparable vehicle for his marvelously theatrical voice. Rifkin's conversational tone heightens the sense of intimacy we feel as these lives are revealed."

One day in 1993, a large envelope from agent Sam Cohn came in the mail. In it was a copy of Arthur Miller's play *The Ride Down Mt. Morgan*—at that time unpro-duced in America. Soon after, a call came. "It's Arthur Miller," said the gruff Brooklyn-accented voice at the other end of the line. "You're a pretty good actor, kid."

Just as Baitz had been sold on Rifkin after seeing him in a Miller play, Miller sought out Rifkin after seeing him in *The Substance of Fire.* Rifkin did a reading of *Mt. Morgan* with Dianne Wiest and Natasha Richardson, but didn't care much for the play or character. Miller then said he had a new play Rifkin should look at, a drama set in the 1930s called *Broken Glass.* Another reading was put together, again with Dianne Wiest. This character Rifkin liked. He played Phillip Gellburg, a well-to-do Jewish Republican who is blind to the troubles besetting his family, his faith, and his own soul. Proudly employed at the WASPy Brooklyn Guaranty and Trust, with a son at West Point, the self-loathing Gellberg has spent his life dodging or masking his Judaism, to the point of repeatedly distancing his name from the more Jewish "Goldberg." The play's central drama is the unexplained illness of Phillip's wife Sylvia, who has been felled by hysterical paralysis since reading about Nazi atrocities against Jews in Europe (the *Kristallnacht* of the title).

Broken Glass would prove a bumpy ride. Wiest was not available to play Sylvia, and Amy Irving was cast instead. Then Ron Silver, who played Sylvia's

Photo by David Rodgers.

Ron Rifkin in the Bay Street Theatre
Festival production of Jon Robin
Baitz's *Three Hotels*, in Sag Harbor,
Long Island, in the spring of 1993.

doctor, Harry Hyman, left during the play's spring 1994 pre-Broadway run at New Haven's Long Wharf Theatre. He was replaced by David Dukes, who spent many performances with script in hand. Perhaps most troubling, Miller and director John Tillinger were undecided as to the ending. Miller wrote fifteen new pages during the second week of performances. On some evenings, Gellberg lived; on others, he died.

The Broadway production that followed—Miller's first with a new play since *The American Clock*—opened at the Booth Theatre on April 24. It was Rifkin's first Broadway role since *The Goodbye People*'s one-night stand. The temperature of New York's critical establishment, long cool to Miller's talent, rose only incrementally for *Broken Glass*. Still, it was a noteworthy achievement for Rifkin. He had created the role in an Arthur Miller play. And the reviews extended his run of positive critical notice.

Asked if *Broken Glass* represented a career high point for him, Rifkin answered with the mournful cast of his eyes barely altered. "I don't think there are high points for me. I don't feel a high point. I feel this is where I am." When pressed, he accepts the following definition of "high point": "A time of more than usual pleasure and less than usual worry."

During this period of praise and advantage, Rifkin knew that *Broken Glass*, *Three Hotels*, a string of film jobs including roles in Mike Nichols' *Wolf* and Woody Allen's *Husbands and Wives* and *Manhattan Murder Mystery*—all opportunities that *The Substance of Fire* had brought him—were only parts of the latest chapter in a career that was hardly over and could change at any moment.

"People think because you won an award and have your pick of parts now, that it's going to be easy. It's never easy," asserted Rifkin. "When you think you've come to the next plateau, you discover that you haven't. Then you think you've come to the next plateau, and someone says, 'Watch it, Ron.' Then you come to the next one, and they say, 'Who cares?'

"It's an enormous responsibility, because even at my age, when you think you don't have to go to the other side, the demons come, they grab you and pull you back, and they say, 'We're here. We're back. Watch out!'

"I would never tell someone to become an actor. You shouldn't do it unless you can't do anything else. If you can get through the day without doing this, you shouldn't do it, because it's too hard. Especially if you're not born looking beautiful. It sounds odd, and it sounds negative, but it's not. In our work, it's not about talent, mostly—especially if you want to work in television. It's never about talent. It's about a combination of things. That's part of the reason why I stopped acting. I had no control of anything: The way you look; the way you sound; the way you remind them of this person that they hate, or of their mother; or you're too Jewish, too ethnic, not ethnic enough, too fat.

"The lows are very low—there's no recourse. It's important for anyone who seriously considers becoming an actor that it is because there is indeed nothing else that person wants to do."

Through the Wringer Again During the first twenty-five years of Ron Rifkin's film career, he had never risen above supporting roles—and relatively minor ones at that. With *The Substance of Fire* and the fierce advocacy of its author in his corner, he was handed all the wonders and nightmares that are part and parcel of starring in a film.

Movie producers had long been interested in Baitz's play as a property but had floated other stars of proven Hollywood merit as Isaac Geldhart. Rifkin didn't want to keep Baitz from a career as a screenwriter and told him to go ahead without him and make the film with this star or that. But the playwright stood firm.

Ron Rifkin starred in the 1996 film version of *The Substance of Fire*, with Tony Goldwyn (left) and Sarah Jessica Parker.

"This is what I write about," Baitz said. "All my plays deal with these issues— morality, excellence, passion. How can I do this and hold onto my system, my beliefs?"

Baitz won. The film was shot starring Rifkin. Sarah Jessica Parker repeated her role. Her two brothers were played by Timothy Hutton and Tony Goldwyn. Dan Sullivan directed.

The producers thought they had an art-house hit on their hands, an award-getter. They sent the film to festivals around the world and Rifkin along with it. It was shown at a couple of the festivals. At each, Rifkin and other actors from the film along with members of the creative team sat at a conference table while journalists from different countries were shuttled through, at fifteen-minute intervals, pelting them with questions in various languages. Back in the states, a press junket was arranged in New York City—more interviews, more reporters. Rifkin carpeted the rest of America, flying to Houston, Boston, Atlanta, and other cities, each time blinded by a new rush of flashbulbs. He appeared on talk shows, including *Late Night with Conan O'Brien*. He was happy to do it all, but found the experience "wrenching."

The producers of *The Substance of Fire* released the film for one week in 1996 to qualify for the various film awards. The reviews were good, particularly for Rifkin. The stage was set. The producers sat back and waited. The awards from the smaller critics' organizations were announced. Neither the film nor Rifkin were among the winners. So they waited for the nominations from the larger award groups, the Golden Globes, the Academy Awards. Still no honors. The producers despaired and abandoned *The Substance of Fire.* They postponed the rerelease until months later. By then, whatever attention the positive press had generated had dissipated. The film quickly came and went.

Rifkin had dedicated several months of his life to the promotion of the film. It would take many more to recover from the experience. "It was very frustrating to me. It's just crazy making. But there was such press, and they were so excited about it.

"You spend so much time and you work so hard, and you adjust to the fact that you'll never be a leading man in film. That's okay. There are a lot of things I get to do. Then you do a movie, and it turns out really nicely. The reviews are wonderful. The people distributing it take out ads every day in the trades: 'Please consider da-da-da for best actor.' They send you all over the world. Then, when you don't get nominated, it's over. They drop it. The movie never gets opened, really. And it's over. And you say, 'Wait, wait, wait! What happened?'"

A Small Price Rifkin would return to film, of course. Soon after *The Substance of Fire*, he played the role of the district attorney in a film which *would* win numerous prizes, *L.A. Confidential.* He would also return to television, playing the city coroner in the short-lived 1997 drama series, *Leaving L.A.* And he would continue to find his best roles where he had always found them: on the stage. One of the better ones was Herr Schultz in the Roundabout Theatre Company's 1998 revival of *Cabaret* on Broadway—Rifkin's first musical in more than thirty years.

"I am more comfortable onstage than I am at home," the actor admitted. "When I am onstage, whether it's in rehearsal or in performance, whether I'm fucking up or forgetting lines, whether I'm frightened or think I'm going to be terrible, there is something about my connection to it—whatever it is—that makes me feel that this is my *home.* This is where my body performs. This is where I experience myself at my best, at my most vulnerable, at my most creative. On the stage.

"Every actor brings his own life experience to it. The thing about actors is, there is no one way, because every actor is unique. Whatever it is they have is incredible, because it's theirs, and it's different from everybody else's. I think it's important for people to know that they don't have to be like Al Pacino or Dustin Hoffman. They don't have to be like *anybody.* Just get off on what makes you *you.*"

Cabaret had begun in London as director Sam Mendes' stark reinterpretation of the classic 1966 John Kander–Fred Ebb musical. When the Roundabout expressed interest in bringing the production to New York, they had to meet Mendes' strict demands that they duplicate the environmental staging he had created at London's Donmar Warehouse. That meant combing the city for a space which could be transformed into the musical's fictitious Berlin nightspot, the Kit Kat Klub.

The Roundabout and Mendes finally settled on the Supper Club, a 1930s–style dinner and dancing night spot on West 47th Street. After deciding that question, the Roundabout called Rifkin's agent and asked if he'd be interested in the role of Schultz. Rifkin had been keeping his voice in shape, and the audition for Mendes went well. "I'd been dying to do a musical. I could sing in musicals for the rest of my life," he said. Suddenly, however, the arrangement with the Supper Club fell through and the production was postponed while the theatre began a second search for a home for *Cabaret*.

After the Roundabout and Mendes agreed on the former Henry Miller Theatre on West 43rd Street, the role of Schultz was offered outright to Rifkin. *Cabaret*, starring its original London cast members Natasha Richardson and Alan Cumming, as well as Americans John Benjamin Hickey, Mary Louise Wilson, and Rifkin, finally opened on March 19, 1998, to the best reviews of the season. It soon became a harder ticket to come by than the Disney hit, *The Lion King*.

Cabaret dominated the Tony nominations when they came out—including one nod for Rifkin, his first. A specific, New York-centric brand of craziness soon consumed his life. "I've been in plays where everyone expected me to get nominated for a Tony and I didn't," he said. "And there was that sense of Tony fever before the nominations. During *Cabaret*, it wasn't just Tony fever, it was Tony malaria."

Rifkin sailed through the next month, attending a variety of Tony-related events. He did not get his hopes up for the prize, however: "Every newspaper in New York predicted that John McMartin [of the musical *High Society*] would win. Not only would I not win, I wasn't even mentioned as a possibility. I was quite content with that. It was a trip to be nominated.

"The Saturday before the Sunday of the Tony ceremony, Natasha Richardson came into my dressing room and did her speech for me. And she asked, 'What about yours?' I said, 'Natasha, I don't have one. I'm not going to win.' So she said, 'You should have one ready.' So in my head I thought—if I were to win—what would I say."

On Tony night, to the surprise of many—and no one more than Rifkin—his name was called. "I thought it was a mistake. I literally thought it was a mistake. I gave my program to Iva, and we connected for maybe a twelfth of a second and that was all I remember." Onstage, he grasped his award and forced out a few words, visibly stunned.

The successes of *L.A. Confidential* and *Cabaret* would not cure Rifkin of his occasional bouts of melancholy. Nor would he like to be rid of them. They come with the territory, in his estimation, and, yes, they make their not inconsiderable contribution. "I like experiences of sadness and loneliness," he reasoned. "It makes me feel human and alive. Loneliness, I feel, is a small price to pay for my experience as an actor. When I'm in it and doing it, nothing could be better."

Index

About the Author

ROBERT SIMONSON's writings on theater and the arts have appeared in *Time Out New York, The Village Voice, Back Stage, Stagebill, Jazziz,* and *Brooklyn Bridge.* He is also the author of several plays—including *Cafe Society, Conversation, Wittenberg, George and Gig,* and *Some Friend*—which have been produced by such off-Broadway companies as Expanded Arts, Nada, The Present Company, Manhattan Playhouse, and Theatre Studio, and by Theatre Three, on Long Island. He is currently senior editor of the theater news service, *Playbill On-Line.* A native of Wisconsin, he lives in Brooklyn with his wife, art critic Sarah Schmerler.